D0466863

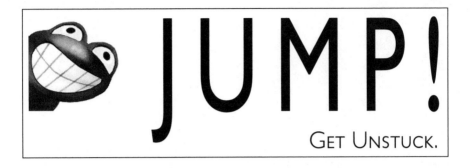

**JUMP!**

GET UNSTUCK.

FIRST PRINTING

# FOR:

## DEBI TIPTON
### AND
## DAVE ELLISON

In so many ways, and at so many times,
you have helped me get unstuck.

I am eternally grateful and very blessed
to have each of you in my life.

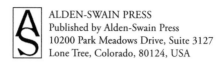

ALDEN-SWAIN PRESS
Published by Alden-Swain Press
10200 Park Meadows Drive, Suite 3127
Lone Tree, Colorado, 80124, USA

Copyright © 2010 by Robert S. Tipton

All rights reserved. No part of this book may be reproduced, scanned or distributed in any printed or electronic form without permission. Please do not participate in or encourage piracy of copyrighted materials in violation of author's rights. Purchase only authorized editions.

Most Alden-Swain books are available at special quantity discounts for bulk purchase for sales promotions, premiums, fund-raising, and educational needs. Special books or book excerpts also can be created to fit special needs.

For details, write ALDEN-SWAIN PRESS, Special Markets, 10200 Park Meadows Drive, Suite 3127, Lone Tree, Colorado, 80124, USA.

LCCN: 2010901067

ISBN 978-0-9825900-0-3

Printed in the United States of America
1 3 5 7 9 10 8 6 4 2

EDITED BY: KATHY NELSON
COVER ARTWORK BY: AC CANALES
GRAPHICS BY: ALDEN-SWAIN PRESS
BOOK AND COVER DESIGN BY: ALDEN-SWAIN PRESS

All copyrights and trademarks are property of their respective owners.

References to *Monsters, Inc.* © 2001 and *Finding Nemo* © 2003 used with permission. Destination ImagiNation® program name and logos used with permission from Destination ImagiNation, Inc.

While the author has made every effort to provide accurate reference information to website addresses, telephone numbers, etc., at the time of publication, neither the publisher nor the author assumes any responsibility for errors or for changes that occur after publication. Further, the publisher does not have any control over and does not assume any responsibility for author or third-party websites or their content.

The leadership fable is a work of fiction. Names, characters, businesses, organizations, places, events, and incidents either are the product of the author's imagination or are used fictitiously. Any resemblance to actual persons, living or dead, or actual events is entirely coincidental.

# APPRECIATION

As the old saying goes, "It takes a village to raise a child." The same could be said about the process of writing this book. I have been blessed with an amazing group of collaborators, editors, reviewers, and an overall support network that helped me refine the message, shape the story, drive the model, and generally bring JUMP!'s potential to its maximum level.

Thank you doesn't seem to be a powerful enough thing to say, but know when I say the words I mean them sincerely.

Thank you to Debi, Amanda, Parker, Spencer, and Grace for your advice, love, and support during this crazy adventure. I appreciate that you have believed in me from the time JUMP! was just a hare-brained thought from your crazy husband / father.

Thank you to Kathy for your wise, patient, and professional editing. You know me well, and you have the gift of helping to retain my voice while making me sound smarter than I think I am.

Thank you to Amanda and Robin for your candid, thorough, and objective reviews of the first complete draft. Your perspectives not only helped to improve JUMP!, but also affirmed my vision for it.

Thank you to AC for your creativity, your vision, and your understanding when it came to my never ending requests to tweak this, change that, try this, do that, etc. The images came out great.

Thank you to Alex, Alicia, Alison, Amanda, Brian, Carol, Chris, Clint, Connie, Daryl, Dave, David, David, Debi, Gerry, Jeff, Kathleen, Jack, Jo, Joe, Keith, Keith, Kris, Larry, Lester, Lily, Lisa, Lynne, Mary Ann, Nahid, Nora, Parker, Robin, Skip, Steve, and Trevor for your positive energy, guidance, unvarnished opinions, and clear suggestions for improvement.

I appreciate you. Each of you. Thank you for being part of my village.

# Contents

## JUMP!: The Model

## JUMP!: Epilogue

## JUMP!: Appendix

# Reader's Guide to *JUMP!*

I don't think it's my place to tell anyone how they "should" read this book—but I *want* you to read it and to get the *most out of it* as you do. Therefore, there's probably a "best" way for you, personally, to read it—which might not be the same way as the person in the next office, the one sitting next to you on the plane, or your neighbor next door. Therefore, consider this to be *your* reader's guide to *JUMP!*

Early readers have told me that they've approached *JUMP!* from basically three different perspectives:

1.  I love inspiring and motivating "two-flight" or "one-evening" stories—where I get the message quickly and succinctly.

2.  I like business-related stories, but I also want to understand the rationale behind them. I like to see the process models as well.

3.  Stories are okay, but I really love to dig into the approaches, methods, and tools side of things. Show me the details!

Now, you may not see yourself exactly in one of these three categories above, and that's okay. However, I'm going to use those three choices to help you chart a course in your JUMP! experience. That said, any approach to reading *JUMP!* will work. It's up to you. No one is watching over your shoulder to make sure you read one page after another. Skipping around is just fine.

### Recommended Approaches For Reading *JUMP!*

*1: I Love a Great Story—Let Me Get to It!*

Jump straight beyond the Introduction, go directly to page 3 and begin reading the leadership fable. I've been told the fable all by itself is the perfect "vacation business book." Beware, though, I've also been told it's hard to stop reading the fable once you've started it! Once you've completed the story, go back and read the Introduction if you'd like to learn more about the ins-and-outs of what you've read in the fable. After reading the Introduction, you can decide whether or not you'd like to devote any time to the process model. You might decide to do so, you might not. If not, I promise not to take it personally.

*2: I Like Good Stories, and I Like to Understand the Rationale Behind Them*

Continue to page xv and read the Introduction. It sets the stage for the entire book. Then, continue on to read the fable, followed by the model. If you read it in this order, you will be reading *JUMP!* in the manner in which I primarily intended it to be read. I think it flows more coherently this way, but don't get smug about it and think you're reading it the "right" way. Readers 1 and 3 might get annoyed.

*3: Stories Can Be Kind of Fluffy—I Have to See the Details First*

Again, I'd recommend that you continue to page xv, and read the Introduction. It does talk a bit about the leadership fable, but more importantly, it gives context to the process model section of the book. Then, after reading the Introduction, jump to page 185 and read the model. One note, however. I do reference relevant aspects of the leadership fable in each section of the process model. I do this to show examples of how the model might be used. Therefore, I wrote the model assuming you would have read the fable first. I hope you'll be okay with that approach—if not, it's okay to send me emails to complain. Either way, I hope you take a look at the fable at some point. It's not too fluffy. I promise.

Here's one last thing to consider—the fable is rich in both content and in the number and diversity of characters. To help you "keep track" of who's who in the book, I've included a character summary in the Appendix (pages 243 – 246). For some it will be helpful to read these pages before starting the fable, while others may find it useful to refer to the character summary while you read the fable. Either way, or not at all, just think of the character summary as a tool to help keep you connected to the action in the fable.

# INTRODUCTION

I have a two-part mission for you as you read this book.

First, I want you to foster and develop a new relationship with the status quo, the "old friend" who dependably provides you with the same results. Sometimes the status quo is a good thing, like for those who run nuclear power plants or manufacture food. We want safe, predictable results there. However, in many cases, the status quo is an unwelcome anchor to the past—a major inhibitor toward moving in new, positive directions. It is in these situations where I want you to develop a new relationship with the status quo.

Second, I want you to feel as if you are armed with new insights, new approaches, and better tools as you move forward, farther, faster in creating more satisfaction, better results, and higher levels of significance in your life and in your organization. I want you to feel powerful and motivated to change.

Why?

Because the pace and degree of change in the world shows no sign of slowing, and as a result, the "target" (survival, success, significance—whatever you're looking for) is moving faster, higher, and farther out of reach. It's not that we don't recognize the need for change (some of us are clueless, but not most). Many of us are working very hard at change. However, meeting and then getting ahead of the pace and degree of change is often unattainable because we have ineffective relationships with the status quo (in some cases, it borders on dysfunctional!), and our old, incremental approaches to change are letting us down.

To illustrate this dynamic, there's a story I heard once about a man who was walking down a street and fell in a hole. Hours later, he managed to climb out. The next day, he walked down the same street and fell in the same hole. Again, hours later, he struggled out. The following day, he walked down the same street—stopped at the hole, looked at it, and fell in again. More hours passed, and he finally got out. The next day, he took a different street.

You've probably heard this story and thought it was about someone else. However, I see this story repeated and repeated and repeated. The status quo bias is incredibly difficult to overcome for most people. It isn't until you decide that things will be different—a single decision, made by a single person—that the energy field associated with change is activated. Until then, the universe is giving you exactly what you're desiring: sameness. You have created a well-oiled machine to give you exactly what you have.

Think about it: How do you feel when someone parks in *your* space at work (assuming, of course, that you don't have reserved parking)? Observe yourself—just once—brushing your teeth. Most likely, you start in exactly the same place and brush the same number of strokes (give or take a very small number) each time. Do you sit in the same seat in the conference room for the weekly staff meeting? Eat at the same restaurants? Do you have your "Tuesday shirt" or "Wednesday blouse"?

We're often stuck in the same, old approaches even as we recognize the world is moving forward. Quickly. Let me use a picture to describe what I'm saying. It's a classic "consultant chart" (yes, I'm a consultant, but please don't hold that against me!) where I show *Time* on the X axis and *Demands and Your Ability to Meet Them* on the Y axis. Then . . . there are the three curves.

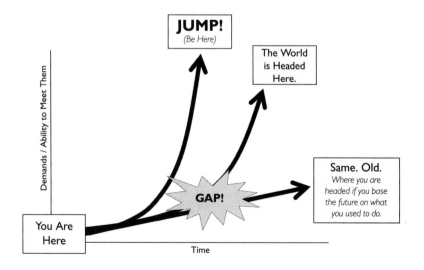

1. Same. Old.: This curve is a slow, incremental curve (so slow, in fact, it appears to be a straight line). Everything here is safe, predictable, and proven. If you follow the Same. Old. curve, you wind up with the same, old results. Now, if you're flying a jumbo jet or are making pharmaceuticals, we want you to have the same, old, predictable results. But if you require a breakthrough in your thinking, your actions, or your results, the Same. Old. curve is a deadly place to be.

2. The World is Headed Here: This curve represents the pace of change in the world at large. Due to globalization, climate change, economic turmoil, relentless competition—whatever the stimulus—the world continues to become more complex and, frankly, further out-of-reach for organizations, groups, families, and individuals that keep doing the Same. Old. things. The pace of change in the world is going higher, faster than ever, and it's showing no signs of flattening out.

3. JUMP! (Be Here): This curve represents the outcomes you will enjoy after implementing the model shown in this book. Massive changes are possible, not only in results (financial, quality, safety, sustainability, and such), but also in leadership styles, interpersonal relationships, quality of life, self-esteem, and overall personal satisfaction.

Not to discourage you, but I need to be clear. For those of you who are in denial and are waiting for the return to the ways of the past where you had time to call meeting after meeting, where you could consider all your options for months on end, you will be left in the dust. In addition, just getting ahead of the "Where the world is headed" curve is only the beginning. *Staying ahead* of that curve is vital and not optional. That's where JUMP! comes in.

## *JUMP! Innovative Change Model*

In my day job as a designer and facilitator of innovative change for individuals, groups, and organizations, I play the role of change coach. I can't decide for anyone what their most desirable future will hold, but I assist them in getting clear about it. Getting clear includes helping them understand the dimensions and shapes associated with their decisions. Further, I help them inspire themselves to make it through the process of changing their relationship with the status quo and to become comfortable with uncertainty, to look for ways to leverage paradox, and to actively embrace the power and benefit of change.

As a by-product of the way I construct and conduct my consulting work, I formulated and distilled the JUMP! Innovative Change Model that is the basis for this book. You'll become intimately familiar with the model as you read the book, but before I give you more details about the model, let me describe some of the model's foundational elements. The JUMP! Innovative Change Model is steeped in a variety of disciplines:

- Principles of quantum physics
- Wisdom of ancient philosophy
- Spiritual practices
- Sound leadership models

I don't know what your first reaction might be to seeing the list above. Some of you may feel immediately positive, some of you may be neutral, and some of you might be turned off by one or more items. For those who might be feeling somewhat off-put or negative about certain items on the list, here's your first chance to change your relationship with the status quo. Be willing (right here, right now!) to move beyond your own biases, and stick with me, and I'll explain how all these disciplines come together.

The bottom line is this: In my experience, the combination of quantum principles, ancient philosophy, spiritual practices, and sound leadership yields powerful, meaningful, and sustainable results in transformational change. And, bringing these seemingly disconnected principles together represents another of the central aspects of JUMP!: making unexpected connections. Sometimes when you make unusual or unexpected combinations, the world begins to shift in amazing ways. I see it all the time! So can you.

### Quantum Principles

I would bet that many of you just read the two words "quantum" and "principles" and felt a bit queasy over the prospect of getting a science lesson. Never fear. The next couple of pages describe a "quantum engine" that I use (and that you can use, too) to help make innovative change happen in powerful and rapid ways. However, just like most of us have no clue as to how the internal combustion engine in our car works, we trust that engine to get us to work, to school, and to the beach. If you'd like to learn more about the quantum engine contained in JUMP!, read on. On the other hand, if you'd like to treat the quantum engine like the engine in your car and just know that when you turn it on, it's supposed to work, go ahead and jump to the Ancient Philosophy section on page xix. Then, maybe, after you've read the whole book, come back to this section on quantum principles, read it, and see if you have more interest in knowing how the quantum stuff works.

Over the course of the past few years, I've developed a beginner's understanding of the world of the quantum—the small, weird, unpredictable, and chaotic world of the sub-atomic stuff. I use three quantum concepts in JUMP!: collapsing waves of probabilities, non-locality, and tangled hierarchies. I'll explain more about them using "real words," I promise.

Before I could begin to understand quantum stuff, I needed a refresher on the Newtonian physics I didn't study very well in high school. I was more into music, girls, and other "don't tell Mom about it" activities than I was into science in high school, but as an adult, I found a reason to want to understand physics. It comes from my desire to understand the universe and then to use that as a platform to try and understand people.

You see, the manner in which Newton and Einstein expressed theories of the "big things" in our universe is similar in nature to the historical ways we've looked at the same old approaches we've used with change. We first develop the formulas (processes) to express the answers (outcomes) we anticipate. Then, through an iterative model, we simplify the formulas (refine the processes) so that predictability and accuracy are ensured (continuous improvement, total quality management, etc.).

On the other hand, when you reduce your view of physics to the very small (the sub-atomic realm), you begin to see that the world is a substantially different place. Or maybe I should say "insubstantially" different, because nothing is certain at that level; everything exists in waves of "probability" rather than as predictable "things." Moreover, things are relative. For example, it is possible to have something exist both as a particle and a wave at the same time. Or for something to exist in two places simultaneously. It isn't until we choose to "observe" something at the quantum level that the thing appears. We "collapse probability waves" into things by observing them.

Okay, maybe I've lost about 98 percent of you here, so let me describe this dynamic another way. In the vocabulary of quantum principles, we are the observer in our own lives, and what we "choose" to focus upon eventually becomes our "reality." Our lives are driven by our choices in the same way the observer in quantum physics makes waves collapse into particles. Make sense? This principle is vital to the JUMP! Innovative Change Model. Our choices drive our future. As such, what are you choosing and why? We'll go back to that theme many, many times.

Now, at the risk of making some of you even more confused, I need to share with you the quantum concept of "non-locality." The weird world of the quantum indicates that stuff exists in "fields," where everything is connected and can influence everything else. Some things in the quantum world seem to travel faster than the speed of light and across massive distances. This means it is possible for the same thing to happen in two places at once, without the need to transmit a signal, excrete a chemical, release a hormone, or do anything else typically associated with non-quantum means. We'll look at the principle of non-locality using social media concepts, technology, prayer groups, and such within the book as a means to create "entrainment." Think of entrainment as the dynamic that happens when a school of fish *immediately* organizes and swims in a new direction. It happens so fast and so completely that something non-local has happened. Again, more about this concept later.

Finally, the third quantum principle I'd like to share has to do with "tangled hierarchies." Stick with me on this. The most classic case of a tangled hierarchy is the question, "Which came first, the chicken or the egg?" It's impossible to have one without the other, and the same thing is true about JUMP!. Which came first, the inspiration for the story, or the story itself? The answer is both: The process of writing the story inspired the story. I found myself fully engaged in the JUMP! model even as I was writing about it. I was both inside and outside the experience. I was inside the book by writing it, but I was also influenced substantially by being outside the book as a participant in the JUMP! model. That's a tangled hierarchy.

Yes, it may be hard to understand if this is your first introduction to these principles, but again, the world of the quantum is weird indeed. And, if anyone out there can say with complete assurance that they *totally* understand the world of the quantum, well, they just haven't dug in far enough. The further you go, the stranger it becomes. Rest assured, what I've just shared with you is as far as I'll go into quantum stuff in this book. But even for the skeptics out there, I've come to fully believe that we can make things that seem impossible possible when we expand our thinking to include quantum principles.

As such, these three quantum principles (collapsing waves of probability, non-locality, and tangled hierarchies) are central to implementing the four stages of innovative change within the JUMP! model.

*Ancient Philosophy*

The scientific method depends upon observable proof, but the role of the observer often contaminates the very quantum experiment that's being tested. As a result, because some quantum things exist only in formulas and calculations and therefore cannot be directly observed, only postulated, some scientists consider certain aspects of the quantum to not be provable.

Thus, enter the world of philosophy. If something cannot be proven, is it science or philosophy? This question (and others, too) gave me a compelling reason to delve into the timeless wisdom of history's great philosophers. And I found some fascinating things. There's an often-misquoted statement from George Santayana in his book *Reason in Common Sense, The Life of Reason, Vol.1*. He said, "Those who cannot remember the past are condemned to repeat it." His message, rooted in the philosophies of Socrates, Plato, and Aristotle, has been used repeatedly as a reminder that we need to learn lessons once. We need to learn the lessons as individuals (don't put your hand on the burner of a stove) and as groups (getting and then sharing the answers to a test in advance only diminishes everyone's ability to benefit from the learning).

Without seeing the value in, or learning the lessons from, the past, I'm sure I've personally relearned thousands of lessons that humanity has dealt with billions or trillions of times already. Instead, what if we had a way to tap into the collective wisdom of the entire human race, including everyone who has ever lived? Now there's a question! I guess I was about 35 or so before I realized asking for help was a sign of strength and not an admission of weakness. Before that realization, I was one of the most self-reliant, opinionated, pains-in-the-neck you'd ever want to meet. Then, some life-altering experiences showed me just how much I was missing by not actively seeking help, answers, insights, suggestions, input, and perspectives from others. It was then that I discovered that the human condition has been pretty constant throughout history, regardless of geography, religion, or such. We've been wrestling with the why associated with life forever, and there are great lessons to be learned from philosophy. Maybe, just maybe, one of the most powerful things for us to do is to ask the right questions.

A lesson I've learned after studying the great philosophers is this: If we ask good questions, we'll have the chance to develop great answers. Great questions? Amazing answers. We just need to get very specific, and very clear. Therefore, asking the right questions is another central aspect of the JUMP! Innovative Change Model.

Finally, one of my favorite philosophies has to do with creating a powerful, compelling vision for something. The status quo bias is a formidable foe when it comes to change; however, a compelling vision overcomes even the most powerful deterrent. The story goes like this:

> *Teaching people to build boats by showing them plans and giving them tools and materials like wood, glue, and nails will have limited benefits. To deliver outstanding results in boat building, instead instill within them a love for the sea.*

## Spiritual Practices

Whoa. Here's another challenging topic. First science, then philosophy, and now spiritual stuff? Rest assured. I'm not going to get "religious" on you, and I definitely won't try to convince you of anything one way or the other. Frankly, I've never been much good at organized religion. I've tried. But I just can't seem to get my head around all the rules associated with different approaches to religion. I also tend to see that religion is more often about beliefs than practices. That's been a problem for me, too. As an example, Jesus never said "Worship me" (i.e., believe what I say and be "right" as a result). He did say "Follow me" (follow my example and do what I do). My personal difficulties with organized religion aside, I consider myself to be an extremely spiritual person, and I incorporate spiritual practices into my daily routine. Further, I believe spirituality is a critical element in building powerful, sustainable, and transformational approaches to change.

Why?

All of history's great spiritual leaders have set examples for us for doing the right thing, even when it is hard or inconvenient or requires taking a long-term view of things. As such, the followers of Jesus, Buddha, Abraham, Moses, Muhammad, etc., have been asked to do things in harmony with nature, with other human beings—and with the universe as a whole. After all, Mother Nature is unforgiving. Try to take shortcuts with the environment, with crops, with weather systems, with flood control, or with mining and drilling, and she will deliver harsh punishments. Therefore, if our decisions and actions are grounded in spiritual practices, we are living in connection with nature, with our creator, and with the power of the universe.

On the other hand, it fascinates me to see the number of "get rich quick" or "lose 30 pounds in 30 days" scams out there. The world is full of schemes that make it seem that getting something at someone else's expense or without earning it creates success. In reality, without spiritual grounding, an approach, scheme, process, or method will ultimately fail. Anyway, I am reminded of a simple, yet very quantum piece of scripture in the New Testament:

> *Matthew 7.7 says, "Ask, and it will be given to you; search, and you will find; knock, and the door will be opened for you."*

Roll that around for a moment . . .

Again, if we go back to the role of the observer in quantum physics, where the outcome of the experiment is changed simply by observing it and where everything exists simultaneously in a series of probabilities, what are you asking for? What are you searching for? Which door(s) are you knocking on? Actively deciding what we are asking for means we need to be accountable for the outcomes. This piece of scripture informs many precepts: Be open to new possibilities, be clear about your questions, and be accountable for the outcomes. All three of those things are central to the JUMP! Innovative Change Model as well.

## Sound Leadership

The final principle upon which I have based JUMP! is sound leadership. To describe what I mean here, I've included excerpts from a book I wrote in 2003 entitled *Untangling IT*. It is a book about leadership, written mostly for an audience familiar with the world of information technology, but it has some passages that are directed at everyone. Here's one passage about leadership:

*I believe all human beings are deeply, subconsciously, and passionately searching for leadership. However, leadership is an elusive quality that appears only when it is real. "Realness" takes time, character, risk, objectivity, pain, trial, failure, and love. Real leadership is a rare, brilliant gem that surprises us when we are in its presence.*

*Unfortunately, because real leadership appears infrequently, our thirst goes unabated. We often substitute popularity, money, or a loud voice for leadership. You know what I mean: Whoever is most popular with the boss, has the most money, or speaks the loudest tends to become the leader of the group. We confuse management, direction, or control with leadership—and as such, we expect our managers, directors, and controllers to lead. Many times, this is an unrealizable expectation.*

*We also confuse leadership with power. Power is something given, not exerted. In America, we let our government be in power because we've given them the power, not because they've taken it. Other countries may not follow this same approach at times, but given enough time, even the most "powerful" dictators and extremist "leaders" will eventually fall. All of them have, since the beginning of time.*

*Therefore, do not confuse leadership with the ability to be powerful over someone else. In fact, I look at it in the opposite way. True leaders are the best servants. Another point of distinction here: Do not confuse service with being subservient. These are two different things. Servant leaders look out for the needs of whomever they are serving and provide assisting service. Subservient persons give away their personal power to others and live life as a doormat. Remember, great leaders are great servants first.*

I will refer to real leadership several times in this book. It is a foundational element in preparing a group to make substantial change and in ensuring that the change ultimately becomes manifested. Without real leadership, results are often undesirable, superficial, and short-lived.

I've just described the four disciplines of quantum principles, ancient philosophy, spiritual practices, and sound leadership that form the basis for the JUMP! Innovative Change Model. With that as a backdrop, let's take a quick look at the individual stages of JUMP!. (No worries here; for those of you who need the details, I'll spend considerably more time describing the entire JUMP! model in *The Model* section—pages 183-230.)

*JUMP!—The Four Stages of Innovative Change*

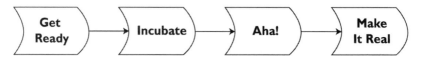

STAGE ONE: Get Ready

Stage One is often the most difficult of the four stages of innovative change in the JUMP! model. And, just to make it more interesting, it is also the most important stage to do well. Why? Good preparation yields great results. Great preparation yields excellent results. Excellent preparation yields transformational results. To begin by using an agricultural metaphor (you'll see it show up here and there throughout the book), getting ready is like preparing the field—a process of removing the stumps, the weeds, the rocks, and other impediments to successful planting, growing, and harvesting. In addition, this stage includes adding the right nutrients, ensuring the correct season for growing, and having the confidence that your preparation will result in a successful outcome.

OUTCOMES: *Overcoming the "status quo bias." Getting your mind right. Opening up to new possibilities. Thinking differently. Breaking down old barriers. Rewriting your internal dialog. Replacing negative energy with positive energy.*

### STAGE TWO: Incubate

Continuing with the farming analogy, the incubation stage is where we trust that the seeds will germinate if we provide the right growing conditions: water, nutrients, sunlight, and pest control. Indeed, we don't really know what happens inside a seed that causes it to germinate: We can observe it, predict it, and tell stories about it—but the detailed process remains mysterious. We have to trust that it will work.

OUTCOMES: *Finding "the zone." Allowing what wants to happen. Inviting uncertainty. Removing your ego from the situation. Nurturing the climate for creativity.*

### STAGE THREE: Aha!

Here's where the planting and harvesting comparison falls down a bit. Nature does occasionally create some Aha! moments. For example, some scientists believe that some significant shifts in evolution are not represented by corresponding fossil records. They suggest the reason we can't find the fossils is because the fossils don't exist! Now, I don't know about this notion myself; I'm not a scientist, nor am I willing to enter into a debate about evolution, creationism, or intelligent design. But all of us have experienced some type of Aha! in our lives when we move right over the linear, step-by-step learning process. These moments might come in a dream, or they might come when we're walking the dog or taking a shower, but for the vast majority of us, Aha! moments are very real indeed.

OUTCOMES: *Leaps in consciousness. Strokes of insight. Moments of genius. Unexpected connections. Answers seeming to come from thin air.*

STAGE FOUR: Make It Real

We can return effortlessly to the agricultural metaphor here. Nature's motivation to create, to make things real, is incessant. We as a species are biologically motivated to go forth and multiply, as are all other living things. Even the lowly dandelion is compelled to create, to implement. Life is a powerful force. It's just when our human frailties betray our innate tendencies to create do we fail to live in harmony with nature's plan and we become stuck in the status quo.

Moving out of the status quo, getting in front of the pace and degree of change curve—all those things eventually require us to act. Preparing, incubating, and collecting Aha! moments are irrelevant if we don't do something with them. The process of action requires both courage and passion. However, before we just run with each Aha! moment as it comes, the first thing we need to do in the Make It Real stage is to evaluate the best fit for a potential idea. Why? Sometimes uninspired Aha! moments masquerade as powerful Aha! experiences. Having courage and passion won't help a bad idea turn into a good idea.

OUTCOMES: *Courageously making decisions. Choosing the most appropriate "right" answers. Developing unqualified commitment to ongoing improvements. Demonstrating unequivocal expectations for success.*

## *JUMP!—The Book*

Okay, we're done with the background. Now it's time for me to give you an overview of how I have incorporated quantum principles, ancient philosophy, spiritual practices, and sound leadership into the four stages of innovative change. I knew from the start that I'd need two pieces of the book to satisfy both sides of my own personality. Part of me wanted to understand JUMP! at an emotional level, and I found I needed a story to help me with that. Then the "Mr. Spock" side of me needed to see JUMP! described as a process. Therefore, there are two parts in JUMP!: a fable and a model.

- The fable is just that—a fictional account using fictional characters designed to tell a story that has a point of view. Some books of this kind use case studies, but I decided to use a fictional story because my clients tend to get miffed if I share the details of their specific situations! So, I created a fictional situation based upon work I do as a change coach.

- The model is a process-oriented depiction of the JUMP! model I use in my consulting practice. Those of you who like process maps and flowcharts will love it!

## More About the Fable

The fable is a story about the Falcon Foundation for Families, a fictitious non-profit organization headquartered in Loveland, Colorado, a city of about 65,000 approximately an hour north of Denver. The founder, Franklin Falcon (whose given name of Ferencz Solyom was changed by his parents after they moved to America when he was a boy), is the son of Hungarian immigrants.

After building a lucrative career as a civil engineer, he leveraged much of his personal fortune in an effort to support other immigrant families who had come to America. He felt extraordinarily fortunate and blessed by the opportunities offered to him and his family in America, and he wanted to provide a mechanism to support other families in finding and developing similar opportunities.

Franklin is a private, passionate man who believes in the best in others but can't always tell who has his best interests in mind. He also wields tremendous personal power and can make many around him feel intimidated. His optimism, strength of personality, vision, and commitment are all qualities upon which he capitalized in creating his foundation, which historically has a powerful track record in delivering exemplary benefits to countless worthy recipients.

However, Franklin's strengths are also his weaknesses. After four decades of serving his "kids" (the term of endearment he uses to describe all of the families his foundation has served—he never liked the word "client"; it sounded too clinical, too far removed), his foundation was faltering, teetering on the brink of potential failure. Trusting the wrong people, not inviting feedback, doing things that were not within his core strengths, and substituting "outcome" for "opportunity" caused the Falcon Foundation to find itself in crisis.

The fable continues with the steps, decisions, insights, and heavy lifting needed to not only save the foundation but to move it forward in new, innovative, and sustainable ways. Ultimately, Franklin Falcon and his team of servant leaders amaze themselves with what they are able to accomplish in a matter of just a few days.

## More About the Model

> W. Edward Deming: *"If you can't describe what you're doing as a process, you don't know what you're doing."*

I smile when I think of Ed Deming's statement when I apply it to things like decision-making in the US Congress, or budget planning in church committee meetings, or how people drive, or even how strategic planning is accomplished within most organizations. I ask myself frequently as I watch these things unfold, "What's the process they're using to describe what they're doing?" Often it's mystifying, and unfortunately, too many individuals, groups, and organizations are not able to describe what they're doing as a process—and therefore, it's obvious they don't know what they're doing.

Consequently, I needed to include an overview of the JUMP! model "in process form" for you so you can follow the steps that Franklin Falcon and his leadership team use to ultimately "Wright" their ship (this apparent misspelling will make sense later). I purposely resisted the idea of having one of the characters act as a consultant leading the Falcon Foundation through the JUMP! Innovative Change Model. While I'm a big believer in using consultants to assist individuals, groups, and organizations with innovative change, I felt it would make for a better story if the characters in the fable experienced "the model" together—growing, exploring, and discovering the power of the process. I suppose you'll be the judge of whether my decision was a good one or not!

The model is straightforward, and I have not attempted to put all the details into this book. Why? The model is in a state of constant evolution: I "eat my own dog food" here. In other words, I'm constantly innovating and changing, all with the result of improving the model. Therefore, in the model section, I reference the "Our JUMP!" community website (see page 249 for more information), where more details about the model are available and where you can download templates, process maps, and other tools for your own use. There's also a section where others continue to share their own "JUMP! Stories." It's left-brained heaven!

## Let's JUMP!

As you read the story of the Falcon Foundation for Families and come to understand the four stages of innovative change, I hope you are inspired and moved and have the conviction to do what it takes to get ahead and then stay ahead of the curve. I also hope you build a new and improved relationship with the status quo!

I find myself living (mostly) in a constant state of JUMP!, and I'm convinced the same can be true for you, too. With regular practice, it is possible for you to be perpetually preparing and incubating. You'll also find Aha! moments will become far more numerous, giving you many opportunities to implement powerful change.

With that, let's JUMP!

# STAGE ONE:
# GET READY

"If we listened to our intellect,
we'd never have a love affair.
We'd never have a friendship.
We'd never go into business,
because we'd be cynical.

Well, that's nonsense.

You've got to jump off cliffs all the time
and build your wings on the way down."

—*Ray Bradbury*

# FRANKLIN FALCON

## Monday: About 8:30 A.M. MST

### *(Loveland, Colorado)*

Week 1

| SUN | MON | TUE | WED | THU | FRI | SAT |
|-----|-----|-----|-----|-----|-----|-----|
|     | 8:30 A.M. MST |  |  |  |  |  |

Franklin Falcon sat with his head in his hands, Angela Liu's application on the top of the pile in front of him. How could things have turned ugly so quickly? It was as if he had somehow entered into someone else's life—and his own life had evaporated spontaneously. Normally a confident man, Franklin was just barely functioning as the news from within his organization continued to worsen. He'd seen tough times before, but through hard work, determination, and self-reliance, he'd developed a massive list of past successes and a long list of A players in the world as former clients.

But this was different than anything he'd experienced before. Far different.

"Their expectations are unreasonable," he said in a strained whisper to no one in particular. He'd begun talking to himself as he sat at his desk, somehow expecting a solution to form from the thoughts floating above him. Minutes passed. When his hoped-for answer didn't appear, he shouted, "They just aren't playing by the rules!" The volume and ferocity of his last statement surprised even him—as if a great balloon had been punctured, and the sudden release of air pressure created a far louder-than-expected explosion. His assistant of nearly 11 years, Behrokh Aghassi (most people called her Betty), cautiously opened his door and peered in.

"Is there anything I can do for you, Mr. Falcon?" she asked, hoping to hear his normal, optimistic answer of "Thank you, Betty. All will be well."

She'd heard that statement from him hundreds of times: *All will be well.*

"Betty, please clear my calendar for today and for tomorrow morning. I need some time to think; Jo and I are going to the cabin."

Betty blushed slightly as she realized she'd been staring open-mouthed at Franklin's response. "Oh, yes, certainly, Mr. Falcon. Right away." She hurried to her desk, trying to think of a plausible story she could use to express Mr. Falcon's regrets at canceling his appointments. She was not having much luck.

"$80 million . . . might as well be $80 trillion. There's no way we can find that much money in less than a month," Franklin muttered to himself as he dialed Jo's cell phone. He needed her counsel. Through the 55 years they'd been married, she was the only person to whom he confided everything.

Franklin Falcon, born Ferencz Solyom in 1935, had an early life full of change and uncertainty. His family emigrated from their native Hungary to Ohio in the late 1930s to escape the growing tyranny of the Nazi empire. Even though his father, Henrik, was a skilled carpenter and his mother, Ibolya, was a highly competent administrator in their homeland, the language and cultural barriers the Solyom family encountered in their adopted home forced Franklin's parents to work at menial jobs for low wages for many years. However, because they were committed to succeeding, they were willing to take some extreme measures to do so. Within the first year, his parents made the difficult decision to change their family name of "Solyom" to the English translation of "Falcon" and to translate all of their given names as well. Thus, Franklin's parents became Henry and Violet Falcon, and their children, Ferencz and Karola, became Franklin and Caroline.

Even in the face of their crushing financial struggles as a family, Franklin thrived in America and was the first member of his family to complete a college education. He discovered he had a passion and aptitude for engineering, and his high school teachers encouraged him to apply for several scholarships. He eventually received a full scholarship in civil engineering from Colorado State University in Fort Collins. Upon graduation, he rose rapidly among his peers in civil engineering, working for a large Midwestern engineering and construction company designing innovations to public infrastructure. Eventually, he specialized in compact, affordable water treatment systems, ultimately receiving a patent on a ground-breaking design to eliminate bacterial contamination (*E. coli*, Salmonella, etc.) from entering the water supply in small, rural water treatment systems. He became a mini-celebrity in the world of water treatment and found himself earning princely sums of money as a result.

Ferencz Solyom was the embodiment of success in the American Dream sort of way. Through a combination of hard work, self-reliance, determination, along with some luck, some help, and a good idea, he found himself labeled a success. But, living as Franklin Falcon, he also never forgot his roots. After witnessing the challenges his parents had overcome and leveraging the strong sense of optimism and work ethic their example set for him, he knew success—on its own—was a hollow ambition and that true significance in life came from enabling others to reach their dreams. Even as a young man just starting in his career, he became driven to provide opportunities to other immigrant families. He became expert at building relationships, raising money, encouraging commitment, and inspiring success in others.

During his undergraduate college career, he'd fallen in love with the Front Range of Colorado, so he moved back to Loveland—a small city of about 65,000 located between Denver and Fort Collins—to create his foundation, the Falcon Foundation for Families. Loveland was a perfect spot to find highly educated, motivated, and altruistic staff members; it was close enough to Denver International Airport (DIA) to allow travel to or from most anywhere; and the weather was a vast improvement over what he'd experienced in his native Hungary and in Cincinnati where he'd grown up. Franklin soon became addicted to the 300+ sunny days each year in Loveland.

But . . . today . . . he found himself lost and confused. Maybe some time with Jo at their cabin would make the future seem brighter. Maybe.

# Ernesto Martinez

Monday: About 11:00 A.M. CST

*(Chicago)*

Week 1

| SUN | MON | TUE | WED | THU | FRI | SAT |
|-----|-----|-----|-----|-----|-----|-----|
|     | 11:00 A.M. CST |     |     |     |     |     |

He'd made up his mind. The speculation from the bloggers, the tone of the emails and Facebook conversations involving other recipients of Falcon's generosity, and the general chatter in the world pushed him to action. Ernesto had to go see Mr. Falcon. Now.

"Falcon Foundation a House of Cards—Here Comes a Tornado" read one headline. Another suggested, "Franklin Falcon Building a Catastrophic Failure?" Each of the stories was long on speculation and nearly devoid of specifics. No surprise there. Franklin Falcon was one of the most private individuals in the world, someone who shared few details about his foundation or his personal life. But the guessing game was starting to make more sense, and the facts that were surfacing, if indeed they were facts, were troubling. The Falcon Foundation appeared to be in major financial distress and was potentially at risk of defaulting on millions of dollars—maybe tens of millions—of payments coming due. Families would be devastated as a result, and Franklin's reputation would forever be stained.

Franklin based his Falcon Foundation for Families on his core belief that everyone—no matter where they came from—deserved an equal opportunity to succeed. Franklin didn't believe in equal outcomes. No, he was passionate about equal opportunities. Consequently, rather than offering handouts, he focused on acquiring dignity through work and opportunity through vision. Franklin transformed his foundation's core beliefs into mandates: Overcome cultural and language barriers; provide decent housing, affordable health care, and quality education; and leverage the sense of optimism and hope embodied by those seeking a better life. After more than four decades of exemplary support to motivated and successful families, everything seemed poised to implode.

Ernesto found he still had the foundation's phone number committed to memory. Although he hadn't used it in a dozen years or so, in college he'd used it on a near-monthly basis. He dialed the familiar number.

"Good Morning, Falcon Foundation for Families, developing the future leaders of tomorrow, how may I direct your call?"

"Mr. Falcon's assistant, please," he said to the business-like receptionist.

"One moment."

As Ernesto waited on hold, the recorded voice of Franklin Falcon gently spoke to him about the responsibilities and opportunities offered to Falcon's Families.

". . . call or write for more information. The Falcon Foundation for Families—helping . . ."

"Betty Aghassi. How may I help you?" Even though she'd been in America for more than 20 years, her voice still bore traces of her Iranian heritage—including the guttural "gh" she used when saying her name. Her family had escaped the revolution and war that tore her country apart in the late 1980s. Once she answered, he discovered he'd been holding his breath for several seconds, as an audible sigh is what greeted her from Ernesto's end.

"Hello?"

"Oh, sorry," he stammered. The stress he was feeling was acute. Ernesto just didn't know what he'd find when he got to Falcon.

"Ms. Aghassi, my name is Ernesto Martinez. I don't think we've met before—my family is a Falcon Family—we were selected when I was about 10 years old, I think."

"Ernesto—oh, my. Yes, I know your name, but I'm not sure we've met either. I do know about your accident; we had the newspaper clippings on the board here for a couple of years. My goodness, you were lucky to have been found—and in very good health, too, if I remember correctly. What can I do for you?"

The accident. A quick flashback to Iceland and the disastrous snowmobiling trip he'd taken on the Langjökull Glacier. The second largest glacier in Iceland was notorious for rapid and potentially dangerous weather changes, and the snowmobiling group he was part of had become engulfed in a freak blizzard. The group lost their leader (who had the only GPS in the group) when he apparently fell into a deep fissure. Only three of the total of nine members survived to be rescued two days later. Ernesto was one of the lucky ones.

"I'm planning a trip to Colorado within the next week or so, and I want to drop in and spend some time with Mr. Falcon if he's going to be in town."

Ernesto was in a good position at work to take a few days off. He had no short-term client-related commitments, and he could do what he needed to do from anywhere. In fact, much of his work as a quantum mechanics consultant could be done in cyberspace. He often wondered how people survived for so many centuries without the Internet.

"Ernesto, I'm sure he'd love to see you. Having one of our kids visit is a highlight for all of us. What about Thursday? He's available for lunch and maybe for a bit during the early afternoon, too. He's planning a family vacation in Hawaii next week and will be gone for about three weeks. So it's Thursday or about a month from now. Is that . . ."

"Perfect," Ernesto replied just a little too quickly. He caught himself, relaxed, and said, "I'll be there before noon, and I'll plan to take him to lunch. Is there a restaurant he prefers?"

"He loves the Black Steer—it's just a short walk from here. Ernesto, I'll put you down in his calendar and make the reservations for lunch. If there's any problem from your end, please call and let me know."

"Thank you." He hung up.

Ernesto wasn't sure he felt much better about things, but at least he'd started taking action. Movement felt positive. It reminded him of one of the lessons he'd re-learned in Iceland: "Nothing changes until something changes." Memories surrounding that statement suddenly came flooding back to him—Mr. Strickland, physics class, JFK High School. Ernesto didn't appreciate Mr. Strickland's wisdom as a 17-year-old junior; in fact, he thought his teacher was downright weird. But, as Ernesto found his groove in college, he became captivated by the world of science, and he decided to make a career out of trying to understand how the universe fits together.

One of his clearest memories of Mr. Strickland was of him saying, *"It might sound obvious, but without a first step toward something else, energy remains in a state of equilibrium. The forces of inertia are at play (an object at rest tends to stay at rest), and nothing happens."* No-thing happens. Ernesto knew his decision to do something about what he was feeling about the Falcon Foundation was by itself the first step in transformation.

Ernesto checked the web for the best price on flights from Chicago to Denver. After all, Thursday was just three days from now.

# Thinking Too Much

Tuesday: About 8:00 A.M. MST

*(Red Feather Lakes Road, Colorado)*

Week 1

| SUN | MON | TUE | WED | THU | FRI | SAT |
|-----|-----|-----|-----|-----|-----|-----|
|     |     | 8:00 A.M. MST |     |     |     |     |

The previous afternoon, Franklin and Jo had driven to their cabin near Red Feather Lakes in comfortable silence. Franklin and Jo had married while they were still in college and had grown up, and grown, together. Jo Falcon was extraordinarily compassionate, but she had a bit of Winston Churchill in her. Saying she could be direct—well, that was clearly an understatement. However, Franklin, who tended to brood, valued her forthrightness and decisiveness.

Franklin needed her help, especially with the deciding part. He was doing an excellent job on his own with the brooding part.

They'd owned the cabin for more than 30 years and enjoyed spending as much time there as they could, that is, when their two sons and their families weren't using it. Their grandchildren especially loved the place, but their school schedules allowed only weekend use this time of year. Upon their arrival, the cabin had been ready for Franklin and Jo, immaculate and quiet. Perfect.

They were avid cross-country skiers, and before dinner last night, they had taken Maggie on a five-mile trek. Maggie was a loyal companion, part Australian Shepherd and part Great Pyrenees. She was a master at making sure things were under control, but in a calm, friendly, canine sort of way.

Franklin appreciated her organizing instincts, but he long ago had wished Maggie knew more about the stock market, hiring practices, and public relations. She listened well, but her advice was lacking in details.

At dinner Franklin said, "I'm not sure what to do. I could really use . . ."

Jo cut in, "Are you ready to admit yet that the foundation is in trouble? If you're not, there's nothing to discuss." She paused. "We don't have enough money to pay our bills, and this is in large part due to some of your decisions, right?"

He blinked once, then twice.

"Jo, you always know how to get right to things . . ." His voice trailed to a whisper, his eyes filling with tears. There. It was out in the open. This was the central issue, and he knew it. He'd just had trouble admitting it. "Yes. I realize the foundation finds itself in a difficult spot, and I'm thinking about some steps we can take to get things turned around." He looked absently out the picture window. Tonight he wasn't seeing the view that usually inspired him.

Jo reached for his hand and squeezed. "You know, my father always told me, if you find yourself in a hole, stop digging!" Jo was very fond of simple, straightforward philosophy.

Stop digging. The words echoed in Franklin's brain as he swirled the wine in his glass.

A pause. She caught herself. "I'm sorry. I know how hard you work, how much of yourself you give to others every day. But you are only one person. How can you expect to have all the answers?"

He glanced up at her, caught her eye ever so briefly, and returned his gaze to his empty plate. Speaking to the china, he said, "Yes—again, you're right."

"Freddie, maybe it's time to look at things differently. Maybe it's time to share more details with more members of your executive team. They're a pretty talented bunch, no? And what about the board? I know you hate those meetings, but maybe you could trust them enough to involve them, too." She was the only person on earth now who called him Freddie—it was the name his mother had called him—a nickname coming from his given name of Ferencz. Hearing the name "Freddie" always had a way of anchoring him, of reminding him that he has always been loved.

His mind retreated inwards. "Share more details? Hmm . . . I'll have to give it some thought," he promised Jo, although he really didn't know what to do first.

She smiled. "There you go—thinking again!" Her voice was teasing, but her message was direct.

They'd turned in early, and much to Franklin's surprise, he'd slept soundly. But the morning arrived without new insights. They'd made and enjoyed a breakfast of fresh fruit and whole grain cereal, and now they were in the process of doing the dishes as Maggie walked into the kitchen.

"Answers. I need answers," Franklin implored the big white dog as he reached to scratch Maggie behind the ears. Her tail wagged enthusiastically, but she remained mute.

Jo was packing the remaining food as Franklin reached for his phone. "Betty—good morning! Yes, yes, we had a great evening. The hummus was delightful; thank you for thinking of it. . . . Oh, yes, Jo's great. We're headed back to Loveland in about 35 minutes or so, and I should be in the office by noon. . . . Okay, I'll drive carefully. No, I hadn't heard about the weather forecast. Anyway, thank you, Betty!"

Once the kitchen was clean, he took out the well-worn checklist he'd created more than 20 years ago to ensure everything was "just so" after cabin visits. He ran over the list at least twice each time they left, and today was no different.

"Come on, Freddie, we need to get going." She shook her head and walked up to him and hugged him. "You know, I bet you never colored outside the lines when you were a kid," she kidded him.

"Huh . . . I'm sorry, Jo. I'm almost done. What was it you said?"

"Never mind. Come on, Maggie; let's go load up the car!" Jo opened the door, and Maggie responded by rushing out to the silver SUV and whining impatiently to be let into the backseat.

As he finished the second pass on the checklist, Franklin's subconscious spoke, "God, I really miss Marty. I know he'd have the right answers."

Franklin set the alarm, closed and locked the cabin door, and tossed his bag into the back of their car. He climbed in, started the engine, and switched on the wipers to clear the accumulating drizzle from the windshield. It appeared the weather forecasters were right: The early bands of a potentially large weather system would be coming over the foothills today. Colorado was notorious for blizzards in March, and the storm models suggested a sizable storm could be on the way.

He certainly felt as if a storm was building.

# THE MUCKRAKER

Wednesday: About 10:00 A.M. EST

*(New York City)*

**Week 1**

| SUN | MON | TUE | WED | THU | FRI | SAT |
|-----|-----|-----|-----|-----|-----|-----|
|     |     |     | 10:00 A.M. EST |     |     |     |

"Do we have any other families lined up? Preferably some with kids who have big eyes—and with something special in their story? Terminally ill parents would be a great angle."

She was running through her mental list of story preparation notes, towing her entourage of junior staff hangers-on in her wake. Marissa Grant, the host of *The Grant Report*, a nationally-syndicated cable "news" show, was fully into her attack mode, sensing that the story at Falcon was far bigger than even she could imagine, and she had a powerful imagination.

A particularly intense member of the entourage blurted enthusiastically, "Let's see . . . yes! There's Angela Liu, a high school senior from Eden Prairie, Minnesota. Falcon Family for nine years now. Beautiful girl! She'll look great on camera. Daughter of Liu Tao and Liu Ping who emigrated from the Jiangxi region in China when Angela was just a baby. Father diagnosed with inoperable brain cancer a few months back. Mother had to quit working to care for him. No health insurance; family is basically surviving on handouts and government assistance."

"Jiangxi. Isn't that where that earthquake happened—lots of kids killed while in school—back in 2004 or 2005? Fantastic images. Big story."

Before anyone on her team could answer her, she was on to the next detail.

"Brain cancer. Inoperable. Big debts. I'm guessing they need the health benefits from Falcon, and Angela's status gives her a virtual guarantee of six-figure employment opportunities when she graduates. They'll be suffering pretty badly if Falcon fails, won't they?"

Again, another rhetorical question.

"Get her story. Now! If it's everything I think it might be, I'd like to go meet her—with a full production crew, of course."

# ANGELA LIU

## Wednesday: 11:50 P.M. CST

### *(Eden Prairie, Minnesota)*

**Week 1**

| SUN | MON | TUE | WED | THU | FRI | SAT |
|-----|-----|-----|-----|-----|-----|-----|
|     |     |     | 11:50 P.M. CST |     |     |     |

The call from the producer at *The Grant Report* had shaken her. Her mind was cycling, repeating the producer's words over and over: "Did you know the Falcon Foundation is about to fail? What are your family's plans? What are your family's plans? What are your family's plans?"

Angela's family had been selected as a Falcon Family when she was nine. Since then, she'd spent years studying, sacrificing, and serving and had earned enough points within the Falcon measurement system to ensure complete funding for all her college-related expenses. In addition, through community service and other volunteer work she and her family were committed to doing, Falcon had been providing other benefits to her family, most especially health care for her father.

She had been accepted to study civil engineering at Colorado School of Mines in Golden beginning in the fall semester, and everything appeared to be falling into place for her. But the rumors about the Falcon Foundation were troubling at best. The blogs were full of people sniping about the future of the foundation. Add the fact that Marissa Grant herself was planning to come interview Angela, and that clinched things for Angela. The foundation was indeed in trouble.

"Angela . . . it's after midnight. It's time to log off and get some sleep," came the quietly compassionate voice of Angela's mother. "Worrying about it won't help."

"I know. I'm just looking at my dorm options in Golden." Truth was, Angela was looking for any shred of positive news she might find online about the foundation. "I'll turn the light out soon."

Her mother retreated from the door, paused to brush away a tear, and walked slowly down the hall. Mrs. Liu wasn't particularly good at following her own advice about not worrying. "This is so unfair!" she muttered, a little more loudly than she intended. "Nine years of work—of planning, of dreaming. For what?"

"Mom? Are you okay?" Angela queried through her door.

"Yes, I'm fine. I just stepped on the cat," her mother lied.

Angela fretted for a few more minutes, read a couple more posts coming from members of other Falcon Families, and decided her mother was right. Worrying wasn't going to change anything. However, her intuition was telling her that she was going to have to make substantially different plans for her college career.

# The Foundation Is Cracking

Thursday: Exactly 9:00 A.M. MST

*(Falcon Boardroom, Loveland)*

Week 1

| SUN | MON | TUE | WED | THU | FRI | SAT |
|-----|-----|-----|-----|-----|-----|-----|
|     |     |     |     | 9:00 A.M. MST |     |     |

Jennifer Boyle was leading Falcon's weekly senior staff meeting, which took place every Thursday morning from 9 A.M. to 11 A.M.—like clockwork. They'd had the same agenda for years, and almost everyone felt comfortable in the routine. Elaine and Nicole, the two newest members of the executive team, believed most of the staff meeting time was so unproductive that watching the fish swim in the lobby tank would be more interesting and beneficial.

However, they would never think to challenge "Mr. Falcon," so they instead endured the weekly meetings with as sincere a smile as they could muster. Everyone loved Franklin, but he could be the most exasperating person at times.

"Mr. Falcon, we're expecting Ernesto Martinez today," reported Jennifer. The fact she still referred to him as "Mr. Falcon" was indicative of his old-fashioned adherence to the formalities of the past. "He should be here just about the time our meeting is wrapping up."

Jennifer's voice was tired, yet it contained a trace of nostalgic expectation. She had been on staff at Falcon for more than 20 years, beginning her career as a case manager and helping those who had been selected as Falcon Families to continue to be successful in their lives, in their studies, in their growth as a family, and in their service to others. One of her cases included

Ernesto Martinez's family, who had emigrated from Oaxaca, Mexico, where their ancestors had spent centuries scraping together simple, dignified lives.

Jennifer reflected for a moment upon Ernesto, a quiet, "scary-smart" young man with a huge capacity to serve others. Ernesto had a knack for understanding the big picture while at the same time seeing how the tiny pieces of things fit together. He'd excelled at MIT in theoretical physics and was viewed as an international expert in his field of study. Jennifer wasn't sure about the word "quantum," but Ernesto certainly seemed to have a strong handle on what it entailed.

For just a moment, Jennifer wished she'd never left the ranks of case managers, where the real work of Falcon was done. She was now executive director of the foundation and one of Franklin's most trusted advisors. She felt the debilitating weight of the responsibilities she had—now more than ever.

"That's marvelous!" Franklin gushed. "It's always a treat for us to have the chance to see one of our kids again."

Franklin always referred to members of Falcon Families as kids. Parents, children, it mattered not to him; they were still "his kids." The smiles around the table showed that everyone agreed. It truly was one of their joys as a leadership team to have one of Falcon's kids visit. They were proud of their kids and were not afraid to express it.

"And then . . . tomorrow. We're expecting a 'visit' by *The Grant Report*, and Marissa Grant has requested to interview you, Mr. Falcon." Just the mention of the name caused the air to be sucked out of the room. No sound. No movement, other than eyes darting from one person to another along the long, rectangular, Formica-topped conference table. Marissa Grant? Oh, my. She never took the time to tell the whole story; instead, she'd made a name for herself by developing sensational headlines based upon sketchy facts and then adding graphic images that captivated audiences.

If Marissa Grant was on the trail of the developing story at the foundation, the executive team's efforts to keep a lid on things weren't working. Marissa was a disrespectful, ego-driven muckraker. Nothing good could come from meeting with her.

Breaking the silence, Franklin spoke to everyone, "We need to remember our agreement here—to keep the content of our conversations confidential. And let's not forget our proud history. Our reputation is spotless, and our track record of success is unblemished. We've weathered some significant storms in the past, and no doubt we'll make it through this one as well."

The team exchanged looks—skepticism, fear, defeat, paranoia; virtually every negative emotion was on full display. Hope? Not present. Franklin had just the day before shared the full dimension of the spot in which the foundation found itself. Before that, only three people knew the details: the chief financial officer, Jo, and himself.

While the executive team now understood the size and scope of the problem, they still had difficulty coming to grips with how it all happened. Because of some bad decisions, incredibly bad timing on a couple of events, and the actions of a small number of unscrupulous individuals, the rug had been pulled out from under Falcon's funding. Throw into the mix one of the most significant financial meltdowns in history, and disaster seemed imminent. Unemployment was skyrocketing, home foreclosures were commonplace, and the government's ability to serve was severely hampered by far lower-than-expected tax revenue.

The needs of their kids were accelerating at unprecedented rates, and the sources of funds were evaporating like free beer at a fraternity mixer. Falcon was hemorrhaging cash and found itself about 72 hours away from defaulting on its quarterly obligations to health care providers, colleges and universities, and the myriad other service providers subsidized by Falcon. Never in their history had they missed a payment. Making matters worse, Franklin (on his own) had decided to mortgage most of their hard assets in an attempt to keep the cash flowing.

Their $80 million shortfall in funding was a massive hole. The implications were even more significant: Not only would Franklin's personal reputation be destroyed, the foundation was likely to fail—and the future for hundreds of families would be put into peril.

The timing of Marrisa's visit couldn't have been worse if she'd planned it, which, of course, she had. Exquisitely.

"Perfect," thought Jennifer.

Sure enough, as had happened every Thursday for years, at exactly 11 A.M. Franklin asked Jennifer to adjourn the weekly staff meeting. The team closed their binders and moved their chairs back. But just as everyone was standing, it was as if he'd tasered the entire executive team because they were stunned by what they heard.

"Please be back here no later than 1:30 P.M. I'd like for you to meet Ernesto Martinez and to hear about his survival journey from him directly. Maybe he's got a pearl or two of wisdom to share with us. Clear your calendars for the afternoon. Nothing is more important than this. Thank you."

Franklin never called spontaneous executive meetings. Ever. Unless ideas had been suggested at least 72 hours in advance, had gone through a rigorous "agenda planning session," had been vetted thoroughly, and then placed on everyone's calendar at least a day ahead, the items just weren't discussed. He was a firm believer in preparation and process.

An extemporaneous meeting? Maybe some things were changing.

# New Members

## Thursday: About 11:50 A.M. MST

### *(Falcon Offices, Loveland)*

| Week I | | | | | | |
|---|---|---|---|---|---|---|
| SUN | MON | TUE | WED | THU | FRI | SAT |
| | | | | *11:50 A.M. MST* | | |

Franklin's secrecy during the past few weeks about their funding crisis meant that by the time the executives heard the details, all they could do was react—and hope if they dared. They were smart. They were dedicated. And they were resourceful. But not one of them could perform magic.

Franklin, for all of his strengths, had one significant flaw. As much as he reinforced the notion that Falcon Families needed to be accountable as they worked to leverage the benefits they received from the foundation, he lived much of his own life as if it were an old-time western movie, where everything turned out okay in the last reel. Unfortunately, "real life" wasn't "reel life." Real life required real solutions.

For all of their talking, hand wringing, and mental gymnastics, the group had failed to find workable solutions. Most distressing of all, trust was quickly eroding within the executive team, something that Franklin worried about most of all. He knew the growing lack of belief in each other made the prospects of success all the dimmer.

Joining Jennifer and Franklin on the executive team were Greg Sullivan, Falcon's CFO, a 12-year veteran of Falcon; Elaine Gustavson, the VP of human resources, a new member with about 18 months of tenure at Falcon; Terrence Kennedy, the VP of client services, a member of a Falcon Family (one of the kids) and a seven-year staff member at Falcon; and Nicole Fargas, the VP of development, another new member of the team—brought in only four months ago with HIGH expectations to create results, and fast.

No one was feeling the pinch more than Nicole, because in the language of non-profits, the term "development" has a different meaning than, say, in a construction company. Development for a non-profit is all about donations, planned giving, annuities, trusts—basically all the activities needed to keep the organization supplied with sufficient, sustainable funding.

In her role as VP of development, Nicole Fargas was the one who was ultimately responsible for ensuring uninterrupted cash flow. Only in her late twenties, the label "prodigy" had been placed on her as a result of her success in development for other non-profits. She was raised in a tough Philadelphia neighborhood—where survival was possible only if you were strong and resilient.

While the results of her efforts were still in question, Nicole's resolve was not. Described as the ultimate optimist, she had a way of finding the positives in all but the most hopeless situations. Even then, she'd still drag out a cliché, or a quote from a famous person, or even more often a scene from a children's book or movie, and would use it to tell an uplifting story designed to make the situation more hope-filled.

Elaine Gustavson, the next-newest member of the executive team, was an HR professional with nearly 30 years of experience. Her Midwestern upbringing had instilled a strong work ethic, a belief in people, and a passion for a long-term vision. She had been hopeful that today's staff meeting would be different from the others she'd endured during the past 18 months since she'd joined Falcon. She'd most recently worked for another non-profit where decisions came quickly, technology was leveraged to support actions, and the organization moved with urgency. Elaine had struggled with her decision to leave her previous employer, but ultimately chose to join the foundation because she believed in its mission.

She'd been personally recruited by Franklin with the intention of instilling a new culture—one of flexibility, decisiveness, and confidence. In the past year and a half, she'd come to realize just how impossible those goals were. Like many executives for whom she'd previously worked, Franklin Falcon knew what he wanted. He claimed to want to fill in some of his blind spots, but his actions betrayed his stated desires. He was fully engaged by his comfort zone and found few opportunities to truly take a different path.

Elaine's growing frustration with Franklin's inaction and secrecy was wearing on her. She had been seeing the all-too-familiar signs of organizational failure everywhere around her and was seriously beginning to consider updating her resume. She'd more than once in the past few weeks spent time on the Internet job sites, and she had become more than casually interested in a couple of positions. She loved Colorado and was quite fond of Mr. Falcon, but she'd been beaten down too many times in the past when HR was asked to "wave their magic wands" and fix organizational catastrophes caused by poor leadership decisions.

Even though Elaine and Nicole came from different backgrounds, they had become friends and allies; they shared similar beliefs about what "could and should" be happening and frustrations about what was actually going on. Specifically, today they had believed the two new business additions to the agenda, Ernesto Martinez's and Marissa Grant's visits, should have dominated the morning's conversation. However, even with those major issues looming, the meeting crawled along before they finally got to discussing new business. By this time, it was already after 10 A.M., meaning they had less than an hour to discuss Ernesto's and Marissa's visits because Jennifer would absolutely, positively end the meeting at 11 A.M. sharp.

Bizarre! Nicole and Elaine felt like time was standing still, and the actions by the rest of the executive team indicated they thought that by remaining connected to their "normal" routine, things might improve through osmosis or something. In reality, Nicole and Elaine believed the full effects of the Falcon Foundation ceasing to exist might take a few years to completely manifest, but the damage to individual families, to their kids, would be profound and immediate. The two women believed the other members of Falcon's leadership team weren't acting in a manner consistent with the crisis in which they found themselves. How could they sit and discuss the equivalent of "which flowers should we plant this spring" when there was a PR-related tsunami looming?

Then Mr. Falcon had shocked them by calling a meeting at 1:30 P.M. After busily working to rearrange their afternoon calendars, the two women were leaving the building to eat lunch together (a habit they'd taken up recently) when they noticed a well-dressed man of about 35 walking slowly into the reception area while brushing the snow off his jacket.

"That's Ernesto Martinez?" Elaine wondered as she and Nicole stepped out into the growing snowstorm. He looked pretty ordinary to her. Nicole thought he was sort of cute, in a bookish kind of way.

# The Survivor Arrives

Thursday: About 11:50 A.M. MST

*(Falcon Offices, Loveland)*

**Week 1**

| SUN | MON | TUE | WED | THU | FRI | SAT |
|-----|-----|-----|-----|-----|-----|-----|
|     |     |     |     | *11:50 A.M. MST* |     |     |

To ensure he would arrive in time for his lunch meeting with Mr. Falcon, Ernesto had to take the 6 A.M. flight to Denver from O'Hare, rent a car, and then drive the hour and fifteen minutes or so to the Falcon Foundation for Families building, which was located in Loveland's historic downtown district. Ernesto had first visited Falcon when he was in elementary school. He'd been back a couple of times since, but it had been at least 10 years since his last visit.

Fortunately his United flight was uneventfully on schedule, the folks at Hertz found it in their hearts to upgrade him to a small SUV, and the 4-wheel-drive Toyota helped him navigate through the early spring snowstorm bearing down on the Colorado Front Range. Ernesto found himself rolling up to the familiar building on Fifth Street with a few minutes to spare. As he sat in the idling car looking at the doorway, the heater was slowly losing the battle to calm the growing chills he was feeling as he reflected on the first time he'd been there and when he'd met Mr. Falcon.

He was about 10 years old and had been nominated by his school to be a potential recipient of the Franklin Foundation for Families "future leader" college scholarship. As part of a small group of about 200 students from all over America who would eventually be selected that year, he and his family had traveled to Loveland to be interviewed and to learn more about the exclusive benefits and responsibilities of a future leader recipient.

At the time, Ernesto thought he was traveling to the Old West from his home in Chicago and that somehow going to Colorado would include seeing stagecoaches and six-gun shootouts. He hadn't been prepared for just how modern everything was, nor was he prepared to meet Mr. Falcon. He was both charming and subtly threatening, and Ernesto found himself wanting to do more, BE more, just by being in his presence. Those feelings resurfaced as Ernesto prepared himself to once again spend time with Mr. Falcon. He was both apprehensive and eager, but most of all he was resolved to do what was necessary.

He shut down the RAV4, rechecked that he had his notebook and cellphone, mechanically opened the door, and began a slow walk from the visitor's space toward the front door.

Upon entering, Ernesto felt as though he had been transported back to his youth. The décor of the reception area had changed very little in the 25 years since he'd been there first: dark wood, chrome-legged chairs and tables, faded lithographs of several foreign countries, and the all-encompassing push-pin map showing the homeland locations of all the former "future leader" recipients. Somewhere on that map he knew a pin represented Oaxaca, Mexico.

Ernesto walked to the reception desk and said, "My name is Ernesto Martinez. I have an appointment with Mr. Falcon today. He should be expecting me."

"Welcome, Mr. Martinez. One moment . . ."

# Birds of a Feather

Thursday: 11:55 A.M. MST

*(Jennifer Boyle's Office, Falcon Foundation, Loveland)*

Week I

| SUN | MON | TUE | WED | THU | FRI | SAT |
|-----|-----|-----|-----|-----|-----|-----|
|     |     |     |     | 11:55 A.M. MST |     |     |

Had the members of the executive team taken the time to survey the walls in the modest boardroom as they left to return to their offices, they would have seen dozens of 11x14 color portraits of their kids. Families representing every conceivable nationality; some with no children, some with many; some biological, some adopted. While the faces were different, the expressions were similar; all the photos portrayed one central feeling: gratitude. The Falcon kids felt truly blessed to have been selected by the Falcon Foundation for Families, and their faces reflected the joy and hope in their hearts. It was a shrine to the altruistic and powerful history of Falcon, and nestled in the left corner, behind Mr. Falcon's seat at the head of the table, was the picture of Terrence Kennedy and his family.

Terrence, Falcon's head of client services, had joined the foundation immediately upon graduating from Pepperdine University with a law degree. He was (like Franklin) the first member of his family to earn a college degree, a degree funded fully by the foundation largely due to the commitment he and his family had shown to others in need. The Kennedy family owned a small farm in rural Georgia, and Terrence's father was a descendant of the sharecroppers who first owned his family's land at the end of the Civil War.

The Kennedys took nothing for granted yet shared what little they had generously. Franklin always considered the families of former slaves to be "forced immigrants" to America and waived the normal first- or second-generation-only requirements for their families to be eligible for Falcon Foundation benefits.

Terrence was obviously connected to the Falcon Foundation in ways that other members of the executive team were not. He and his family had benefited significantly from Mr. Falcon's vision, and as a result, he was an ardent supporter of Franklin. In his role as VP of client services, it was his job to oversee the selection of candidate families and to direct the activities of all the case managers. Given his background, he had difficulty remaining objective about the foundation's activities and its finances.

He considered his job to be a blessed activity and couldn't imagine doing anything else for a living. The fact that the funding to support his responsibilities had somehow disappeared was unimaginable. He'd ignored Greg's reports about the impending financial doom until just about a week ago. By then, he had subconsciously developed a full arsenal of excuses, thoughts of denial, and other means to deflect himself from dealing with the reality of the situation. However, "something" was trying to break through his defenses—a nagging suspicion that his world as he knew it was about to change radically. His stomach was churning.

"Jennifer, do you have a few minutes?" Terrence asked as he walked uninvited into her office. Upon seeing Greg Sullivan, Falcon's CFO, sitting on the couch reserved for Jennifer's guests, Terrence went on to say, "Oh, sorry. I didn't know you and Greg were in a meeting."

"No worries, Terrence. I was feeling the need to chat with Jennifer, too. I actually just got here myself," said Greg in an accent that strongly hinted of his youth in Belfast.

"Hold on," said Jennifer in a distracted tone, "just let me finish this sentence," as she returned to her keyboard.

Greg Sullivan joined Falcon about a dozen years ago, starting as a junior financial analyst and working his way up to chief financial officer, a promotion he received under stressful circumstances. He replaced Marty Wright, Falcon's original CFO, who was considered a legend within the halls of the foundation. Marty was fearless, intrepid even, because he was one of the few (maybe the only) members of the Falcon staff who would actively and regularly challenge Franklin—in public, in private, it didn't matter.

If something didn't "feel" right to Marty, he'd say it. And most amazing to everyone at Falcon, Franklin would listen—and would eventually agree with almost every one of Marty's suggestions.

Internally, these events carried the descriptor of "being Wrighted." Greg, although coached by Marty his entire career at Falcon, just didn't have the conviction in himself to challenge Mr. Falcon. When Marty died three years ago, and Greg followed him as CFO, the entire organization lost the balancing and "Wrighting" effect offered by Marty. Over time, Falcon found itself, and Franklin found himself, more and more off course as a result. Secretly, Greg thought everyone blamed him for not being more like Marty.

"What's up?" asked Jennifer as she swiveled her chair to face them.

# What's "Wanting" to Happen?

Thursday: Exactly 12:00 P.M. MST

*(Franklin Falcon's Office, Loveland)*

Week I

| SUN | MON | TUE | WED | THU | FRI | SAT |
|-----|-----|-----|-----|-----|-----|-----|
|  |  |  |  | 12:00 P.M. MST |  |  |

It was exactly 12:00 noon when Ernesto walked into Mr. Falcon's office. He looked different than Ernesto had remembered.

The Franklin Falcon he had met as a fifth-grader was an imposing person—not tall, not muscular—but nonetheless big in an energy-related way. He radiated. He was the embodiment of passion. The man Ernesto saw before him that day was not, at least not at first appearance. Franklin Falcon, however, was a survivor, and his slumped frame and weary eyes transformed as he regarded Ernesto standing in the doorway of his office. Rising to his feet, the glow in his face a mask to the stress underneath, he strode to meet Ernesto and embraced him in his characteristic "kiss on each cheek, and then a vigorous two-handed handshake designed to test the connecting tissues in every joint between your wrist and waist" manner. Just meeting the man for the first time put one on notice that you were in for an experience, not simply an interchange between two people.

Again, the thought of Mr. Falcon ultimately being a survivor reconnected Ernesto with his own past. As such, more images from his time in Iceland materialized, and the trials he'd experienced started flowing through him again. The fact that it was snowing hard today brought even more power to his memories of surviving Langjökull Glacier. The key to his survival? Adapting as quickly as possible to his new situation. The past was just that—the past. Ernesto had to look around, understand, and accept his new situation—and then establish ways in which he would be able to succeed.

Now. Here. Not back home in Chicago; not even in his hotel room at the Fosshótel in Reykholt. Mr. Falcon's greeting snapped him back to the present.

"Ernesto. How wonderful it is to see you again! When Betty told me that you'd asked to meet with me today, I have to admit I was surprised—and thrilled."

"Mr. Falcon, it's so good to be here. I'm glad you were able to meet with me, particularly given the fact you'll be headed out of town shortly for an extended vacation."

Franklin's eyes shifted slightly to the right and down, breaking contact with Ernesto's. An awkward silence ensued, the first of several they would endure over the next few days. Stammering something about lunch, Ernesto looked at his watch and said, "Betty made reservations at the Black Steer; she said it was one of your favorites. We probably ought to get moving; the weather isn't the best today." Normally it would be only a ten-minute walk from Falcon's offices to the restaurant, but the blowing snow made walking unappealing. "I can drive. My car is still warm from the trip up from Denver."

"Oh, yes. Well . . . that would be nice. Thank you."

Ernesto put the Toyota into gear and slowly backed out of the visitor's space. His mind was "pinballing" through the various questions he'd mentally prepared to ask Mr. Falcon, but he found he couldn't sort out the best opening question. Instead of trying to force the "right" question to come, he decided to trust his instincts, to open himself up to "what wants to happen," and to stop pushing forward on what he thought "should" happen. This was another of the key lessons he had learned in Iceland: to quit trying to "make" things happen. Instead, look around, open yourself up, and focus on what wants to happen. If you do that, you can make plans that have a far better chance of actually succeeding. This thought calmed him.

They drove in silence, found a parking space on the street in front of the Black Steer, and made their way into the restaurant.

# Stirring the Pot

### Thursday: About 1:00 P.M. CST

*(Minneapolis Airport)*

Week I

| SUN | MON | TUE | WED | THU | FRI | SAT |
|-----|-----|-----|-----|-----|-----|-----|
|     |     |     |     | 1:00 P.M. CST |     |     |

"She's an impressive young lady." Marissa Grant's matter-of-fact statement resulted in enthusiastic head nodding from her entourage. The morning interview with Angela Liu and her family had been a complete success, but in reality, the only thing impressive to Marissa about Angela was the fact that the Liu family represented damaging evidence to the Falcon Foundation. Marissa got the human interest angle she wanted, and her brain was already twisting portions of the interview to enlarge the scandal. Scandals—real or invented—were the fuel that made her fire glow.

Her team was busy with details—checking emails, answering text messages, posting Tweets, returning calls—but Marissa was constantly five steps ahead of them. Pleased as she was with the trip to Minneapolis, Marissa was silently fuming because the airlines serving the Denver airport were beginning to cancel flights. Their 3:30 P.M. Southwest Airlines flight to Denver still showed "On Time," but the word "Canceled" appeared next to the late afternoon Frontier and United flights to Denver. Her stress was increasing because she just knew the crazy early spring weather in Colorado was going to interfere with her carefully crafted assault.

"We need a plan B if we can't get to Denver tonight," she directed. "I really want to lead tomorrow's show with Franklin Falcon—on camera— telling the world that he's sorry for causing so many so much pain."

Marissa fully intended to use the tsunami of suspicion related to the Falcon Foundation to force Franklin Falcon into a rare television interview. Franklin had never consented to an on-camera interview and shied away from television cameras even when he was part of a good news story. He guarded his privacy, and his persona, with Fort Knox–like methods.

Just then, the gate agent for Southwest Airlines made the announcement Marissa dreaded: their flight had been canceled. In fact, the agent said, it was a strong possibility that the entire Denver airport might be closed and they would not be able to begin rebooking flights until Friday morning at 8 A.M. at the soonest. Her crew started their whining in earnest. "Great! Now what?" came the complaining. Marissa tuned it out.

Rather than wallowing in her anger, Marissa was undaunted; in fact, she could use the cancelation of the flight as a benefit if she looked at it the right way. Any obstacle was just another opportunity to learn, a chance to explore options and to ultimately create new solutions. She thought to herself, "Let's get back to the studio and put together a human interest piece: lots of tears, heartstring pulling, touchy-feely stuff. We'll build the image that Franklin Falcon has completely lost touch and is actually hurting people instead of helping. We'll fly out to Denver on Sunday, maybe Saturday if those local yokels can figure out how to get rid of the snow, and we'll interview Falcon then. He'll have some big questions to answer by that point; there'll be lots of public outcry. We can run his interview on Monday. That way we'll have all week to replay it. Done right, all the cable newsies and bloggers will pick up on it as well, and *The Grant Report* (and I!) will be the big story next week." Marissa's mind, once on a track, was impossible to derail.

"Get us back to New York now!" she barked to her traveling administrative assistant. "And let's get every clip we have with the Falcon Foundation teed up for a production meeting. Tonight! We'll be working late, so make sure your neighbors are feeding your dogs and cats." Her staff looked at her, almost blankly for a moment as their conversations about the weather, travel disruptions, and so on were interrupted. The moment passed, and within a nanosecond, they were back on the phone making new plans.

Marissa didn't have the time or inclination for pets. She wanted to be completely free to do what was necessary when it was necessary. Her statement to her staff about their pets was a private joke; she thought those with animals were somehow inferior to her.

"I'll bet Franklin Falcon has a dog," she thought to herself. She smiled.

# Asking for Help

## Thursday: About 12:10 p.m. MST

### *(Black Steer Restaurant, Loveland)*

Week 1

| SUN | MON | TUE | WED | THU | FRI | SAT |
|-----|-----|-----|-----|-----|-----|-----|
|     |     |     |     | 12:10 P.M. MST |     |     |

Formal as ever, Franklin insisted on using the coat-check. He firmly believed that those who work have noble tasks, even if they spend their days matching up claim checks to coats and working hard to keep the mismatched gloves to a minimum. The person behind the coat-check desk needed to support her family, too, and Franklin always respected those who worked.

As they handed their coats across the counter and collected their numbered tags, a cheerful man of about 60 came around the corner and visibly lit up when he saw Franklin.

"Mr. Falcon! How great to see you. We've missed you around here," the restaurant manager playfully scolded Franklin. It was clear the two had a long and friendly relationship. However, if pressed, the manager wouldn't be able to recall any significant details about Franklin, other than what he normally ordered for lunch. Franklin was cordial, positive, and courteous. He always used good manners, but he offered little insight into himself to anyone.

"See you in a moment," whispered the manager to Mr. Falcon, as he rushed off to check a detail in the kitchen.

"Reservation for two. Martinez," Ernesto said as the hostess asked how many were in their party. "This way," she said as she efficiently and quickly moved them to their table. It's obvious she was new as she showed no recognition of Franklin. Probably a freshman at CSU, Ernesto thought. The restaurant was quiet today, far emptier than normal according to the seating hostess when he asked her about it. She wasn't sure if it was due to the weather, the economy, or both. Secretly Ernesto was glad for the privacy the virtually empty restaurant would allow.

The menus she gave them provided a temporary barrier between Franklin and Ernesto, who took the moment to settle himself down and connect to his inner source of power. He had learned over the years that the more he tried to "think" his way through situations, the more he limited himself to potential choices. He settled himself, told himself to be "fully present," and to trust his intuition. The answers would flow if he let them. That said, even without being able to make eye contact with Franklin, Ernesto could tell Franklin was nervous about meeting with him. He was shifting in his seat, clearing his throat repeatedly—almost too urgently—and flipping the menu back and forth. He was distracted and really not focused on reading the menu at all. He was using it as a shield.

The manager reappeared and came to the table to take their order. Ernesto ordered a salad with steak strips, and Franklin ordered chicken-fried steak. "Comfort food," he rationalized to the manager as he laughed nervously while placing his order. Now with the food ordered, the drinks arriving, and the menus gone, it was time for discussion. A momentary silence ensued, and both of them found themselves rushing to fill the gap.

"Great to see you," Franklin blurted, just as Ernesto offered, "I'm glad your schedule was open today!" Neither of them really understood what the other said, but they laughed at the fact they'd simultaneously spoken to each other. The tension eased.

Another pause—this one much calmer.

"Mr. Falcon . . ." He waited for a couple of seconds, knowing that a short space was necessary for the right words to come to him. "I am very glad you were available to meet with me today. I've gotten better over the years when it comes to paying attention to my feelings, and I've been concerned about you, the foundation—really everything."

Franklin interrupted, "Ernesto, your visit is very timely. Thank you for coming."

They smiled quietly at each other, but Franklin broke eye contact first and looked down at his iced tea. Absently, he stirred the lemon in the glass, a distance growing in his eyes. "Ernesto, we are so very proud of you. And, to think we nearly lost you . . ." His voice trailed off, and looking closely Ernesto thought he could see traces of wetness in his eyes.

"Thank you, Mr. Falcon. Yes, I've faced some difficulties, and while I wouldn't want to repeat things like my accident in Iceland, I'm glad I had the chance to learn from those kinds of experiences. And, I can't tell you how important you and the foundation have been to me and my family; you've made such a difference to so many over the years. I don't know if you hear 'thank you' enough."

Again, Franklin spoke over Ernesto's last few words, "Iceland," he said simply. "We followed the news, read the articles, kept the clippings."

"I really appreciated your providing the tickets so that my parents could travel there to meet me at the hospital; money for them was . . ."

"A difficulty," he said.

"Yes."

Ernesto had been blessed with excellent business opportunities after graduating from college. Although his parents would never accept charity from anyone, they did "allow" Ernesto to help with some of their expenses and to assist them in building some level of financial security. But the economic situation today was wearing on everyone. It was hard, and Ernesto wasn't sure how to broach the subject of the foundation's rumored financial crisis with Mr. Falcon.

Another shift in his seat. More time spent poking at the lemon.

"Ernesto, I've always wanted to ask you about it. The accident, I mean," he struggled. "Really, I want to know if you thought about 'not making it,' the potential of dying out there." Ernesto waited. Franklin's eyes shifted to the door and then back to Ernesto. "Why do you think you survived and the others didn't?"

There. The question was out. Why? It was something Ernesto had asked himself repeatedly for years. A few people had also asked him, but none quite so directly and so quickly as Mr. Falcon. Ernesto's eyes drifted down, and suddenly a wave of fatigue hit him. He rubbed each eye slowly as he recalled the lessons he'd learned on the glacier.

"Mr. Falcon, I didn't understand it at the time, but after looking back at the experience, I've come to a few conclusions." The faces of his traveling party appeared before him, mostly strangers whom he had just met that morning as they selected their snowmobiling clothing, boots, goggles, gloves, etc., but also a couple of very good friends who had traveled to Iceland with him to present at the Central European Workshop on Quantum Conference. One friend survived, another didn't. That fact haunted him still.

"Accepting the fact that we were miles from civilization, that our guide—who had the only GPS and radio in the group—had suffered a catastrophic equipment failure with his snowmobile and had vanished into a massive crevasse in the ice, and that we hadn't brought more than just the basic first aid kit–type of survival equipment took time to sink in."

More images from the glacier crowded into Ernesto's mind . . . "A few weeks after I'd been rescued, I recalled that in reality, some in our group never accepted the fact that things were different. A couple wandered off on their own, fully believing that help was just 'one more hill away.' Their bodies were found during the summer thaw two years later. Others believed that it was just a bad dream, something they'd eventually wake up from, and that someone else would take care of fixing things.

"These individuals gave no support to the group, did nothing to prepare, sought no new answers, and suffered the consequences once it became clear that inaction would eventually result in death. When others of us decided it was time to make decisions based upon the facts at hand, those who were stuck 'waiting for someone else to fix things' decided they'd stay where they were.

"Not long after we were discovered, huddling in a small cave, the rescuers came upon the clump of those who were 'stuck.' They'd literally become frozen physically after freezing mentally. The amazing thing was that they were no more than about 100 feet from us. Never more clearly in my life did I have a chance to see that escape, survival, and 'life and death' decisions sometimes are very close together."

He found the memories flowed more freely now, that he was recalling details he'd not thought about for years. Franklin sat forward in his seat, paying close attention to Ernesto's words, some of which were registering deep within him.

"But those of us who clearly understood that our survival depended on adapting to our new situation—and quickly—were the ones who eventually made it."

A full five seconds elapsed before Mr. Falcon spoke. He maintained eye contact the whole time, and then while continuing to look at Ernesto, he said in a voice hinting at self-contempt and uncertainty, "Ernesto." He looked down at the table and continued, "I understand the part about it taking time to accept that a new situation is very different from what you've experienced before."

He regained eye contact with Ernesto. His eyes grew more serious, his chin was set, he focused more intently on Ernesto as his voice became steady and quiet. "I believe I may have made some decisions that have created a potential catastrophe for the foundation. I'm hoping you might help us." His eyes burned into Ernesto's.

Time stopped. Ernesto's thoughts crawled, and the room felt as if it went dark. He looked down at the table, hoping for inspiration to come from the salt and pepper shakers. Five, six, seven seconds elapsed, and then the words came to Ernesto as insight filled the vacuum.

"Mr. Falcon . . . don't worry. All will be well."

It's something he remembered from his youth at summer Bible camp. The phrase "Do not be afraid" (or variations of it like "Don't worry") appear in the Christian Bible 365 times. Ernesto didn't remember why this had stuck with him, but he'd found comfort in it when he was young. He offered it to Mr. Falcon as a message that came through him, not from him. The fact his message also included Franklin's favorite saying of hope, "All will be well," clearly wasn't a coincidence, and Ernesto witnessed Franklin's immediate connection to it.

Quietly, slowly, the protective cocoon with which Franklin had shielded his feelings, his fears, and his perceived weakness began to fall away in small pieces. A light started to flicker within him, a realization that no matter how much he'd wished for things to "be as they were," it was clearly time for him to begin to adapt to his new situation. Now. Not in 10 minutes. Now.

Franklin's transformation had begun, and Ernesto was slowly beginning to understand why he'd come: He was not there so much to respond to Franklin's request for help but instead to help Franklin find a safe place to say what he'd just said and for him to remember that, indeed, "All will be well."

"Mr. Falcon, anything I can do to help, I'd be honored."

Again, Franklin cut Ernesto's sentence short as he said two small words to him, a nearly imperceptible quiver in his voice, a tiny outward sign of his building emotions. "Thank you."

Their food had materialized quite unnoticed by either of them, and between bites, Ernesto shared the impetus for his visit. The news, the blogs, the rumors—and his sense of needing to do something. Mr. Falcon listened intently but remained mostly quiet. He had walked up to the cliff; his act of asking for help was profound in its simplicity and rarity. A proud, self-made man who valued his clear-headed decision-making, strong relationships, and an inner sense of right and wrong, he rarely found himself needing to ask for anything. The fact he'd asked for help was a massive step in the right direction. Ernesto found he respected him more because of it.

When their meal was finished, and as he put a $5 bill into the tip jar for the coat check-attendant, Franklin said, "Ernesto, I've asked the senior leadership of the foundation to meet us back at the office. They'll be waiting for us."

"Yes," Ernesto's voice cracked. He finished silently, "They'll be waiting."

# Resistance, Futile It Is

## Thursday: About 12:15 P.M. MST

### *(Falcon Foundation, Loveland)*

Week 1

| SUN | MON | TUE | WED | THU | FRI | SAT |
|-----|-----|-----|-----|-----|-----|-----|
|     |     |     |     | 12:15 P.M. MST |     |     |

Jennifer's office was similar to that of all the others within the executive group. It wasn't particularly large nor especially well-furnished. It was competent. Conservative. It reflected a sense of professionalism, a focus on family, and a long-term feel, as if the person working there had been part of the organization for a long time and expected to be so long into the future. Jennifer sat at her keyboard and was finishing a response to an email from a reporter with the *Denver Post*. She frankly wasn't looking forward to another complaint session with Terrence and Greg.

Mildly distracting to her was the flat-panel TV mounted behind her desk that she used to monitor the local and national cable news outlets. Today the TV was tuned to a local Denver channel. The snow was no longer simply falling—it was smothering everything in its path. Accumulating at the rate of two or more inches per hour, and with winds blowing at 15-20 mph, the National Weather Service indicated a Blizzard Warning for the Front Range of Colorado was imminent.

"The area from the Palmer Divide to the Wyoming state line will receive upwards of 30 inches of snow during the next 24-36 hours, with drifts in the five- and six-foot range. Travel is discouraged," droned the immaculately coiffed TV weather guy.

"Discouraged," thought Jennifer. "Impossible was more likely." But just as she began mentally bemoaning the fact that getting home to the northern Denver suburb of Westminster (normally a 30-minute drive) would take hours, if she could get there at all, a germ of an idea sprouted. It might be possible the weather would stop Marissa Grant from coming to meet them. But was that a good thing? If we can't defend ourselves directly with her, what might she . . . Before she could finish the thought, Terrence's urgent voice cut in.

"Just how bad is the situation?" Terrence asked. He wasn't one to dwell on small talk. He was angry, and he wasn't shy about sharing it.

"The snow?" asked Jennifer.

"No! Not the snow! No, what might happen to our kids in the next few weeks?" Terrence questioned.

"Things could get ugly—with a capital UGLY," said Greg. His manner was cynical, and his tone of voice reflected the weeks of stress he'd endured. Greg was tired.

"Terrence, Greg . . . wait. We've had this conversation before. We need to be careful not to jump to blaming anyone. The other members of the executive team aren't the enemy. They, well, haven't been here that long," Jennifer started.

"And they've failed." Greg's tone was adamant.

"Failed?" asked Terrence.

"Yes. They've failed to continue the legacy of this foundation. Their new approaches to reaching potential donors haven't worked." Greg reported things as he saw them. However, in doing so, he continued to deny that he had played any role in the situation. In fact, rather than owning his position as the chief financial officer, he instead acted as if he were more of a controller, an "executive bookkeeper," if you will. He was reluctant to provide a financial and moral rudder for taking the right actions. Instead, he rushed to blame others.

The story's rerun had begun. Same players, same script. Jennifer was ready for a different ending but found it difficult to be optimistic about that. Terrence's view of reality was clouded by his own experience: He was so grateful to Mr. Falcon and the foundation that he suffered a loss of objectivity at times. He wasn't viewing the situation from the foundation's viewpoint; he was, instead, already grieving the losses to current and future Falcon Families should the foundation fail. He'd jumped quickly beyond the disbelief stage in Elizabeth Kübler-Ross's grief cycle and was fully committed to being pissed off.

Greg, on the other hand, was a person who often chose the role of victim. Jennifer joked with her family about Greg at times, saying he had a fully matched set of Teflon suits in that nothing would stick to him. It frustrated Jennifer, particularly because she had been so fond of Marty Wright, Greg's predecessor.

Marty Wright. Just the name conjured up snippets of previous interactions with him. Jennifer retreated mentally again and asked herself, "What would Marty choose to say right now? He seemed to always say the right thing, no matter the situation."

While she was only partially paying attention to the whining and complaining coming from Terrence and Greg, one thing came to her, the word "appreciation." She remembered it was Marty's favorite word; he loved to tell everyone he could about the word.

"Appreciation," she surprised herself by speaking the word aloud.

"What?" came the joint response from Greg and Terrence. Reflecting her verbal non-sequitor, their expressions looked as if they'd expected to take a drink of milk but found orange juice in the glass instead.

Catching herself, she said, "It was Marty's favorite word, remember? He loved talking about that word because he said it had two meanings, both of which were positive." Jennifer became nostalgic as she spoke.

Marty Wright had passed away three years ago, but his influence on the Falcon Foundation was still powerful, particularly with Franklin and Jennifer. He'd been their confidant, advisor, coach, and occasional butt-kicker. He was not a large man—quite the reverse. No matter who was in the room, he seemed to need to look up to make eye contact, and his belt appeared to be the only thing keeping his pants from sliding down his thin frame. He was fair and optimistic about life, and he had no issue with holding himself and others accountable for results.

Jennifer was remembering one situation in particular in which she had been wrestling with an ethical decision. It must have been 15 years ago, but it was vivid in her mind. She'd gone to Marty's office to ask his advice, and as was his normal custom, he'd dropped everything he was doing, turned to face her, and gave her the benefit of his full attention. Most people commented on the fact that Marty was an exceptional listener and that they felt better just being in his presence. He didn't need to actually say anything. Jennifer was struggling with a decision related to one of the foundation's families. It involved plagiarism. One option meant devastation to the family; the other meant the foundation would be compromising its values. Jennifer was fully engaged in her internal conversation with Marty when Terrence's voice interrupted.

"To see the value in, and to increase the value of," parroted Terrence, not trying in the slightest to hide his impatience with Jennifer's decision to bring the memory of Marty Wright into the conversation. "What's that got to do with anything right now?" he challenged.

"Terrence," she sighed. She stood and walked slowly across the five-foot space separating them as she spoke. "As much as anyone, I know we talk about 'being Wrighted' a lot, and I've felt many times that Marty's words have almost become a cliché."

Greg rolled his eyes slightly and crossed his arms. Once again, he felt as if he was being compared to a ghost.

"But Marty was one of the wisest people I've ever met, and I, for one, miss some of his advice." She stopped and placed her hand on Terrence's shoulder. He briefly met her eyes and then looked away.

"I think Marty would tell us to appreciate our situation—and to not continue dwelling on problems. He'd also say that problems are like rabbits. Left on their own, they reproduce like crazy. Stop focusing on problems, and start looking for solutions!" Nearly fully manifested physically, the memory of Marty Wright permeated the office. Jennifer had mimicked his voice, his accent, even his mannerisms. He had a way of connecting with you—until he was fully into your personal body space.

"Appreciate," she repeated.

"I don't know," said Terrence. "I'm just so disappointed . . . and frustrated." The normal timbre and resonance of his deep baritone wavered.

"Great," chimed in Greg. "The ship is sinking, and now we're supposed to 'appreciate the journey,' right? I don't feel much like seeing the positives in a very bad situation. Sorry, but no singing around the campfire for me. I need to look at finding some solutions to our problems. You two can stay here and share a moment with each other, but I'm heading to my office to see about some bridge financing or getting an angel investor or two. Someone needs to be prepared when Mr. Falcon asks us what we're going to do."

Greg stormed out, leaving Jennifer and Terrence in silence.

# Defining the "Right" Problem

### Thursday: Exactly 1:30 p.m. MST

*(Falcon Foundation, Loveland)*

Week 1

| SUN | MON | TUE | WED | THU | FRI | SAT |
|-----|-----|-----|-----|-----|-----|-----|
|     |     |     |     | 1:30 p.m. MST |     |     |

Over the years, Franklin continued to be amazed at the timing of Jo's calls, emails, and, recently, text messages. Maybe the old saying about married people starting to look like each other over the years (Jo was clearly not in agreement with that idea!) was only part of the story. Franklin was a firm believer in the notion that life partners, soul mates—committed, loving individuals who truly devoted themselves to each other—actually began thinking and feeling like each other. It was hard to explain, but Franklin just knew what Jo needed and vice versa. Today was no exception.

What had started as a simple conversation letting him know that she wanted him to drive safely as the weather deteriorated had moved into one of Jo's famous Zen lessons. She'd studied all sorts of philosophy over the years, but she was in particular a fan of the short, thought-provoking messages in Zen philosophy. Just before saying goodbye and telling Franklin she loved him, Jo related her story of the day.

"You know, Freddie, your situation reminds me a bit of another Zen lesson."

Franklin smiled to himself. Some of these stories were really good, and some were kind of silly, but he did look forward to hearing them.

"A traveler meets up with a family—a father, a mother, and their two children, all of whom are enlightened. He asks if the road ahead is difficult.

The father says, 'The road is hard.' The mother says, 'The road is easy.' The first child says, 'The road is neither easy nor hard.' And the second child says, 'The road is both hard and easy.'"

Jo paused as she finished the story, and then offered, "Your road is what you make it, Freddie. I love you."

Franklin understood both the power and simplicity of her message. While he had been dreading the meeting with his executive team that afternoon, he also was convinced it was the right thing to do. "I love you too, Jo. I'll call later!"

With that he hung up, gathered his papers, and headed to the boardroom.

"I'm glad you were all able to clear your calendars for this afternoon's meeting." Franklin opened the meeting. Most facial expressions said, "Yeah, right. Like we had a choice in the matter!"

Elaine and Nicole glanced at each other, and each smiled ever so slightly. Their lunch conversation had centered on the opportunities for transformational change offered by Falcon's current crisis. Each of them had come from organizations that had experienced significant challenges, one of which survived (actually thrived!) and one of which failed.

Specifically, one of Nicole's earliest non-profit employers had experienced a formidable operational and financial challenge back in the late 1990s and early 2000s when they lost 80 percent of their funding. The foundation's primary source of revenue came from a dot.com millionaire whose fortune vanished as rapidly as it had arrived. His heart was still committed, but his bank account was depleted. They'd discovered, though, that asking themselves the right questions—powerful, focused, outcome-driving questions—created strong forward movement. It was through this process of reinvention—a shift in funding and revenue planning—that Nicole Fargas's rock-star status in non-profit development had germinated.

Using many of the skills she'd developed as a teenager in surviving the streets, she had built a reputation (and track record) that Franklin found irresistible. He recruited her heavily and eventually won her over through the power of his personal commitment. Nicole just didn't know the depth of the financial crisis into which she had stepped. Maybe the crisis would be a galvanizing event and would bring the leaders together at Falcon the way it had with her last organization. Nicole prayed that it might.

Elaine's experience with a recent employer was quite different. When that organization found itself in trouble, instead of focusing on defining the problem clearly and then asking the right set of questions, the company degenerated into politics, finger-pointing, and butt-covering activities. Ultimately, the entire "ship" sank, destroying even those who'd worked so hard to make sure their personal "deck chair's territory" had been clearly marked. Elaine knew that HR was often the group in a company that carried the bucket and shovel behind the elephant of bad decisions, and her experience at that organization reinforced her vow never to find herself in that position again.

Her Swedish heritage underpinned her no-nonsense, direct, and clear-headed approach to things, and she'd built a reputation of bringing clear leadership to employee development. She looked at each person as a vital resource, fully worthy of extensive investment. Elaine was an early adopter of the philosophy that an employee's real value in an organization has nothing to do with positional authority or tenure.

Instead, she preached that feeling valued for one's capabilities (along with a commitment to training and education) and knowing that one's activities are directly connected to helping achieve organizational goals is real value. People who feel the greatest sense of belonging and who clearly know how they help to create success are the happiest, most motivated group.

Elaine had tried hard to instill at Falcon a philosophy of employee development, where new ideas were welcomed, open dialog was fostered, and creative solution-finding was commonplace, but she found the entrenched culture fully resisted the notion of outside change. Maybe the looming crisis would force the issue. Regardless of her own sense of futility caused by months of banging her head into the "we've always done it this way" wall, no matter how ugly things might get in the next two or three hours, Elaine had vowed to ensure the conversation related to issues and not personalities. Her conviction would be tested.

"We have much to discuss this afternoon, but before we get to that, I'd like to introduce our guest." All eyes shifted toward Ernesto. "For those of you who haven't met him yet, this is Ernesto Martinez," Franklin stated with a paternal sense of pride. "His visit is particularly timely, especially given the weather. He may be stuck with us for a week! I hope he brought enough clean socks . . ."

The group smiled and chuckled. Franklin's attempt to break the ice was somewhat effective, but the uncertainty and resistance within some of the team was firmly established.

A subtle hand gesture told Ernesto it was time for him to say something. "Yes, I'm Ernesto, and I'm really excited to be back here in Loveland. I haven't been here for about 10 years. It's amazing how much it's grown." He smiled, and he looked at each member of Falcon's executive team as he spoke. Some expressions were open, quite eager to hear what he had to say, a couple were pretty much blank, and a couple of faces were showing nothing positive: not quite hostile, but certainly not neutral.

He continued, "I'm sure you all know that my family is a former Falcon Family, and I—like all of your kids [he smiled at Franklin]—have a great sense of loyalty to and pride about the foundation." Terrence beamed, and Ernesto returned it. "There, behind Jennifer, second row from the top, third picture in, that's me and my family. Gosh, look at all the hair I used to have!" More smiles, more laughing. "I'm really pleased to be here."

Franklin cut in, "Ernesto contacted Betty earlier this week and asked whether I had some time to meet with him. He didn't elaborate on the reason he wanted to meet, and I wasn't sure why he wanted to come, but you know how much we look forward to visits from our kids. It's just about the best thing about doing what we do!" Franklin's energy was contagious, and that combined with Ernesto's obvious pride in the foundation's work had a calming effect on the room. Some of the concern, uncertainty, and negative feelings were dissipating.

"But," continued Franklin, "Ernesto and I just returned from lunch, where we had . . ." He stopped, glanced down at his hands, paused for a heartbeat, and said, "a remarkable conversation. I now know why he's here."

As if cued from a reality TV show, Franklin waited. He took the time to look each member of his executive team in the eye, one by one. Curiosity reigned.

Terrence shattered the silence, "Mr. Falcon, why *did* Ernesto come?" His voice was huge in the small room; while some people might be described as having an "outside voice," Terrence was told he had a "stadium voice." The volume and urgency with which he asked startled the group.

Franklin's demeanor showed confidence, a sense of knowing. His eyes softened, and he shifted toward Terrence. Franklin nodded slowly.

Ernesto squirmed, and wrung his hands together. In reality, he was nervous. He didn't want to be perceived either as a full-time know-it-all (someone who swoops in and saves the day) or as a fear monger, who was there to assign blame and take names. He and Franklin had not discussed the answer to Terrence's question in advance, and Ernesto, too, was anxious to hear Mr. Falcon's answer. He waited.

"At lunch, Ernesto told me he'd come because he was concerned about the news, the rumors, the theories that are swirling about the health of the foundation. He was concerned, and he felt a personal sense of responsibility to offer anything he had to help us, if help was needed." Heads swiveled. Ernesto's steak salad suddenly wasn't digesting well.

"The last time I checked," Franklin smirked, "Ernesto may have done very well for himself financially, but he doesn't have an extra $80 million lying around, just looking for a home . . ."

Eyes popped. Franklin had everyone's attention now, especially Greg's.

"What Ernesto does have," started Franklin, "is a powerful story, one that all of us would benefit from hearing." He looked at Ernesto and asked, "Would you mind?"

Ernesto jumped in, "Of course not," and for the next 20 minutes, he recounted his story of survival on the glacier in Iceland.

Upon finishing, Greg had one question for him, "What the hell does that have to do with our situation? We need to look at raising cash, not feeling good!" he stammered.

The glares were instant, the energy in the room began a free fall, and Greg was greeted with silence. His confidence retreated, and he shut his mouth.

Jennifer's quiet words soothed the tension, "Now's not the time for arguing. There's too much at stake."

Ernesto was sensing that a moment of clarity—of real transparency—was at hand for the leadership team. They were getting close to seeing that they'd been working on the wrong problem for the past few months. Yes, the foundation needed a huge influx of cash to cover its obligations in the next six weeks, but the real problem wasn't related to their lack of funding. The real problem was something altogether different.

Just as he was about to suggest that they'd been working on solving the wrong thing, Franklin spoke again.

"Yes, there's a great deal at stake, including the very future of the foundation. We've dug a pretty big hole. According to Greg's cash flow analysis, it looks as if we'll have to default on some payments for the first time in our history. Then, if our creditors jump into the middle of it, they might call some of our loans due, and we'd be forced into bankruptcy."

The group was somber, although Greg was looking smug, like the cat who had just swallowed the canary. He was fully expecting Mr. Falcon to ask for some ideas related to rapid sources of liquid capital, and he made sure his research papers were on the top of the stack in front of him. He was ready to share his preparations with the group.

Franklin shocked the group, "But, I think we've been looking in the wrong direction for the past couple of months. Instead of just looking at new ways to replace our lost funding, I've come to the conclusion that we'd be better served if we addressed the reason behind the fact we can't raise additional capital."

Greg's frustration boiled over. "But Mr. Falcon," he blurted, "If you'd just let me share . . ."

Right then, Betty poked her head into the boardroom, got Franklin's attention, and said, "There's an urgent call for you." Franklin nodded and stared in Greg's direction.

"Jennifer, what about a break?" he said, thinking that a short time-out might be a good thing. "Let's reconvene in 30 minutes. Say, 2:30?"

As Franklin made his way into the hallway, Ernesto saw Betty approach him and overheard her as she said, "Mr. Falcon, the weather's really looking crummy this afternoon. I let the rest of the staff leave early. I hope that's okay with you. I'd planned to stay to help with whatever you might need this afternoon."

Franklin smiled as he grasped her shoulders with his hands. "Oh, that's great! You always know the right thing to do. Thank you."

Ernesto was hoping Franklin, too, was doing the right thing by interrupting the meeting and that the moment wouldn't be lost. Ernesto hoped Franklin's intuition was right.

# Transparency Will Set You Free

## Thursday: About 3:00 p.m. CST

### (Liu Home, Eden Prairie, Minnesota)

Week 1

| SUN | MON | TUE | WED | THU | FRI | SAT |
|-----|-----|-----|-----|-----|-----|-----|
|     |     |     |     | 3:00 p.m. CST |     |     |

"Mr. Falcon," started Liu Ping, "I hope I'm not interrupting anything."

"No, it's never an interruption to hear from one of our families, Mrs. Liu." Franklin's tone was gentle and paternal, and he did an admirable job of masking the tension he was feeling. "To what do I owe the pleasure of speaking with you?" Franklin asked.

"Well, I'm not entirely sure how to start." Mrs. Liu was telling the truth. During the past hour, she'd partially dialed the Falcon Foundation's number at least a dozen times as she'd tried to steel her nerves and find the right opening statement.

A beat. Franklin waited. "It's a difficult time for us, and I guess rather than pacing the house anymore, talking to the cats, I thought I'd call you directly and ask what's going on," she said, all the while building momentum.

"On?" was Franklin's quiet reply, but once her low self-confidence veneer had been breached, Mrs. Liu found herself able to power forward. She ignored his question.

"You can't read anything related to the Falcon Foundation right now without sensing all kinds of fear and doubt about your situation; I mean, it's like there's only bad news right now. It's a growing sense of dread, that something horrible is about to happen."

"Mrs. Liu?" Franklin offered. It was as though the earpiece of her telephone was somehow blocked. She was not listening.

"You know, Angela's father isn't doing well. We've been struggling to make ends meet, but, please, please don't think we aren't appreciative of everything you and the foundation have done and are doing for us. We thank you—very much. But, it's the fear about what's next. Angela's so excited about school; it's tough to watch her try to remain optimistic amid all the rumors. She wants, well, we all want to remain positive, but without more specific information . . ."

He raised his voice, ever so slightly. "Mrs. Liu?"

He was greeted with silence. Almost. Franklin thought he could hear a faint sniffle, as if she was crying. He waited for her to speak.

"Yes, Mr. Falcon, I'm so sorry. I got carried away. The stress . . ."

"Yes, Mrs. Liu. I understand. There seems to be a fair amount of stress going around these days."

He wasn't sure what he'd say next. The "voice of reason" (as he called his normal approach of keeping everything to himself) was screaming for him to say only "All will be well" to Mrs. Liu and get off the phone without sharing anything more. But there was another voice that had gotten a bit more assertive and louder since his lunch conversation with Ernesto. This voice was saying, "Listen to your heart. The right thing to do right now is to trust Mrs. Liu. Share with her." This voice was unfamiliar to Franklin, but he found it offered a calm source of power to him, as opposed to the power-sapping, fearful, small voice that wanted him to retreat.

Remembering Ernesto's words about adapting quickly to a new situation, he decided to open up—just a bit—to Mrs. Liu and to relate some specific information about Falcon's situation.

"Mr. Falcon?"

"Oh, sorry." He shook his head to himself, "I was lost in my thoughts for a moment. Mrs. Liu, I have a few things I'd like to share with you. Is that okay?"

"Absolutely," she gushed. Then catching herself, she said, "I mean, yes, I'd appreciate that."

"First," he said, "I want to tell you again how much I appreciate your call. Having the chance to speak with you right now is both timely and, frankly, therapeutic as well. Some of what you're reading or hearing out there as rumor is in fact true. The Falcon Foundation finds itself in a place where our finances are not as strong as in the past."

Again, the voice of reason was speaking, but this time it was congratulating Franklin: "That's it, Franklin. Use some carefully chosen words that don't betray reality." The other voice also weighed in: "You have a chance to do something important here. Don't waste it."

Grimacing for a moment, Franklin continued his internal struggle. However, rather than continuing the charade of PR-speak, he squared his jaw, narrowed his eyes, and said, "Actually, Mrs. Liu, we're working hard to avert a financial crisis. Things have been going downhill for a while, and I must admit, my stubbornness in wanting to keep things quiet, really my desire to handle things myself, has made our situation even more dire."

He winced, preparing himself. He expected her to lash out, to pour on the negative feelings, to condemn him for his poor leadership and lousy decision-making and even worse approach to managing the foundation. Her reply rocked him.

"Oh, my. I am so sorry, Mr. Falcon. I hope my call hasn't made you feel worse about things. If there's anything we can do to help you, you know we'd do whatever we can for you!"

He sat slack jawed. Nothing could have prepared him for her answer, but the second voice in his head was now speaking again. It said, simply, "Ask her." Not waiting for the voice of reason to reappear, he went on gut feel.

"Mrs. Liu, there is one thing," he began. "Would you send some positive thoughts our way? In fact, if you're a spiritual person at all, would you offer some prayers for us? You did catch me in the middle of an emergency meeting, and we have some extraordinarily important things to do this afternoon. Your help with positive energy and prayers would be powerful."

"Of course," came her immediate reply.

Her next question stopped him again. "What, well, um—what would help you the most right now? What specifically should I pray for?" she asked.

What exactly, indeed? With all the potential options available out there, what would be of the most value right now? This afternoon? What should he ask her to do, specifically, to help him and the executive team? The second voice returned and gave him one word this time.

"Possibilities," came his reply. "Ask that we are open to possibilities, rather than continuing to do things the same old way."

"Okay. I can do that. I'll start immediately."

"Thank you, Mrs. Liu. Your call has been a delightful, unexpected pleasure. I appreciate your . . ."

She cut in, "No. Thank you, Mr. Falcon. Knowing that I can help is very good news. I feel so much better after our conversation. All will be well," she said. "That's one of your sayings, isn't it?"

He smiled.

"Yes, all will be well, Mrs. Liu. Thank you." He hung up.

Calmly, he folded his hands into a tent, rested his chin on them, closed his eyes, and let his mind wander. In Franklin's experience, he knew that getting the right problem on the table was vital to ensuring the best solutions would present themselves.

His father had a saying related to that: "Define the 'real' problem that needs to be solved, rather than the problem you *think* you should solve, and magic will happen."

Recalling his father's wisdom was energizing. For the past several weeks, Franklin had been fully absorbed in the wrong problem. He was focusing simply on raising more cash—a great deal more cash, and quickly. Not surprising to him now, as he recalled his father's saying, he realized that running on the treadmill of previous solutions had just made him tired, and it hadn't produced the results he desired.

However, as a result of Mrs. Liu's serendipitous call, he was clearly feeling more upbeat and confident than he had in days. He was eager to share his conversation with Mrs. Liu, and the insights he gained as a result of it, with the rest of the executive team. He wanted to share with them that the "real" problem needing to be solved, right now, was exploring new possibilities, as well as escaping the traps of the past. But how open would they be to exploring new possibilities?

# Accelerating the Energy

## Thursday: About 3:15 p.m. CST

### *(Liu's Home, Eden Prairie, Minnesota)*

Week I

| SUN | MON | TUE | WED | THU | FRI | SAT |
|-----|-----|-----|-----|-----|-----|-----|
|     |     |     |     | 3:15 p.m. CST |     |     |

"Hi, Mom."

"Angela?" It always made Angela smile to hear her mom on the phone. She knew it was Angela, but for some reason, her mom needed to verify things, often, on the phone. Even when Angela's mom called her, sometimes she'd lose track of who had dialed whom. It was a private joke between them.

"Yes, it's me, Mom. You called me, remember? What's up?"

"Oh, yes. Hey, I decided to do something this afternoon, take matters into my own hands, that kind of thing. I'd been wandering through the house, talking to the cats. You know how they look at you when you talk to them? Sort of like a combination between a question, 'Is she going to feed me, and should I stay here with her or head off into another room,' but . . ."

"Mom!" Angela was used to her mother's ramblings, and she usually let her go on for a bit, but she was with a couple of friends and wanted her mom to come to the point.

"Sorry. You know I can go on and on. I called him." She stopped.

Angela sighed and continued, "Who, Mom?"

"I decided to call Mr. Falcon at the foundation and ask him about the rumors. I just couldn't take the uncertainty any longer."

"You . . . called . . . Mr. Falcon? Mom! Why did you do that?"

Mrs. Liu interrupted, "Angela, it's okay. He told me he appreciated hearing from me, and he asked for my help."

"Mom, I can't believe you did . . ."

Again, Mrs. Liu cut in, "He did say something about some financial difficulties the foundation is having, and a big meeting they're having out there in Loveland today, but most importantly, he asked me if I'd pray for him—and for his executive team, too. Isn't that amazing?"

Shaking her head slowly in disbelief, Angela nevertheless found herself proud of her mom. It was a big step for Mrs. Liu. Normally, she'd continue to fret and would become ever-more paranoid about things.

"Wow, Mom. You actually talked to him? What else did he say?"

"Like I said, he asked me to send some positive thoughts and to pray for him. When I asked about his specific request, he said one word: 'possibilities.' He asked me to ask that the Falcon Foundation executive team would be open to new possibilities and not be stuck in the past."

Angela's mind was gearing up. She was confident that her mom had already said a prayer or two or three before she called Angela and that she would likely be in prayer for much of the afternoon. Angela also knew that her mother would be on the phone with her prayer group at church before the day was out. Before midnight tonight, there would be dozens of people throughout the Twin Cities praying for Franklin Falcon and his foundation.

However, Angela believed she could get thousands—maybe tens of thousands—of people involved in offering positive thoughts for Falcon's situation by the time her mom mobilized one or two dozen.

"Mom, that's just excellent. I'm really glad you called both Mr. Falcon and me. Now, I've got some work to do, and I know you do, too. I bet you'll be on the phone with your prayer group shortly, and I want to talk with a few of my friends about helping Mr. Falcon as well."

"Well, now that you mention it, I had considered calling the prayer group. How'd you know?"

Angela said, "I just know you, Mom. And I love you. I'll be home around dinner time. Talk to you then."

They hung up, and Angela huddled with her friends. Neither Franklin Falcon nor Liu Ping had ever personally used Facebook, or Twitter, but a tiny fraction of the collective power of the world's social networking capability was about to be focused on helping the foundation's leadership to be open to new possibilities and to not remain stuck in the past.

Angela was about to begin a major exercise of the "Six Degrees of Separation" principle.

# WHAT IF?

## Thursday: Exactly 2:30 P.M. MST

### *(Boardroom)*

Week 1

| SUN | MON | TUE | WED | THU | FRI | SAT |
|-----|-----|-----|-----|-----|-----|-----|
|     |     |     |     | 2:30 P.M. MST |     |     |

By the time Mr. Falcon returned to the boardroom, everyone else was already there. In fact, it was obvious they'd been there awhile because an uncomfortable and somewhat unnatural silence fell over the room as soon as he entered.

Sitting red-faced, Greg was perspiring. Jennifer's arms were tightly crossed in front of her, and Elaine appeared to be captivated by her PDA, a defeated look etched on her face.

"Hmm . . . seems I've interrupted something," Franklin suggested.

They looked at each other, almost challenging someone to break the silence.

"Things have gotten, well, a little tense," Ernesto said.

"A master of understatement," added Greg wryly.

Rather than responding to his sarcastic remark, Franklin simply walked to the front of the room, pulled out his chair, and sat down slowly. He sighed deeply and began speaking while moving his gaze from one member of the executive team to another.

"I've just had the most interesting phone call."

The executive team had settled and was concentrating on Franklin's words.

"Mrs. Liu, from Minnesota, woke up this morning and felt compelled to call me, to ask . . . ," he hesitated, ". . . to ask about the foundation. She'd heard some rumors about our financial difficulties and wanted to verify things for herself." They nodded their heads slightly. "It seems she's been working herself into a bit of a tizzy. Do you know their family story?" he asked.

Without considering the others who had slowly raised their hands, Terrence started, "Yes, Mr. Falcon. I do," and he proceeded to give a well-organized summary of the Lius' situation, sharing both the high and the low points.

"Thank you, Terrence, that's an accurate description," Franklin offered.

"What did you tell her?" blurted Elaine, showing sudden interest in the conversation. She returned her PDA to its case. It was clear the others in the room were also now giving Franklin their full attention.

"I started to give her a message our PR consultant would have been proud of, telling her we'd reached a tough spot, but that we were fully in control of the situation, don't worry, something like that."

Jennifer subtly shook her head, expecting to hear that Franklin had once again found a way to remain guarded in his response. In fact, Jennifer was surprised that Franklin had taken the call at all.

"But, you didn't do that?" Ernesto suggested, his mood starting to brighten immediately.

"No," stated Franklin. "I didn't. I sensed her phone call was an opportunity, an opening, really, for me to do something different today."

Greg was clenching his jaws, his breathing shallow. He nearly shouted, "You didn't tell her anything specific, did you? We can't have any details emerging outside of this room! What about asking her to sign our confidentiality agreement? We have to manage . . ."

"Greg," Franklin said loudly. Franklin paused, looked directly at Greg for a moment, then continued in his calm, fatherly manner of speaking while once again making eye contact with everyone in the room.

"I told her we are in trouble."

It was as if the dust stopped falling. The ticking of the clock on the wall echoed through the room, and everything became still. The group was sitting forward, waiting for the rest of Mr. Falcon's confession, as it was obvious he wasn't done speaking.

"I also told her that I personally have made many bad decisions that got us here, including the decision to keep things to myself for far too long." He stopped.

"Oh, my God," started Greg.

"Greg . . . please. Let Mr. Falcon speak," Terrence said, all eyes suddenly shifting toward him. "What did Mrs. Liu say when you told her that?" he asked.

"That's the strange and amazing thing," said Franklin. "She apologized to me! To me," his eyes moistening, his voice cracking, "for giving me more difficult things to think about."

He recovered, straightening his tie before continuing.

"She felt bad that her call had somehow upset me. What it did, however, was wake me up. It's time to look at our situation with a new set of eyes, to explore new choices and to be hopeful about our future. I know I've been in the dumps for weeks. It's been a very challenging time for me on a personal level," Franklin confided.

Looks of agreement circled the room, and the mood was becoming lighter by the moment.

"Nothing changes until something changes," Ernesto said, quoting the conversation he had been having with himself a few days earlier.

"That's exactly right, Ernesto," Franklin agreed, "but that's not where Mrs. Liu's conversation ended with me. Yes, I felt a change within me, but more importantly, I sensed that something within the entire foundation needed to change as well. It's time to own our situation, not to continue to bob and weave and use well-crafted messaging to continue the charade that we're in control. We aren't."

Anger clouded Greg's face.

"It wasn't until she asked me what she could do to help—imagine that? With all the challenges her family is facing, her response to my, well, confession, was that she asked me how she could help!" He waited a moment, searching the faces and seeing expressions of surprise. "I wasn't sure what to tell her. But . . . then . . ."

"What?" Jennifer showed her impatience.

"A small voice in my head—one that I haven't listened to for years—spoke to me. The voice told me to ask her to send positive energy, to pray for me, for us actually, to be open to new possibilities as we continue our work this afternoon." By this time he was speaking to the ceiling and no longer looking at anyone.

More silence. Greg was beginning to think the old man had cracked, that the pressure had gotten to him. After all, admitting fault, asking for help, and invoking a request for prayer, well, those were clearly the traits of a "leader" who was no longer in control. Greg was seconds away from asking his fellow executive team members to take a vote of no confidence in Franklin's ability to lead when Nicole spoke.

"Possibilities," said Nicole. "What a magical word!"

"Funny you should say that," offered Franklin. "Because as I was on the phone with Mrs. Liu, I was reminded of something my father told me repeatedly as I was growing up. One of his favorite sayings was, 'Define the *real* problem that needs to be solved, rather than the problem you *think you should* solve, and magic will happen.' Magic indeed."

Franklin stopped momentarily, smiled, and looked directly at Greg as he spoke again.

"Ladies, gentlemen, we've been trying to solve the wrong problem. Rather than the single-minded focus that I, and others, have had to simply raise as much cash as possible as soon as possible," Greg blanched, and Franklin looked away as he continued, "we need to use new approaches, to be open to new ideas, to new solutions. It's time to look at things through a new lens."

Ernesto sensed that hope was beginning to replace worry, but the group was clearly not yet united in its view that Franklin was right.

# The Law of the Harvest

## Thursday: About 4:00 p.m. CST

### *(Living Room, Liu Home)*

**Week 1**

| SUN | MON | TUE | WED | THU | FRI | SAT |
|-----|-----|-----|-----|-----|-----|-----|
|     |     |     |     | 4:00 p.m. CST |     |     |

Angela's mother had indeed called her prayer group. Motivated by her genuineness and urgency, all those in the group who were available decided to come together face-to-face that afternoon. They did this on occasion, but it was a process they reserved for very special circumstances. They couldn't explain why, exactly, but when the situation called for powerful outcomes, they seemed to "create" better results when they were able to be in the same room.

"Thanks for coming right over," Liu Ping began. "I appreciate your willingness to be here. You know we think the world of Mr. Falcon and his foundation; they've been wonderful to us."

Murmurs from the group affirmed her statement, and the group of 10 (made up mostly of retired folks) became quiet again.

Mrs. Liu continued, "It was, well, just so surprising. It took all the courage I had I think to actually call Mr. Falcon. I must admit, I thought he was sort of intimidating; after all, who am I to question him. He's been . . ."

"Ping," one of the prayer group started, "I'm not sure I would have been able to call him like you did."

"Well, that's the amazing part. Again, like I told all of you on the phone, Mr. Falcon actually asked me to pray for him. He asked! I thought to myself, well now, Ping, that's something you're actually quite good at. I began looking at different ideas, and immediately I thought to call you, and . . ." She was fully into rambling now, and her friends smiled warmly as she talked and talked for the next few minutes. Ultimately, she had somehow detoured into talking about a new recipe she was trying that evening, and that snapped her back to why her friends had come over.

"Oh, gosh, sorry for getting off the subject. I don't know how that happens," she chided herself, "but let's prepare ourselves to be ready to help Mr. Falcon and everyone who is attending their big meeting this afternoon."

The group had developed a specific ritual for getting into the right frame of mind. They'd discovered over the years that if they weren't able to eliminate their own personal dialog (thinking about to-do lists, recounting conversations, making plans, daydreaming, and so on), it would diffuse their effectiveness. In addition, making the request—the person and the specific need—crystal clear created far better results. None of them was a researcher or a scientist, but they believed their approach was right. Too many circumstances in the past had shown them the value of what they were doing, and how they were doing it, for them to disagree.

As many in the group had come from agricultural backgrounds, including the Lius, their approach mirrored Mother Nature's own process of ensuring a bountiful harvest. Consequently, the first step of preparing the soil—removing all impurities, rocks, dead plants—was the group's way of reminding themselves to clear their own minds before they began.

"Sit comfortably, relax your body, close your eyes, and quiet your minds," recited a member of the group. They had been doing this together for years and immediately fell into the routine. Knowing that the process of quieting their thoughts took time, the group felt no pressure and no timeframe. After about five minutes, sensing everyone was in the right frame of mind, the group knew it was time to add the seed to the soil. The seed was the specific request for the specific person or group of people. Knowing it was her responsibility, as she'd asked for the prayer team's assistance in this case, Mrs. Liu shared her specific request.

"Today we offer our positive energy and prayers for Mr. Franklin Falcon, the head of the Falcon Foundation for Families, and his team of managers. He has asked us to help them to be open to new possibilities as they look to solve their financial trouble. We pray they are open to new possibilities." The group was calm, focused.

Once the seed had been introduced into the soil, the group knew the next step was to add the right conditions for the seed to take root. They each were responsible, in their own unique and powerful way, to ensure they provided the right level of moisture, nutrients, sunlight, and care to keep weeds and insects away. Their approach included remaining focused on the seed itself, in using only positive, hope-filled words, in envisioning the seed sprouting and taking root deep within the well-prepared and cared-for soil, and in seeing the result of their request manifesting itself.

Powerful, focused, transforming energy flowed through the group, and each felt connected to each other, losing a sense of themselves as separate entities along the way. As a result, they knew the seed had sprouted and was now taking root.

# ASK, SEEK, KNOCK

## Thursday: About 3:00 P.M. MST

### *(Falcon Boardroom)*

Week I

| SUN | MON | TUE | WED | THU | FRI | SAT |
|-----|-----|-----|-----|-----|-----|-----|
|     |     |     |     | 3:00 P.M. MST |     |     |

"Possibilities," Elaine said, repeating Nicole's word. Throughout the entire executive team meeting, she had been actively watching, waiting for a chance to share her experience from her former employer. "Surely we need to look at positive, hope-filled possibilities and not dwell on negative ones. I think I've mentioned some of this before, but one of my previous job situations was awful."

Elaine's mind went inward for a moment. She felt her blood pressure rise involuntarily, and her mouth went dry. As she had spoken, recognition showed in some eyes. The members of the executive team had heard her story and had been amazed that Elaine had tried for so long to make things better back then.

Terrence, for one, wasn't sure he would have stuck it out.

Elaine continued, "Instead of looking at a crisis as an opportunity to grow, to reflect on the greatness of our organization, to reaffirm our commitment to it and to each other, we instead began to point fingers at each other. Most of our 'leaders' were personally obsessed with making sure their butts were covered before doing or saying anything, and before you knew it, the thing we feared most happened right before our eyes. The company died. It was if we invoked the most negative outcome simply by spending so much time focusing on it."

Ernesto said emphatically, "Exactly. That's what happened in Iceland as well. Some people literally died because they were looking out for themselves first. By doing so, they sealed their fate."

Heads nodded.

He continued, "In a strange sort of way, invoking outcomes by focusing on them is kind of *the* dynamic upon which I've built my entire career. Not to dig into the details of the world of quantum physics—unless you really want me to [bemused grimaces were nearly universal]—let me just say that in 'quantum-speak,' nothing exists in a state of absolute certainty. Everything exists instead in a state of probability, where all possibilities exist simultaneously. It's not until the observer arrives and begins looking at the quantum stuff that it actually manifests into something that we can see."

Ernesto could see that a few of the team were following him, but he'd lost a couple completely. When he had first started studying the world of quantum mechanics, like most people he thought there were a few things that seemed impossible. Unbelievable, literally. But, some really smart folks over the years had proven that the laws of quantum physics are indeed real, and they have some incredible power to help us do things we otherwise couldn't. Rather than digging into some formulas, he thought he'd try to explain things more simply.

"Okay, I can see I've lost a couple of you already. So let me try a different approach." The others' expressions grew relieved.

He continued, "The idea that every possibility exists as a probability in the world of quantum physics sounds unbelievable at first, but trust me on this, the formulas prove it's true. Therefore, if you accept the notion that all possibilities exist simultaneously, both positive and negative, and that just the process of observing is what causes a quantum particle to manifest, to pop into concrete form, it begs a very interesting question as we start thinking about our possible solutions to the financial challenge we face."

Ernesto paused and took a deep breath before continuing. "As observers to our own quantum possibilities, where every possibility exists simultaneously, which possibilities are we choosing to manifest, right now, and why?"

He'd stopped the group in its tracks. Ernesto didn't believe anyone had really considered the idea that they were completely in control of the process of choosing, of making their quantum possibilities real. No one spoke, but he could see the gears turning in almost everyone's heads.

"That reminds me of something else," Nicole offered after a moment of quiet. "Not quite the same thing, Ernesto, but maybe it's connected somehow." She smiled. "How many of you have seen the movie *Monsters, Inc.*?" she asked.

The tension softened as members of the executive team reflected on the movie.

"I'm watching you, Wazowski," Terrence said, in his best impression of the gritty, busy-body character, Roz. Everyone laughed, even Greg.

"No, seriously," Nicole continued. "The movie has a powerful message about how we approach things." She took a deep breath, "You're going to think I'm nuts, but I think the movie is very philosophical, and I've even thought of renaming it 'The Tao of Boo'!"

Their smiles grew quizzical.

"Okay, so let me explain. The movie starts with the idea that monsters under the bed and in the closet are real. Also, these monsters really are trying to scare the crap out of us, because they use fear to generate and then capture the energy needed to power their world. So, night after night, monsters move through closet doors, a crossing point between their universe and ours, wake kids (the only ones who still believe in the monsters), scare them, and then capture the released energy in containers that cross back into the monster's universe along with the monsters.

"Now, the monsters have strong beliefs that anything from the world of humans that comes across the barrier is toxic, and the monster world has an entire career field dedicated to containing and eradicating any vestiges of human stuff that occasionally 'hitches a ride' across the barrier. Socks make it from time to time [maybe that's where they go when they disappear, thought Jennifer], and other stuff, too, and should it be discovered on the other side, special-purpose monsters dressed in hazmat suits take care of the contraband.

"All is moving along normally when Sulley, the perennial monster-of-the-month, selects a door, goes through, and tries to scare the dickens out of a young girl named Boo only to have things fall badly apart for the monsters. Boo," she paused and smiled, "ironic name for the little girl—no?—actually makes it across the parallel universe barrier herself and winds up in the monster world.

"After some mishaps here and there, the monsters finally discover something profound when they quit trying to do what they've always done." Nicole looked intently at everyone.

"You see, when Boo laughs, the energy receptors calibrated for fear-based energy are unable to contain the amount of energy released. The entire infrastructure of the monster world is at risk of massive overload due to the effects of positive energy, and it's only one little girl who is causing all the potential damage."

Ernesto was the first to speak, "I remember the movie clearly. I'd just never thought of it as being quite so philosophical." He continued, "Indeed, the monsters found a solution to their power problems in a very unlikely source. Something they'd once thought of as toxic and dangerous became powerful and transformational."

"So," Nicole finished, "being open to new possibilities sometimes means you create considerable unexpected benefits—if you're willing to give it a try."

Greg had had enough. First spirituality, then physics mumbo-jumbo, and finally some BS philosophy from a kid's movie. It was time for action, not time for reflection. He decided it was time to call the question.

"Give what a try, Nicole?" Greg glared first at her and then moved his eyes to Ernesto and continued, "More of your untested, untried possibilities, Ernesto? There's only one possibility I see. We need cash. Today. And lots of it. Why are we wasting time looking at possibilities when we could be twisting some arms? And what about the story from *The Grant Report*? What will we tell them when they show up for their interview?"

Had Greg taken the time to look around, he would have seen that he had just separated himself fully from the team. The others had been moved by Ernesto's insights, and they related powerfully to Nicole's reflection of the energy fields in *Monsters, Inc.* They had also begun considering the fact that each of them had not only the power, but the responsibility, to act as the observer as they chose possibilities for their future. New possibilities could be fantastic, and very different, and the chance to explore them was compelling.

Instead, Greg's "saw" had neatly cut through the branch upon which he was sitting. And again, he was beet-red and sweating.

"Greg," cautioned Franklin, "above all else, we need to remain professional with each other. Ernesto is giving us the value . . ."

"Sure. Right," Greg spat sarcastically. "I can see my perspective isn't valued at all. I've been living and dying with our financial situation for weeks now, trying to raise the alarm, and finally when the situation has gotten your attention, Mr. Falcon, you're more interested in voodoo and touchy-feely than hard, practical answers." His spittle found targets throughout the room.

Silence permeated the room, except for the sounds of Greg's heavy breathing. Most of the executive team found solace in the laces of their shoes or in the interlacing of their fingers. No one was making eye contact with either Franklin or Greg.

Rather than reacting to Greg's emotional outburst, Franklin instead decided to once again listen to the voices in his mind. The voice of reason was vigorously suggesting that Greg was right, that the only logical solution to the problem was finding substantial amounts of cash ASAP. However, the other voice was telling Mr. Falcon that Ernesto was correct, that infinite possibilities exist simultaneously. Listening more deeply to this voice caused Franklin to swear he could hear Mrs. Liu's prayer group offering support to him and the executive team in their quest to explore, to discover, to dream.

After a minute of intense, disquieting silence in the room, Mr. Falcon finally spoke. He began asking a question with two of most powerful words any of them had ever heard: He said, "What if . . ."

As Franklin started to ask his question, Greg shot a look of extreme contempt Ernesto's way, packed his things, stood, sarcastically saluted the rest of the executive group, and walked out.

# STAGE TWO:
# INCUBATE

And when the broken-hearted people
living in the world agree,
there will be an answer, let it be.

For though they may be parted
there is still a chance that they will see,
there will be an answer. let it be.

Let it be, let it be, . . .

—*John Lennon / Paul McCartney*

# Making Plans for the Night

Thursday: About 3:00 p.m. MST

*(Falcon Foundation Offices)*

Week 1

| SUN | MON | TUE | WED | THU | FRI | SAT |
|-----|-----|-----|-----|-----|-----|-----|
| | | | | 3:00 p.m. MST | | |

Betty was nervous. The weather was deteriorating rapidly, and travel was getting to be nearly impossible into, out of, and around Loveland. She'd called and made sure all of the staff had made it home safely, but she wasn't sure what to do about the executive team members. Some of them lived near the office, but most drove some distance to get there. A few lived in the northern Denver suburbs, and she herself lived in Fort Collins.

After ruminating about it for a few minutes, and sensing that the meeting going on in the boardroom was not ending soon, she called the La Quinta Inn on Eisenhower and asked about rooms for everyone, herself included. She discovered that other travelers had already nearly fully booked the hotel, but there were four rooms left, each with two queen-size beds. Before thinking about it, she quickly booked the rooms, for two nights (she'd lived through a couple of these storms before), as her intuition told her the whole city might be shut down for a while.

After hanging up, she allowed herself to do a quick calculation and consider how the rooms might be divided. She and Jennifer had shared rooms countless times over the years at various conferences and seminars, and doing it again was a no-brainer. Nicole and Elaine seemed to be compatible and should be able to make it work for a night or two. Then there were Greg and Terrence . . . hmm . . . Ernesto and Franklin. Betty wasn't sure how to arrange the guys, but she guessed they'd figure it out.

If the roads were really bad tomorrow, getting back to the office might be a challenge. They'd used the facilities at Group Publishing (right next door to the hotel) several times for meetings; maybe they'd have space open so the executive team could continue working. Or, there was a small conference center at the hotel. Betty was sure one or the other would work.

Food was going to be difficult; although the hotel did have a restaurant, it probably didn't have a "Franklin Falcon stash" in its pantry. His taste for raw, unprocessed foods required constant planning whenever he left home. Betty had accumulated some of the things Franklin preferred, but she figured a non-organic hamburger wouldn't be toxic to him. He might even remember he liked them at one point.

Her mind moved to handling transportation to and from the hotel. Franklin had his Pathfinder, and it looked like Ernesto had an SUV, too. She thought there were a couple more SUVs available with other staff members. Jennifer? Elaine? She surmised getting to and from the hotel should be okay.

Finally, what about having a change of clothes, toiletries, and such? Ernesto should be fine, as he was already in traveling mode, but what about the others? Betty knew that Franklin kept a small travel bag in his office; he was always ready to get to the airport and head out of town for a day or two. He prided himself on being prepared to meet his kids, whenever and wherever. But Betty wasn't sure about the other executive team members. She herself had also put together some emergency supplies in case Franklin asked her to join him on a spontaneous trip, and Betty hoped the others were prepared as well as she was.

Betty created a short speech for Mr. Falcon about all of her planning and was rehearsing it as the boardroom door opened and slammed shut. She was riveted as Greg stormed past her thundering, "Those idiots. They have no idea about how to solve this problem." Greg continued berating the other members of the executive team as he disappeared around the corner, clearly heading for his office. After only a minute or two, he reappeared, fully dressed to enter the extreme winter conditions, and then pushed open the door and was consumed by the snow.

She grimaced and whispered to herself, "Yes, indeed. The next day or two are shaping up to be something indeed." Mr. Falcon's voice abruptly pierced her reverie. He'd come into the hall and asked, "Have you seen Greg?"

Needing a moment to orient herself to his question, she managed to reply, "Um, well—er, yes, Mr. Falcon. Greg left the office just a minute ago. He seemed quite upset," she added.

Betty immediately thought that the guys would now only need to divide two hotel rooms among the three remaining men. It was obvious that Greg was not coming back.

Franklin sighed. "Darn. I was hoping to catch him before he left. Thanks, Betty." He looked at the door through which Greg had recently left. "Oh, if you've got a moment, would you please join us for a little while?" he asked her.

"Of course. Be right there," said Betty, glancing once again at the door, trying and failing to make out a Greg-shaped shadow among the swirling flakes.

# GALVANIZING COMMITMENT

## Thursday: About 3:15 P.M. MST

### *(Falcon Boardroom)*

Week 1

| SUN | MON | TUE | WED | THU | FRI | SAT |
|-----|-----|-----|-----|-----|-----|-----|
|     |     |     |     | 3:15 P.M. MST |     |     |

Murmurs and side conversations greeted Franklin as he returned to the meeting room, Betty walking in before him as he held the door for her. Before sitting in his familiar chair, he and Betty shared a brief conversation. Betty pulled a new chair up to the table at Franklin's suggestion; he then loosened his tie, returned to his seat, and addressed his team.

"Betty tells me that Greg has left the office," Franklin stated matter-of-factly. "I need to be open with each of you right now," he added.

Everyone's attention was rapt.

"First, I hope he is capable of driving safely. It's a mess out there, and I'm worried about anyone who's on the roads right now."

Shifting attention to the weather caused the executive team to wish there were windows to the outside in their boardroom. But Franklin had intentionally designed the room to be without windows so he could place more photos of his kids on the walls.

"Related to the weather, Betty once again has trusted her intuition and has made arrangements for all of us to stay at the La Quinta tonight, and maybe tomorrow night as well, should the weather really fall apart. She's planned for food, meeting space, etc., and we both hope you've kept a small travel bag here in the office, as she and I have, so that you'll have clean socks and deodorant for tomorrow. Deodorant especially," he quipped. Grins and chuckles met his words.

"However, I need for you to look at moving to the hotel for the next day or two as voluntary, not mandatory. Obviously the work we have at hand is critical, and your participation will be vital to our success. But I need you to do this with commitment, not compliance. Be there and be part of the work because you choose to, not out of any sense of obligation to me or the foundation."

Ernesto spoke first, "You know I'm in. And I've brought several days' worth of deodorant with me from Chicago!" The room filled with genuine laughter, and it lasted for several seconds, almost completely destroying the vestiges of Greg's negative energy.

"Seriously," restarted Franklin, "are the rest of you up for this?"

Without hesitation, most around the table shared their agreement, some saying "Yes!" and others saying "Absolutely." Terrence and Elaine hesitated, and then murmered their agreement as well. It was another moment of transparency for Ernesto. Watching the remaining members of the executive team sign up to work hard, to be out of their comfort zones, and to work together was a powerful indicator all by itself. They were indeed going to explore new possibilities. He smiled broadly, showing the executive team all of the fine dental work for which his parents had sacrificed to pay.

"Okay, maybe it's time for me to tell you that you'll need to share rooms," Betty interrupted. The lightness in the room was somewhat tempered. "They had only four rooms left, so you'll be bunking together. I'm thinking Nicole and Elaine? Jennifer, you and I . . ."

"Absolutely," shared Jennifer, who then added, "I guess the guys will have to make do. But only three guys for two rooms when there's four women in two rooms? Doesn't seem fair to me. But then again, without enough deodorant to go around, maybe three guys in two rooms are too many." More laughter.

Hearing this, Ernesto consulted his cell phone browser. He had a room reserved at the Embassy Suites near the Budweiser Events Center, and he had started the process of canceling his reservation when he heard Franklin speak again.

"Thank you. Everyone. We have much to do, but knowing that we're doing it together gives me a great sense of hope. Maybe Greg will change his mind and come back this afternoon. If not, we will surely miss his perspective and his skill."

Terrence spoke, "Mr. Falcon, I've tried calling his cell phone, but either he wasn't answering or he was out of range. He does live up the canyon a ways. I left a message letting him know I'd like to talk to him and that we'll be staying at the La Quinta tonight. He has to drive right by it to get to his house."

"Good idea, Terrence. Thanks. While I don't appreciate the approach Greg used to try to make us believe he was right, I do care about Greg, and I'm concerned for his safety. However, as I've gotten older, I've become more aware of the fact that we should take the situation seriously, but not ourselves. Greg was clearly taking himself, and his viewpoints, very seriously."

Franklin waited for his statement to sink in. During the pause, Terrence recalled another of Marty Wright's sayings. Terrence spoke up, "Focus on 'what's right, not who's right,' as Marty would say." This time Terrence's tone of voice was sincere; the earlier hints of sarcasm had disappeared.

Heads nodded.

Franklin continued, smiling at Terrence, "Again, I don't agree with Greg's anger and his insistence on his own way, but part of me agrees with Greg's dogged determination that finding large sums of money in a short period of time is required to solve our challenge. However, doing it in the 'we've always done it that way before' manner wasn't working, nor do I believe it will work now. Twisting arms, remaining secretive, not sharing our situation, not asking for help, taking care of things ourselves . . . Speaking for myself, 'I've always done it that way before' is a major reason why we're in the mess we're in."

Jennifer regarded Franklin with a newfound sense of respect. She was seeing a side of Mr. Falcon that he didn't show to others outside of his wife, Jo, and their dog, Maggie. Franklin could be "real" with those at home, but he found it difficult to be vulnerable with those he felt he was leading.

Ernesto spoke up. "Mr. Falcon, it seems everyone has had a role to play in getting things to where they are. Actively or passively, our decisions have made the thing we now call reality, and certainly we need to be accountable for it." He was feeling a part of the team now and began speaking as if he had been actively invited.

"I've got a few tools in my toolbox that might help us move farther forward, faster. With your permission, I'd like to use a few of them in helping us explore possibilities and find solutions." He had decided to go "all in" and share everything he had to share.

This time, affirmation was unanimous, spontaneous, and somewhat boisterous. Even Elaine's and Terrence's energy was growing more positive by the moment. The group had been looking for a chance to release some tension, and his offer to help was met enthusiastically.

As the room quieted, Elaine spoke, looking intently at Ernesto.

"Ernesto, we are lucky you took the initiative to come meet with us. Thank you for your offer, and for your leadership." Elaine had been quiet for quite a long time, as she had been engrossed in a conversation with herself about her future with the foundation.

"I was uncertain if I could really commit again to helping any organization move forward in the midst of a major crisis. It takes a surprising amount of focus, energy, and unity. I have to admit I've been skeptical about whether I wanted to continue to work here, but the past several minutes have been important to me. I'm now drawn to you, to this situation, and to the possibilities we might create."

Ernesto showed his dental work again.

"But, I'm wiped out. What does everyone think about taking a break for an hour or so to get ready for tonight. I may have to walk to the store to get some more personal hygiene products myself," she joked, "but more than anything, I could use some time to relax and to process everything we've talked about this afternoon. I know I'm far more productive after I recharge my batteries."

Elaine's wisdom resonated throughout the room. Franklin was the first to speak.

"Wise counsel indeed," he said. "It's about 3:30 right now. What do you say we meet here in the boardroom at 5 P.M., travel bags in hand, calls made to our families, laptops, PDAs, etc., charged up, ready to load up into some of the all-weather vehicles we have, and then head over to the hotel?"

More agreement, and it was done. 5 P.M. They'd be back, and they'd be ready.

# A Climate for Innovation

## Thursday: About 6:00 P.M. MST

### *(La Quinta Inn, West Loveland)*

Week 1

| SUN | MON | TUE | WED | THU | FRI | SAT |
|-----|-----|-----|-----|-----|-----|-----|
|     |     |     |     | 6:00 P.M. MST |     |     |

The drive to the hotel was mostly uneventful but very slow. Normally, the four- or five-mile trip would take less than 10 minutes, but today it took over 30 minutes. At about 4:45 P.M., the National Weather Service had upgraded the Winter Storm Warning to a Blizzard Warning for the northern Front Range of Colorado, and Loveland was squarely in the crosshairs of the weather's fury. The Public Works Department in Loveland was trying valiantly to stay ahead of the piling snow. However, the 60+ mile per hour wind gusts were covering the streets in mere minutes after they'd been plowed. The driving conditions were quickly changing from simply hazardous to downright dangerous.

Franklin drove his Pathfinder (complete with the factory off-road package), Elaine had a Ford Escape Hybrid, and Ernesto drove his rented RAV4. Franklin had the best-equipped vehicle and was also the most experienced driver in severe weather conditions, so he went first. He attempted to navigate the drifting snow and plow a path for the other two vehicles to follow. Elaine's car, following Franklin's, struggled to keep up. The Escape's low ground clearance and all-season tires made it difficult to navigate the deep snow, even as Elaine tried to stay in the Pathfinder's tracks.

The RAV4 wasn't much better than the Escape, but being third gave Ernesto the advantage of a more "flattened" path. In addition, the front bumper of the RAV4 meshed nicely with the rear bumper of Elaine's car, which he discovered during the eight or 10 times he found it necessary to give her a small push when she got stuck. He hoped Hertz wouldn't notice any scratches.

Massive snowstorms like the one in progress are a strange weather phenomenon in Colorado. When it snows this heavily in the lower elevations, the mountains are often unfazed; they might even be dry, sunny, and warm. That was the case with this storm. As such, the tourists who had come "down the hill" after visiting Estes Park, Rocky Mountain National Park, and the other sites along US 34 were completely unprepared for the weather in town. Some turned around and headed back to the mountains once they'd gotten in the snow, but others, hearing the weather reports, decided another day or two in the beauty of Colorado's mountains was in order and had never left in the first place.

Inevitably, however, there were others who didn't pay attention to the weather, didn't believe the weather report when they heard it, or thought they were somehow impervious to nature's capriciousness. It was that group, those who thought they could get to the Denver airport, or return to Denver or wherever else they'd come from, who were in trouble. And since the La Quinta was the first large hotel or motel they saw when driving east into Loveland, the hotel was teeming with an unlikely collection of stranded travelers.

The three vehicles had inched their way across town from the foundation's offices to the hotel and successfully transported all of them, their luggage (as modest as that was), and some boxes Betty had pulled together from the office. When the Falcon team arrived, the parking lot was jammed, and they actually had to park on the street outside the hotel and walk. They slipped, tripped, and fell repeatedly while trying to help each other get from the vehicles to the lobby entrance. But they worked together, and laughed together, to get it done, albeit ending up a bit wetter, colder, and goofier than they'd planned.

Upon entering the lobby of the hotel, they found themselves to be just a few of the number of people who were looking for a place to stay. From retirees to a troop of girl scouts to a 1980s retro "hair band" to various salespeople, business owners, and a cross-section of tourists from all corners of the world (Japan, the UK, Brazil, and Australia to name a few), the sights and sounds were fantastic in their variation. For all of Betty's careful preparations, it became instantly evident that they were not going to have a warm and cozy conference room to use for their meetings.

The hotel management, rather than turning people away, had instead begun converting the meeting rooms and the events center into impromptu shelters, using every available blanket, pillow, and roll-away bed, couch, and cot they could lay their hands on. The staff's attitude of welcoming, of supporting those in need, was infectious. The hotel was a living mosaic, rich in its diversity and alive with its sense of warmth, service, and invitation. Almost as if pre-planned, the environment at the hotel was one of constant adaptation to new situations: Each new arrival brought sounds of greeting, generous readjustment, and hope for a positive change in the weather.

The staff had set up a computer projector and a large screen and had loaded *Finding Nemo* into the DVD player. The movie was showing a scene in which Nemo's father and his traveling companion Dory found themselves being guided through the East Australian Current with a group of sea turtles. Rather than resisting the current, the turtles were relaxed and content and had surrendered to the natural flow in which they found themselves.

Ernesto took note of the symbolism in the movie and how it fit with their situation. While it had been only a few hours since he and Mr. Falcon had sat down for lunch, they had been trying to surrender to the natural flow all afternoon. Well, except for Greg. He'd decided to swim upstream, out of the current. And unlike the little turtle in the movie, who when he found himself outside the flow decided to jump right back in and was welcomed with "open flippers" by the rest of his friends and family members, Greg chose to stay on the outside.

"That's one of my favorite movies," Ernesto mentioned to Elaine. "It's very quantum, I mean, in relation to choosing possibilities. Especially this scene. It's . . ." He stopped.

Elaine regarded Ernesto a bit like the RCA Victor dog: with a crooked neck, squinted eyes, an ear angled toward him, and a quizzical expression on her face. He was quickly reminded that not everyone looked at the world the way he did. He chuckled to himself, "You're a geek, Ernesto!"

"We should have four rooms. Reservation for the Falcon Foundation," Betty told the front desk clerk. The hotel had indeed held their rooms for them, and they were extremely lucky to have private space, with their own beds, showers, and bathrooms.

While the desk clerk went about the task of creating their keys, they stood there wondering what the right thing to do was. There were so many people in need at the hotel, and they could probably squeeze into two rooms instead of four, but there were so many in need of rooms, how would the hotel choose among them?

"Mr. Falcon," Jennifer began, "using four rooms seems like the wrong thing to do. There are only seven of us. Look at all the others here!" Jennifer's hand panned across the lobby. She was conflicted with the tug at her heart to help others and the challenge of choosing which of those without a room might be served best by using theirs. It was daunting.

Looking at the other members of the executive team, Ernesto believed the unity of the group was about to be tested. He just felt it. It was the same situation on the glacier when the group split into two. In that situation, half of the group took action consistent with the new situation—and half did not. The half that took action made it. It was a permanent lesson for him.

"We have a choice to make, clearly," Ernesto said. "Certainly I prefer to have a more private room—I'm a pretty introverted person—but not helping others here seems to be inconsistent with the mission of the Falcon Foundation. We need to do the right thing."

The test began, and it lasted only a few moments.

"I have a suggestion," offered Terrence "I think the three guys can share one room. I'll offer to sleep on the floor. That'll free up one room." Franklin and Ernesto both immediately protested and offered to sleep on the floor themselves.

Then Nicole chimed in, "And, ladies, what about us sharing one room? We can talk about boys all night!"

"And paint our nails?" asked Elaine. The twelve-year-old in her was rising to the surface; you could see it.

Goofy grins replaced the fretting. The guys started teasing the ladies about Nicole's slumber party references, and the ladies told the guys there had better not be any "doorbell ditching" going on in the middle of the night. The teasing was good-natured, and unlike Ernesto's experience in Iceland, the group decided to bond together as opposed to split apart when faced with a challenge. His optimism continued to grow.

"Excuse me," said Franklin as he addressed the desk clerk. "I know we reserved four rooms, but we have decided we can do quite nicely with just two. We'd like to return two of our rooms."

"For both nights?" asked the clerk.

"Yes, both nights," replied Franklin.

"That's very generous of you. Thank you!" the desk clerk said, clearly showing a sense of relief. She'd had to tell dozens of needy travelers that a spot in a hallway, or on the floor in the lobby or the ballroom, was the best she had to offer them. "I'll talk to our manager. I know there are a couple of families who can really use the rooms."

"It's a small gesture," said Franklin, truly believing it. Just then, the clerk turned to speak to the manager, who had arrived behind the check-in desk. They engaged in a short conversation, and then the manager turned to face Franklin.

"Mr. Falcon?" asked the manager, extending her hand. "I thought I recognized you when you came in. I'm so pleased to meet you." The manager was a bit in shock, and in awe, to find Franklin Falcon standing in her lobby. "Your offer to return two rooms is a generous and timely gesture. We have a couple of stranded families who were coming from a special-needs camp near Estes Park. They have two or three kids with extreme sensory challenges, who are struggling big time with all the hubbub in the rest of the hotel. They'll be thrilled to know they can have private space tonight."

Franklin radiated, but remained mute. Jennifer was the one to speak first; she addressed all of them standing in the lobby.

"Wow," she started. "I was thinking the process of choosing the 'right' folks to take our rooms might be more complicated, or painful. But I'm not sure the fact that there are these two families with special-needs kids who were 'waiting' for us to decide to share our rooms is a coincidence." Her message sank in. "I've been part of this organization for a long time, and years ago we didn't try to help everyone, nor did we get paralyzed because we felt like we didn't have enough to go around."

Terrence's eyebrows knitted.

"Instead," Jennifer continued, "we took what we had and shared it generously. It seems we began getting ourselves in trouble recently when we over-reached and started making promises we couldn't keep."

Elaine finished the thought, "We lost our way."

Terrence wasn't sure he agreed with the women. His baritone filled the small space, "I'm not so sure. Aren't we asked to serve those in need, whenever and wherever the need might exist? I learned that lesson in Sunday School as a boy. Our family lived that way. We still do!"

The battle of values was evident in Terrence's face. His faith told him that everyone who has needs should be served, and he'd committed his professional life in pursuit of that mandate.

"No question that was, and is, a core principle of the foundation," added Franklin. "It's part of who we are. However, we have begun to take ourselves far too seriously in the process. We, okay, I," he rubbed his chin, "started feeling an overwhelming sense of obligation to help those in need. Years ago, we had a fairly rigorous selection process, based upon need, yes, but also on accountability, and integrity."

Jennifer added, "We used to rule out more families that we ruled in. Do you remember that?"

Terrence nodded his head, resigned to the memory.

"Things are in a mess for sure," Jennifer said, "but our commitment to look at new ways to find solutions doesn't mean we should compromise our core values. We just can't serve everyone ourselves."

The sounds from the television, the children, the voices of welcoming for new arrivals, and the general hum in the hotel returned to their ears. They shifted from one foot to another and crossed their arms, seeming to wait for inspiration.

Nicole offered her thoughts, "I for one am ready to help some of these folks here in the lobby feel welcomed into Loveland, Colorado. The issues and pressures related to the foundation can wait until the morning. Let's go put our stuff away in our rooms and come back here. I love *Finding Nemo*, and I'd like to find out how I might be able to help the hotel staff this evening."

"Again, a great idea," said Franklin.

They gathered their stuff, headed to the two rooms they'd reserved, dropped their luggage, supplies, and miscellaneous boxes of stuff, and walked back to the lobby.

"Hey!" hollered the group of girl scouts upon their return. "We're going on a scavenger hunt. Want to join us?"

"Absolutely!" Betty said with enthusiasm, and she was off.

"All will be well," Franklin muttered to himself, and he, too, followed the girl scouts, watching their ponytails swing as they skipped down the hall.

# The Wisdom of the Network

Thursday: About 11:15 p.m. CST

*(Cyberspace)*

Week 1

| SUN | MON | TUE | WED | THU | FRI | SAT |
|-----|-----|-----|-----|-----|-----|-----|
|  |  |  |  | 11:15 P.M. CST |  |  |

Angela had never heard the term "entrainment" before, but she had experienced the awe of watching schools of fish swim in unison, seeing flocks of birds move through the air as if choreographed only by God, and observing how the menstrual cycles of the women close to her came into alignment over time. That night—for some reason—she'd thought about all of that as she watched the text messages, Tweets, emails, and Facebook updates flow, all of them about Mr. Falcon and the foundation. She was completely, utterly blown away.

Thinking back to last night, Angela reflected on how her weeks-long decision to sit on the sidelines and just worry about the Falcon Foundation had drained her of her energy, her commitment, even her motivation. 180 degrees different than that, tonight the simple act of "energizing and trusting her social networking cloud" had done exactly the opposite. As she started posting positive, help-requesting comments about the foundation and Mr. Falcon through Twitter and on her Facebook page, and by blasting text messages throughout her network of friends to everyone she could think of who might want to help, she was energized!

Her message was simple and pure. It had nothing to do with self-interest, casting blame, showing panic, or obligation. It was a genuine request to do something important and filled with meaning.

Angela had typed, "Mr. Falcon told my mom that he's in big trouble, and he asked for our help. He wants us to send our thoughts, prayers, and positive energy to him and his executive team as they look to find some answers. He's done such great things and helped so many others. Would you please help? Send your thoughts, prayers, and energy out toward Loveland, Colorado, and forward this message to others who might be willing and able to help. Thank you; I know we can make a big difference for them!"

Entrainment. The process of aligning energy frequencies sometimes so quickly across distances that it defies the laws of physics. After all, nothing is supposed to be able to travel faster than the speed of light. But for some reason, entrainment happens simultaneously and spontaneously. It happened right before Angela's eyes.

One small question to a few dozen friends had turned into hundreds of messages, then into thousands, into tens of thousands, and eventually into millions of messages in just a few hours. With a small "metaphysical nudge" coming from Angela Liu and her Apple laptop in Eden Prairie, Minnesota, she'd started the process of getting thousands of others throughout the world to start vibrating at a very high level of energy. Contagious energy. Cleansing, hope-filled energy. The energy of possibilities. The energy that was connected to the universal mind—and the source of all energy.

Even when a few suspicious, negative messages crept into the virtual conversation, they were simply ignored. The power of the positive, forward-focused energy was far too aligned to be negated by nay-sayers. What started with a simple word inside Franklin Falcon's own mind, "possibilities," through the power of pure intention and authentic desire had literally grown into a tsunami of potential.

Angela was not at all prepared for the conflagration-like growth of the messages, and she wondered what might happen next.

"What if," she whispered to herself.

# Non-Locality

## Thursday: About 10:15 P.M. MST

### *(La Quinta Inn Kitchen)*

Week 1

| SUN | MON | TUE | WED | THU | FRI | SAT |
|-----|-----|-----|-----|-----|-----|-----|
|     |     |     |     | 10:15 P.M. MST |     |     |

"Mr. Falcon, um, sorry to interrupt you," the shy, Australian-accented voice of a young woman began.

"Oh, yes, what can I do for you?" asked Franklin, momentarily stopping his work of scraping dishes before loading them into the automatic dishwasher.

Rather than focusing further on the challenges of the foundation that evening, they'd been working in the restaurant, alternatively doing their best to follow the directions of the chef to prepare creative dishes with the ever-more limited quantity of food, to run the dishwasher, and to bring food and drinks to their fellow refugees in the rest of the hotel. It was hard work, especially considering the restaurant was part of the events center, and a trip to and from the hotel actually involved icy blasts across the 150-foot courtyard separating the buildings. However, the process of using their hands and their hearts to serve others was refreshing to their spirits. They were tired, but they were still full of energy!

"Please, no, um, I mean, I don't mean to ask for anything from you," she said. "It's just that I was on my computer a few minutes ago, and, well, I must have received messages from 20 or 30 of my friends back home saying that you needed our help."

Franklin was lost. "What? I'm not sure I know what you mean."

She continued, "I'm sorry. It's just that the messages said that you were having some money troubles, and that you had asked someone in Minnesota to help you not get stuck in the past, that kind of thing. So, when I told my friends that you were actually here in the hotel where I was staying, they thought that was awesome."

The dots slowly started to connect, and realization crept into his mind. It was just a few hours ago when he'd talked with Mrs. Liu, and that had somehow transformed into having this young woman from Australia hear from her friends some 8,000 miles away. He could see the connection, but he had no clue as to how it happened.

"Would you," he said, " mind showing me the messages you've received?"

"Oh, sure!" she brightened. "I brought my laptop."

Franklin dried his hands and took her computer gently. He needed a brief introduction into how to navigate Facebook, but he quickly caught on. For the next 10 minutes he read slowly, message after message, about how strangers in a country half a world away might offer assistance to him. In following the string backward even further, he saw that the messages had originated somewhere in the US but had traveled throughout the world. His mind was spinning. How had one phone call with one person earlier in the day become thousands of messages flowing across the planet? While he was unsure of the "how" associated with what was happening, the voice inside his head told him there was limitless power available to him and the foundation as a result of what he was reading.

"I don't know what to say," was all he could muster as an initial response to the young woman. He smiled uncertainly.

She was confident as she replied, "Mr. Falcon, we have some ideas we could share."

"Yes. I see that. My goodness. Sharing some ideas with us would be wonderful," he replied.

The young woman beamed.

"But I'd like to share this with some other folks. Would you mind coming with me?"

"Of course not," she blushed. "I'd like that." Her confident words betrayed her introverted nature. She was out of her comfort zone here, but she felt a compelling force driving her forward.

They left the kitchen, and Franklin felt a twinge of guilt as he left the small mountain of dishes needing to be washed as they left in search of the members of the executive team. He hoped he'd have the opportunity to come back to the dishes sometime later that evening.

# Synchronicity

## Friday: About 3:15 P.M. Australian EST

### *(Town of Oakey, near Toowoomba, Queensland, Australia)*

Week 1

| SUN | MON | TUE | WED | THU | FRI | SAT |
|-----|-----|-----|-----|-----|-----|-----|
|     |     |     |     |     | 3:15 P.M. AUSTRALIAN EST |     |

"I've just heard from Rebecca, I mean, Miss Anderson, and you won't believe this." The small team who made up the school's teaching and administrative group and about a dozen of the older students were meeting at the end of their school day in the tiny one-room school in the town of Oakey, near the city of Toowoomba. Rebecca was one of the teachers in the school and had left for America about a week before. She'd planned a vacation to coincide with the marriage of her older sister, who had moved to the States a few years back. The wedding was in Colorado at an impressive site called St. Malo near Estes Park.

Oakey was located on the edge of the Outback (the "bush" to the locals), and it served this agricultural region of Queensland. The entire school comprised about 100 students, who ranged in age from grade one to grade 12. It was a family atmosphere, where the older kids combined learning with nurturing as they completed their studies and simultaneously acted as role models for the younger kids. The walls were covered in everything from colors, shapes, and simple addition and subtraction equations to the table of atomic elements and detailed anatomy diagrams. It was a rich learning environment and a place where everyone felt a strong connection to each other.

"She's stuck in a huge snowstorm in Colorado, and the amazing thing is that Mr. Falcon is staying at her hotel!" Rebecca's coworker stated, shaking her head in disbelief. "They're refugees together!"

She spent another few minutes describing the details of Rebecca's situation, and the group followed closely. Almost all of the students had personally received some form of electronic communication (including some telephone calls) about the need to help the Falcon Foundation. Mr. Falcon had an amazing reputation throughout the world, and that was definitely true in Australia. Australia was another country founded by immigrants, and a couple of Falcon-like foundations had started there and were doing similar things to help immigrants to the land of Oz. Many of the kids in Toowoomba themselves were first- or second-generation immigrants and had been helped to some degree by these foundations.

So when the need to help Mr. Falcon had come up, they'd been motivated to help. In fact, through much of the day, they'd been busy contacting others within their personal network to spread the word. The teachers found out about the "subversive" text messaging, twittering, and Facebook updates eventually, but rather than shutting it down, the teachers actively encouraged it, albeit during short, coordinated times after lessons had been completed.

"What did she say about Mr. Falcon? I mean, did she give us any more information about what we can do to help?" The group was looking for specifics. The need to send positive energy, prayers, and a hope that the foundation's leadership would be open to new possibilities was a very important thing, but the group of teachers, administrators, and students in the one-room school on the edge of Australia's vast interior wilderness was ready to help provide some answers.

"Actually, she told me she was about to go introduce herself to him. That must be quite difficult for her. She's pretty shy!"

"Okay, but I think we should start looking at some ideas to help Mr. Falcon. It's about money, right?" one of the students asked.

"I think so, but I'm not sure about the details," the teacher offered.

"Well, remember when our scout troop needed to raise some money for a trip to Melbourne? We kept hitting a brick wall. Everyone said they didn't have enough right now, that the economy was bad, the drought had dried up more than just the fields, and most people just didn't feel confident about giving money to us. Remember?" The student was reflecting on a situation from about six months ago.

"Yes, you're right," another teacher said. "Maybe some of the ideas we used then would help now. It was amazing how fast your trip got funded."

The group got to work, and within about 15 minutes, they had put together a list of a few suggestions and sent them to Rebecca's email address. It wouldn't be long before they'd hear back from her.

# As We Become Like Children

Thursday: About 10:50 P.M. MST

*(Room 212, La Quinta Inn)*

Week 1

| SUN | MON | TUE | WED | THU | FRI | SAT |
|-----|-----|-----|-----|-----|-----|-----|
|     |     |     |     | 10:50 P.M. MST |     |     |

Finding the other members of the executive team was pretty easy with the exception of Jennifer. She'd been delivering food throughout the hotel, and during her last delivery, she'd also found out about the exploding Internet traffic related to helping the foundation. When her cell phone rang, she was deep in conversation with the Miller family from San Antonio, Texas.

"Hello?"

"Jennifer, it's Ernesto."

"Oh, Ernesto. I didn't recognize your number. What's up?"

"Mr. Falcon would like for us to get together as a group for a short meeting. Are you able to do that?"

"Um, yeah, that should be fine. I've got some interesting news to share with everyone. Where are we planning to meet?"

"We're in our hotel room—the guys' room—room 212."

"Sure. Meet you there in a couple of minutes, and I'm bringing someone with me if that's okay." Jennifer's eyes questioned Jack Miller as if to say, "that is okay, I hope." He nodded and smiled in return.

Everyone had arrived a few minutes before Jennifer got there, and while they had been waiting, they swapped stories about the other hotel guests and the work they had been doing. Mr. Falcon introduced them to Rebecca, and she shared a story about a pregnant woman in the hotel who was very ready to give birth. Based upon Rebecca's description, they wondered if that mom-to-be would make it through the night. The baby would certainly have an interesting story to tell later in life.

As they told their stories about their volunteering, all of them genuinely felt good about serving others, and the break from wallowing in the foundation's financial mess was both a relief and energizing. Just simply being rid of Greg's destructive energy in addition to actively doing something to serve others helped to quietly and subtly rebuild their relationships as a team.

As Jennifer and Jack Miller entered the room, Terrence spoke up.

"I've finally heard from Greg. He made it home safely, although the power is out up there."

"I'm glad he's somewhere safe tonight," shared Franklin. "This storm is one for the books!"

Terrence went on, "But Greg told me he's 'done.'" He drew quotation marks in the air around the word "done." "He wishes things would have worked out differently for him with the foundation, but he can't support the direction we're heading in, and as such he will be sending along his letter of resignation to you, Mr. Falcon." Terrence imparted the information calmly, but they could tell it bothered him to have to report it. Greg was his friend; they'd spent considerable time together and had become close over the years.

"That's unfortunate," Franklin said directly, "but not unexpected. I'll miss him on a personal level, but it became very clear that he was not open to looking in new directions to solve our problems."

The executive team regarded Mr. Falcon and each other and realized they had made significant progress in coming together. They knew that Greg's influence had been destructive over the past few weeks, but no one had either the insight or the courage to speak up about it. As of now, though, things were different.

Ernesto was particularly amazed at how much they were "together" on things. The events of this afternoon and evening, all by themselves, had a unifying effect on their thoughts and feelings. Not only did they feel far more hopeful about the situation, they also were believing that a solution would be found—and soon. What a change from earlier in the day, when defeat seemed inevitable.

"Mr. Falcon," Jennifer changed the subject. "I'm sorry I'm the last to join our meeting, but I have had the most incredible experience in the past 15 or 20 minutes. In fact, I'd put it in the category of unbelievable!" She was gushing.

She looked at Rebecca and said, "But, oh, sorry, where are my manners? I'm Jennifer." She extended her hand to Rebecca, and they greeted each other.

"I'm Rebecca Anderson. It's nice to meet you."

Jennifer then motioned to Mr. Miller, who introduced himself as well. "My name is Jack, Jack Miller. My family and I are here from San Antonio, and I have to admit, we were completely unprepared for this weather! What is going on?  Right now we have flowers blooming, and I'll need to run my lawn mower when we get home. If we get home!" He smiled.

"We live here," said Betty, "and we are still unprepared for things like this. Crazy weather in Colorado, but it makes it interesting. We'll have to see what happens overnight; sometimes storms like this can go on for a couple of days." The group murmured its agreement.

Jennifer found it hard to be patient and was almost bouncing up and down as she continued, "Okay. Let me finish!"

The group quieted and found small pieces of the floor and the ends of the beds upon which to sit.

"It seems the world—and I mean *the world*—is not only aware of our situation, but thousands of people have been contacted about potentially helping us. I don't know how it happened, but it's amazing!" Jennifer's excitement was growing as she spoke.

"Jennifer, I've had a similar experience, and that explains why I've asked Rebecca here to join us," Franklin said, his energy nearly rising to meet Jennifer's.

"Rebecca," began Franklin, "would you please share with everyone how you and I had the chance to meet?"

With a few nervous glances at everyone, and a quick reassuring hand on her shoulder from Mr. Falcon, Rebecca recounted her story. In the middle of telling everyone about her school, her students, her friends, and the network of connections she had, and how the messages asking to help the Falcon Foundation had been pouring in, her cell phone alerted her that she'd received another message.

"Rebecca, what's happening with you is happening everywhere. It's exactly what I heard from the Millers," agreed Jennifer. "The offers to help are everywhere!"

As Jack Miller shared his story, nearly matching Rebecca's word for word, Rebecca was busy reading her new message.

Once Jack had finished, Rebecca said calmly, "Well, it looks like some of my students have some concrete suggestions about fund-raising. I just got an email from them, and they've put their heads together and used an example of how they quickly changed their situation and raised money for a scout trip last spring."

The team's reaction was quick and intense. It was as if the entire universe had been preparing itself for an answer to the foundation's dilemma. Her announcement made them feel as if they'd tapped into some massive energy field, just waiting to release its energy. They snapped to attention and fixed their eyes on the young woman.

She misinterpreted their response and immediately became reticent. Rebecca thought they were going to be critical. So, in defense of herself and her kids, she said, "But they're just a bunch of kids. I don't know if their ideas would work for you. I'm sure your problems are much more complicated, and you'd need a more sophisticated approach."

"No! No! Noooo!" came the urgent replies from many in the room.

"That's not at all what I think," said Franklin.

"I'd love to hear their ideas," said Nicole.

"Yes, absolutely," added Terrence.

"I'm fascinated," Ernesto added, sounding just a little too much like Mr. Spock. The group laughed at his "logical" tone of voice.

Sensing a moment where he could break in, Jack waved his hand as if to ask permission. The group smiled at him and waited. He said, "Sometimes the best ideas come from those who clearly don't know what's not possible."

He grinned and waited, expecting someone to comment, but when no one did, he continued, "I'm a leader in a group called Destination ImagiNation, or DI as we call it. It's an after-school program for kids that helps them learn the processes and benefits of creative solution-finding, teamwork, innovation, etc." *(Look for more about DI in the Appendix on page 247.)*

"I'm quite familiar with DI," said Elaine. "My kids have been involved in it for years. It's a great program!"

"The best. Period," stated Jack. It was clear he was passionate about DI. "But I've found some of the most amazing benefits from DI extend to the adults who become familiar with it. If it's okay with you, Mr. Falcon, before Rebecca shares the ideas from her students back in Australia, I'd like to tell you more about DI."

"I'd love to know more!" said Franklin.

# A Massive Snowstorm

## Thursday: About 11:30 P.M. MST

### *(La Quinta Lobby)*

Week 1

| SUN | MON | TUE | WED | THU | FRI | SAT |
|-----|-----|-----|-----|-----|-----|-----|
|     |     |     |     | 11:30 P.M. MST |     |     |

The fatigue on the hotel manager's face was evident as she spoke to her staff. The hotel was finally mostly quiet, if the sounds of dozens of people sleeping in close quarters could be interpreted as quiet. The human symphony included soprano, alto, and baritone snoring, staccato drumbeat-like coughing, and the muffled undercurrents of those shifting positions on the floor. It was beautiful if you looked at it with the right perspective. The place looked like a slumber party had exploded everywhere!

"Thank you all for your amazing work today. It's been quite a day," she spoke softly.

The staff nodded their heads in agreement and stifled a few yawns.

"As you've heard by now I'm sure, the weather forecasters are saying this storm is likely to stick around throughout most of tomorrow."

The workers knew that, and by then they had made the decision to continue to serve their guests. They'd committed themselves to helping until the weather changed and the streets were once again passable. They'd each created a small "nest" for themselves in the hotel's offices, using towels, sheets, and other linens not previously given to the guests.

"Yes, we're tired, and we need our rest." Her gaze was mixed with pride and concern. She was proud to be part of this group. "But we also need to have someone available through the night to care for our guests should they need something. I'd like to propose that we work in two-hour shifts tonight, and I'll volunteer to take the first shift. The rest of you . . ."

A maintenance worker interrupted her, "No ma'am. I'll take the first shift, and you go get some rest."

He was emphatic. She tried to protest, but the others on her team agreed with him, and finally the hotel manager gave in. She was amazed at how quickly fatigue filled her body. She and the other hotel workers nestled in, and sleep overtook them.

# PERCOLATION

## Thursday: About 11:45 P.M. MST

### *(Room 212, La Quinta Inn)*

**Week 1**

| SUN | MON | TUE | WED | THU | FRI | SAT |
|-----|-----|-----|-----|-----|-----|-----|
|     |     |     |     | 11:45 P.M. MST |     |     |

Jack's description of DI was both brief and comprehensive. He'd been involved with the program for more than 20 years, and he explained how DI provided a safe, challenging, and fun environment for kids across the world to explore their abilities to solve complex challenges. Hearing about it was motivating to everyone. They wished they had had a chance to learn some of the DI principles early in life.

"Jack, thanks for sharing DI with us," said Franklin. "You presented some vitally important principles. One thing that stuck with me is when you said the creative process cannot be forced."

Elaine spoke next. "I completely agree! One of the concepts I've always used in my life is based on how I make coffee each morning."

Breaking out of a moment of deep reflection, Ernesto asked, "Huh?" Again, they snickered at him. His "intellectual" question stunned the group.

Elaine grinned. "Okay, it's like this. In order to have the best-tasting coffee, I need to start with clean, filtered water. I then add a new coffee filter and freshly ground coffee beans. Next, I push 'start,' and," she paused for effect, "I wait."

"Yeah, that's how most of us who actually make coffee actually make coffee!" teased Jennifer. "Personally, I understand the process, but I totally respect the folks at Starbucks and their ability to make what you request."

They all smiled.

Elaine was undeterred. "Man, you're a tough audience!" she joked. "But what happens after I press 'start' is vital to the process of having the best coffee. I can't rush what happens next. The machine percolates, using the water to unlock the flavor in the beans and the filter to stop unwanted things from contaminating the end result."

Betty made the connection. "Elaine, I think I understand what you're saying. We've reached the point where maybe it's time to let things 'percolate' for a while. I know I'm the type that strives for results, and I have difficulty waiting. But I do like my coffee as well!"

"So forcing a decision isn't a good idea. That makes sense, but I would like to hear the suggestions Rebecca's students came up with," said Terrence.

"I'll bet they have some good suggestions." agreed Jennifer.

After a short pause during which Rebecca looked at Mr. Falcon for assurance, she read the list of ideas coming from the students.

1. Remember *why* you are asking for help. Not the fact that you need money—that's a given. If the person you are asking gets a sense that this is very important to you, they'll be more open.

2. Take the time to connect with the person first. Just asking for money right away is a sure way to get the door slammed in your face.

3. Have people feel like they are part of what you are doing. If they "feel" what their part might be in all of it, they are more likely to want to help.

4. Don't take the amount of money you need to raise and divide it by the number of people you ask. Instead, ask people to give as they are able. For some, a dollar or two is a big sacrifice. For others, they may have a lot of money they'd be willing to share, if they feel right about it.

5. All the money we need already exists somewhere. We don't have to find a way to "create" money, just a way for the money to come from where it is to where it is needed.

6. Genuinely appreciate everyone's gift. Say thank you while looking them in the eye, and mean it.

Rebecca stopped reading, feeling a bit sheepish. Again, the thoughts of having some teenagers from the middle of nowhere lecturing executives in a major organization seemed ludicrous.

"I'm sorry," she started. "I'm not sure . . ."

Franklin gently cut in, "Rebecca. Don't apologize." He sighed and rubbed his eyes. "We've forgotten almost all of these lessons over the past few years. We started doing things because we 'should,' not because we 'want' to. We began to look at the activities of the foundation as obligatory instead of joyful. We bounced from one donor to another, forgetting to say thank you and mean it. We lost our rudder, and your students, well, they should be very proud of themselves. They've become the teachers tonight."

Slow breathing is all they could hear.

Betty broke the silence. "Mr. Falcon, we have all the ingredients we need to make some really good coffee." Her face was earnest, her words direct.

He looked up at her, recovering his energy. "Yes, Betty, indeed we do. Ladies, gentlemen . . . I think Elaine's idea is spot on. Let's take everything we've done, said, felt, learned, and shared today and put it into our personal percolators. I believe there's real value in sleeping on things and letting our subconscious minds work. So once we've gone back to the kitchen and finished those dishes, let's head back here and get to sleep. We have some important work to do in the morning."

They silently groaned about having to go back into the snowy causeway, but they knew that Franklin would go alone to finish the dishes if they didn't go with him. They looked at each other, smiled confidently, and started heading to the door. After all, the beef stroganoff the chef had prepared wasn't getting any easier to scrape off the dishes!

Franklin stopped them with a wave. "But first, two things. Rebecca, Jack—thank you for your help tonight. I really appreciate it. Thank you."

They smiled.

"And if it's not too much of an imposition, would you be willing to be with us in the morning? I'm not sure what time we'll be starting, but we can find each other."

Both Rebecca and Jack enthusiastically nodded their agreement.

"And second, I'm sure the rest of you have probably heard me say this 10,000 times, but all will be well, I'm sure of it."

His words were magical: quiet, reassuring, and confident. They knew he was right.

# Plans Interrupted

### Friday: About 5:30 A.M. EST

### (The Grant Report *Offices, New York City*)

Week 1

| SUN | MON | TUE | WED | THU | FRI | SAT |
|-----|-----|-----|-----|-----|-----|-----|
|     |     |     |     |     | 5:30 A.M. EST |     |

Coffee cups filled most of the horizontal spaces in the production room that weren't stacked with CD and DVD cases. The aroma in the room resembled a Starbucks filled with runners who had just completed a marathon: sweat mixing with Arabica. The production team of *The Grant Report* had just pulled another all-nighter, something that Marissa demanded about a dozen times a year. She was highly motivated to put stories on the air, no matter the obstacles.

They'd heroically stitched together a story, as one-sided as it was possible to create, that painted Franklin Falcon as a reclusive, controlling megalomaniac who had obviously been misleading the world about the Falcon Foundation's motivations. He wasn't interested in helping others. That was just a ruse for him to be able to build his empire. Marrisa's team asserted that his power-hungry ego was insatiable, and having the world fawn over him and his foundation was the fuel that fired him.

They had found just the right sound bites, suspicious-looking video clips, and enough bread crumbs in the newspaper stories from around the world to develop a true-sounding message designed to influence those who had not yet made up their minds about Franklin. Those who were fully in support of Franklin Falcon and his foundation may not be good targets for her message, but the other 60-75 percent of the world (the fence-sitters and those who already were leaning toward negativity) would no doubt be motivated by it.

Her team was used to Marissa's demands, but this story was different. She was different. She was operating well beyond her normal, maniacal taskmaster role as she was driving herself and her team to position Franklin Falcon as a monster. At various times during the past 36 hours, many of her staff wondered if this story was personal with Marissa. Had Franklin Falcon done something to her in the past? None of her team really believed he was a monster, but they weren't going to disagree with Marissa.

However, one staff member raised the question to herself, "Isn't perception 90 percent projection?" Before she was able to continue the train of thought, Marissa erupted.

"What?" Marissa's shrill voice filled the room, which a split second before had been filled with the soft hum of electronics, the rhythmic clicking of computer keyboards, and the deep breathing associated with REM sleep. Two of her staff members had succumbed to their fatigue and were curled on the floor.

"That can't be happening!" she bellowed.

One of the TV monitors in the production room was tuned to CNN, and a reporter was standing outside of an Internet café near Amsterdam. Marissa listened to the story from the reporter: "In an unprecedented manner, cyberspace has literally been overwhelmed during the past 10 to 12 hours with millions of messages to help the Falcon Foundation for Families in finding solutions to their rumored financial difficulties. Help is coming from all corners of the world. The common theme about Franklin Falcon we've seen as we've looked at the commentary throughout cyberspace is that his efforts to serve immigrants to the United States make him extremely well-loved the world over. Really, he is revered as a champion of the immigrant and an advocate for those in need."

Resembling a belligerent two-year-old who was refusing to remain seated "when the seatbelt sign is illuminated," Marissa began a full-on, hysterical temper tantrum. She paced, she ranted, she swore, she screamed, she threw things, she pounded on desks—and she generally terrorized the room, her staff, the equipment, and anything else near her. Her temper was epic, and her staff cowered during her nearly five-minute outburst.

Even as papers she'd thrown were still floating in the air, Marrisa's attention was drawn back to the television. She quieted for a moment and heard the studio talking-head CNN reporter drone, "And in related news, while Denver's purported 'all-weather' airport is still officially open, all airlines have canceled all flights in and out of DIA until at least 8 P.M. Eastern Time this evening. Crews are dealing with drifts over six and seven feet high in many locations as they work to clear the runways."

Marissa knew what that meant. She and her team weren't getting to Colorado today, and maybe not tomorrow. "No wonder they call it 'fly over' country," she thought. "What a God-forsaken place. They can't even handle a little snowstorm. I'd bet some of the crews from LaGuardia or JFK—or even Logan in Boston—could teach them a thing or two. How provincial they are out there."

"This SUCKS!" she spat, and with that, she disappeared from the studio.

They were used to her tirades, but again, this one had more energy. More spite attached to it. While most of her team set about returning the studio to the "pre-hurricane Marissa" state, one of them shouted, "Hey, look at this! It might explain a few things."

The rest of the team gathered around the computer monitor and began reading the story: "*WNBC, June 15, 1999. Family members are considering a lawsuit in response to the news that the Grant family of Brooklyn, New York, had their application denied by the Falcon Foundation for Families. Attempts to reach the Falcon Foundation for comment have been unsuccessful, but sources close to the Grant family indicate that Marissa Grant, their older daughter, was caught in a plagiarism scheme where she purchased an essay on the Internet that she subsequently described as her own original work. Her stolen essay was used as part of the Grant family's application to the Falcon Foundation. Complicating the matter is the fact that the Grant family had been accepted by Falcon, only now to be told they have been denied. The family had made significant plans for the funding and support being offered by Falcon.*"

"That seals it," murmured one staffer. "It is personal."

# Stage Three:
# Aha!

"If you do not expect the unexpected you will not find it,
for it is not to be reached by search or trail."

—*Heraclitus*

# Coffee

## Friday: About 8:00 A.M. MST

### *(Lobby, La Quinta Inn, Loveland)*

Week 1

| SUN | MON | TUE | WED | THU | FRI | SAT |
|-----|-----|-----|-----|-----|-----|-----|
|     |     |     |     |     | 8:00 A.M. MST |     |

Rebecca had been in the US for a week, but her days and nights were still upside down. She envied those in her traveling party who could acclimatize easily (or acclimate as they said in the States), but she was finding it difficult. Rebecca feared that she'd finally feel tired at the right time just about the time for her to return to Oakey. Thus, she dozed on and off throughout the night, her sleeping made even more difficult due to the mass of humanity with which she was sharing part of the hotel ballroom. Fortunately she'd been able to find a spot near a power outlet, and while she should have been quietly dreaming, she was able to share a virtual conversation with her coworkers and students back home.

Rebecca told the gang in Oakey about her experiences with Mr. Falcon, Jack Miller, and the entire executive team of the foundation. Her pride was obvious as she described the reaction Mr. Falcon had when she had read the list of suggestions they'd put together. According to Rebecca, it seemed as if the suggestions were some kind of catalyst, almost a secret force that made Mr. Falcon see the situation in high definition. The positive feelings had started moving forward after she and Jack Miller had shared the news about how many people around the world were actively involved in supporting the foundation, but once she had read the list of ideas from half a world away, she felt a major shift in the energy. Mr. Falcon's face was shining, and other members of the executive team were exhilarated. The "clouds" had parted, and a direction was taking shape.

This morning, Rebecca couldn't wait to see what a night's worth of "percolation" might bring. But she had a big issue of her own to deal with.

Just before signing off of her computer for the last time a few hours earlier, before fatigue finally pushed her toward a short period of deep sleep, she'd casually mentioned to the group back in Oakey that Mr. Falcon and the executive team were quite interested in hearing more concrete, creative suggestions about what might be done for the foundation beyond simply offering positive feelings and prayers. That simple request had somehow transformed itself into thousands upon thousands of messages. She knew this because once the world had discovered that Rebecca was staying at the same hotel with Mr. Falcon and the foundation's executive team, Rebecca's Facebook page had been used as the collection point. She had no idea what she was going to do now. It would take hours just to respond to all the friend requests, read everything, then maybe days more to make sense of it all.

Just as Rebecca was considering what to do, Jennifer walked around the corner and made eye contact with her.

"Rebecca?" Jennifer mouthed the question. Jennifer and the rest of the executive team had been up early. They'd already been to the kitchen to help the staff with preparing what they could for breakfast, and they'd been in touch with their own families. Jennifer had been looking specifically for Rebecca, as the executive team was eager to return to their discussions. Jack Miller and his family had already made their way to Room 212, and they were enjoying a light breakfast with the executive team.

"Oh, yes, good morning, Jennifer," Rebecca whispered. There were still dozens of folks sleeping near the women.

"Would you like to join our conversation this morning?" Jennifer asked quietly.

"Absolutely," Rebecca answered as she stood to walk with Jennifer. Once they'd left the ballroom, Rebecca continued, "Something amazing happened over night. I've received thousands of messages about what you and the foundation might do to help get you out of financial distress. I've only read about 20 or 30 of them, but some messages actually include offers to send money. One in particular offered to share $5,000."

"It's no coincidence," Jennifer stated simply. "We've been overwhelmed with messages sent to our 'catch-all' email address, and Mr. Falcon's voicemail filled quickly over night with more offers to help. We've been thinking this morning about what to do. Some of us have had some great ideas pop into our heads as we slept as well."

The women arrived at Room 212 and could hear the excited chatter all the way in the hallway. The members of the executive team and the Miller family were having a very animated conversation about the massive outpouring of assistance.

"Rebecca!" erupted Franklin. "So great to see you. How did you sleep?"

"Well, I'm still not sleeping well, I must admit. But I'm too excited right now to worry about all of that."

"We've had an interesting morning around here," Betty understated. "Once we settled down last night . . ."

Terrence interrupted, "It was a bit like camping together." He smiled broadly. "I had no idea Ernesto snored quite so prodigiously!" All eyes fell on Ernesto, and his cheeks reddened.

"Runs in the family," he responded. "You should hear my mother!" The room bounced with laughter.

"Aaaanyway," Betty continued, "while we settled down last night and got some sleep, the rest of the world appears to have continued looking at potential answers to our financial troubles."

"I know!" Rebecca shouted. "I mean, for some reason, my Facebook page became a collection point for everything. I'll bet I have 50 million messages." She paused, "Well, not *that* many, but it feels like it!"

"Amazing. Simply amazing. Humbling, too." Franklin quieted the group. "We've received hundreds, maybe thousands, of messages as well, including dozens of voice messages left on my phone."

"I read maybe 20 or 30 of my messages this morning," said Rebecca, "before Jennifer came and got me. When she saw me, I was trying to think what I might do. It'll take days just to read everything!"

Jason Miller, Jack's 12-year-old son spoke. "It's pretty simple, really."

"It is?" asked Elaine.

"Yeah. Facebook has a search engine. Enter some keywords, press Enter, and boom!" Jason was speaking with the confidence only a pre-teen has. To him, the situation was clearly no big deal. The others in the room looked hopeful but also clueless to Jason. Their frowns made him roll his eyes.

"But," said his father, "remember what you do in DI when you're looking at all the ideas you've generated?" Jack Miller had been Jason's team manager for several years in Destination ImagiNation and began offering the perspectives gained through that experience. "Before we can look at any particular idea as being better than another, we need to be clear about the reasons why we might want to use one idea and not another."

"Sounds like we need to 'taste' our coffee," Ernesto said. Squinted eyes, cocked heads, and general expressions of "What?" met him.

"Sorry. Dang. I sometimes just blurt out part of my internal conversations, usually right in the middle of a thought. As Jack was talking, I remembered what we talked about last night. About using the percolator to brew the coffee. I'm really interested to 'taste our coffee,' to hear what everybody else thought about during the night."

"Here's what I thought of," Franklin looked at Ernesto and teased him. "I thought about an infomercial I saw once. The product was called 'Snore-no-more' or something like that."

"I know, I know," Ernesto protested.

Terrence piled on, "Yeah, I was thinking about industrial-grade ear plugs all night!"

Elaine cut in, "Boys, are you finished yet?" Ernesto feigned being hurt, then smiled.

"Okay, I think Jack's on to something here," said Franklin, "And I, too, would like to know what 'sleeping on it' meant to you. I had a giant revelation last night myself."

They all looked expectantly at him, gesturing for him to get on with it.

"Well?" asked Jennifer. "Are you going to keep us in suspense all morning?"

Franklin looked very pleased with himself, twisted his mouth ever so slightly, winked, and said, "What if . . ."

# PLAN B

### Friday: About 10:15 A.M. EST

### *(Marissa Grant's Apartment, NYC)*

Week 1

| SUN | MON | TUE | WED | THU | FRI | SAT |
|-----|-----|-----|-----|-----|-----|-----|
|     |     |     |     |     | 10:15 A.M. EST |     |

Marissa had walked for hours. Her frustration had taken her from *The Grant Report* studios on the Upper West Side of Manhattan, through Central Park, and ultimately to her trendy apartment building in Soho. Along the way she'd consulted her Blackberry, reading stories about the weather in Colorado and seething about more reports on the Internet about what "a great idea" it might be to help the Falcon Foundation. "Pass it on." Pass it on? God. She personally had received dozens, maybe hundreds, of requests from her virtual network about helping Mr. Falcon and the foundation. Each message pushed her blood pressure higher and higher.

The Weather Channel said the storm in Colorado had raged until about 4 A.M. or so, but the massive low pressure system responsible for what the locals called "upslope snow" was already well into the panhandles of Oklahoma and Texas, so the power of the storm was nearly spent. A few bands of snow were still expected, but the bulk of the white stuff had already fallen. The Loveland public works crews had been fighting the drifts all night, but their efforts were hampered by all the abandoned vehicles on the roads. Even without significantly more snow, it would be hours before the major roads in Loveland would be passable; for some of the side streets, it might be days.

Reports from the Colorado Department of Transportation looked bleak as well: The highways from Pueblo to Cheyenne and from the foothills to the Kansas border looked to be closed until late that night. There would be no getting to or from Denver, and DIA, while "open," was effectively cut off from the rest of the world because of the closed highways.

Marissa just had to get to Colorado—somehow—so that she could confront Mr. Falcon. Her only interest in the foundation was retribution and payback. After the humiliation of her rejection as a Falcon Family—she really hadn't done anything wrong; after all, it was a pretty innocent and common practice to take stuff off the Internet, change a few lines here and there, and then turn it in—she committed herself to one day finding the right time and place to make Mr. Falcon pay. And pay dearly. Now, after years of preparation, some meddling teenager in Minnesota had pulled the rug out from underneath her. Marissa wasn't going to stand for it.

She picked up her Blackberry once again. "Get us as close to Loveland as possible. Today!" she spat into her phone as she called her staff back in the studio. "See if Hertz can get us a friggin' Hummer, and we can drive the rest of the way. Just make it happen!"

She hung up and told herself, "More than one of us can use the Internet, Ms. Liu." With that, she connected to the server at the studio, downloaded the video they'd put together last night, and began some "at-home" editing with clips she'd been saving in a secure folder on her personal computer.

# MOBILIZING

## Friday: About 8:30 A.M. MST

### *(La Quinta Inn, Room 212)*

Week I

| SUN | MON | TUE | WED | THU | FRI | SAT |
|-----|-----|-----|-----|-----|-----|-----|
|     |     |     |     |     | 8:30 A.M. MST |     |

"What if . . . ," Franklin said. He repeated it a third time for emphasis, "What if we turned the foundation on its head and looked at things very differently? My evening was full of difficult sleep, prayer, meditation, and ultimately a great sense of peace. By this morning, I'm feeling confident I've forgotten some of the reasons I started the foundation in the first place. And I think I have fallen into the trap of doing things that made *me* feel important, things that were not designed to help others."

He spoke for himself, but they all resonated with his words.

Terrence began, "I feel exactly the same way. I just haven't thought about it using those words. Now that I think about it, for the past year or two I haven't felt the rush I used to get when we had successfully found, selected, and included a new Falcon Family. Getting new kids was a wonderful thing. Recently? Just the thought of another family, deserving and needing our help . . . Well, I'm ashamed to admit it. It's just added to the pressure I've felt to continue to serve them and has stressed me out. A lot! Obligation. That's the right word."

His voice trailed off as he sat, arms crossed, as if to hug himself through the moment. The transparency was obvious on Terrence's face. His admission was from the heart, and it was clear he'd been struggling with this idea for quite a while.

They sat quietly as Nicole spoke, "I realized over the evening just how strong my feelings of failure have been." They objected, but she was adamant, "No, seriously. I've looked at it as my personal obligation to find the missing money, the resources we need to meet our financial obligations. I'm not used to failing."

"There's that word again," Ernesto said. "It's no wonder, really, that once everyone began looking at the work of the foundation as drudgery, as a requirement, as an 'obligation,' that the whole thing started falling apart. Remember, we have been choosing our fate; in fact, we've developed a powerful, predictable machine to deliver exactly what we have."

He wasn't trying to insult anyone, just openly stating the fact that they had the results they deserved.

"On the other hand, it felt so good last night to just serve others. To forget about the reason behind it, to lose ourselves in the work, to just help those who needed our help. I guess that explains what might otherwise be seen as miraculous." Betty summed up the experience for all of them.

"And maybe," Rebecca offered, "maybe that's why we've seen so many people wanting to help. They're coming out of the woodwork."

"Rebecca, you are absolutely right. I think it's time for us to rethink just how we go about doing things with the foundation, and maybe we shouldn't be doing all the thinking ourselves." Franklin's facial expression showed that he was speaking about himself now: "We will be well-served to include others in that process. Specifically, I'd like to get input from more of our kids, both those like Ernesto and Terrence who have used the foundation as a springboard to bigger and better things, and the families we are currently serving, and even some families who are in process to be selected."

"And . . ." Nicole started, but Franklin stopped her.

"Please, let me finish, Nicole." His tone was calm. He wasn't correcting her; he just felt compelled to complete his thought. She nodded respectfully. "And I'd also like to include others in the process, like some leaders at various universities and colleges, some community leaders, some politicians, really a cross-section of folks who represent both those that we serve and those whom we 'pay.' Going back to what Ernesto told us yesterday, I've been operating from the perspective of only seeing a few possibilities, a small number of choices surrounding our dilemma. Just looking at the massive number of choices the rest of the world is offering to us has been a huge wake-up call to me. We have an infinite number of options, but just looking at things the way we used to doesn't seem like a good idea." He stopped.

Jason cut in, "Oh, wow!"

They all gave him a "children are meant to be seen" kind of look, but he was undeterred.

"I think I've totaled this right." He continued, "From all the messages on Rebecca's Facebook page, it looks like . . . Holy Crap!" He shook his head. "That can't be right . . ."

"What?" implored Betty.

"Well, it looks like people are willing to send in about $10 million to the foundation today. Right now, actually."

"Let me see that," said Jack Miller in the way only a parent can. The rest of them gathered around Jason's laptop, eager to see as well.

# BEAUTY

## Friday: About 9:00 A.M. MST

### *(La Quinta Inn Lobby)*

Week 1

| SUN | MON | TUE | WED | THU | FRI | SAT |
|-----|-----|-----|-----|-----|-----|-----|
|     |     |     |     |     | 9:00 A.M. MST |     |

The sun was breaking through in bits and pieces, and its power was making jewel-like reflections on the ubiquitous piles of snow.

"For all the problems this storm has caused, it sure is pretty out there." The hotel manager was brushing the snow off of her jeans as she spoke to the small gathering of staff in the lobby. "And I've seen the plows several times this morning. It looks like Eisenhower is mostly passable by now." Her words were met with expressions of expectation from her coworkers. They'd all been "on the clock" for nearly 24 hours straight, and the effects of too much work and too little sleep were evident. Their attitudes were still positive, but their bodies were tired.

Just then, the manager's attention was drawn back to the television. "Joining us from I-25 and the Longmont exit is reporter Bazi Kanani," announced the stressed-out, tired, and "really" ready-to-go-home weather anchor. "Good news, Kathy," started the reporter. "The snow is over, and life is returning to normal on the Colorado Front Range. From Wellington in the north to Monument Hill in the south, I-25 is reopening in stretches. It is open throughout the Denver metro area, and C-DOT expects the rest of I-25 to be open by noon today."

"I wonder how we're doing here in Loveland," asked the manager, verbalizing the tail end of an internal conversation. She'd been secretly wondering how soon she might be able to head home, take a long hot shower, and get some sleep. The news report was hopeful.

"I've been on the phone with Loveland Public Works," reported one of her staff members, "and they say the major roads are pretty much cleared right now. But we're having some difficulty getting our own parking lot and driveways cleared. Our ATV's plow is doing its best, but it's struggling. And then—it's just amazing. There must be 20 or 30 guests out there helping us, using all kinds of implements: shovels, brooms, wastebaskets, dish tubs, you name it. They're making good progress, but wow! There's a lot of snow."

"I know everyone would like to be on their way as soon as possible," stated the manager, reflecting her own feelings as well, "but we need to continue to make our guests as comfortable as possible, especially those out there on snow removal duty." Her staff returned her smile, and they began returning to the kitchen, to the reception counter, and to other areas of the hotel. She had never been prouder of any group than she was of her staff; they'd handled the situation with professionalism, with compassion, with grace, and with a sense of joy. They did this work because they wanted to, not because she'd asked them to.

Stopped momentarily by that thought, the manager wondered what might happen in the world if it were filled with more "want to" attitudes. Her smile grew and her eyes twinkled.

# We'll See . . .

## Friday: About 9:15 A.M. MST

### (La Quinta Inn)

Week 1

| SUN | MON | TUE | WED | THU | FRI | SAT |
|-----|-----|-----|-----|-----|-----|-----|
|     |     |     |     |     | 9:15 A.M. MST |     |

"Jo, gosh, it's so great to hear your voice. How's Maggie this morning?" Franklin had stepped out of the room to call Jo, as he was particularly concerned about Maggie. She didn't like changes in the weather, and for a dog that was part Great Pyrenees, it always amazed Franklin that Maggie didn't like to have wet feet due to rain or snow.

"She's doing fine. Actually, it's been fun watching her in the backyard. The snow is so deep that she disappears between jumps. It looks like she's having a great time out there."

Franklin smiled as he tried to imagine Maggie leaping from one hole in the snow to another. He loved that dog. But after a few seconds, the mental picture of Maggie drew him back to the present. He was reminded of the hole the foundation was in and their need to jump out of it.

Interrupting his thoughts momentarily, Jo asked, "So what was it like camping with your coworkers? Did you have s'mores?"

Franklin could almost see the mischievous grin on Jo's face. "No. No s'mores. Campfires were outlawed in the hotel last night." They chuckled. Teasing was one of the ways they showed affection for each other.

"Snacks aside, we had a marvelous evening, and amazing things have been happening this morning, too," he said, temporarily pushing aside his anxiety about "what's next." "It's a bit of a madhouse around here, but the hotel staff, our fellow snowstorm refugees—really everyone—came together, served each other, and made a bad situation quite enjoyable. I'll have very fond memories." Franklin caught himself; the sudden rush of strong emotion surprised him. He sniffled.

"Freddie, I just had a feeling that something good was happening over there. But I'm sure you're ready to leave the hotel. Have you heard the news?"

"Yes, it sounds like the street crews deserve a trip to the beach. They must have done some magical things. We probably won't be able to leave for at least a couple more hours. The hotel parking lot is a disaster, and the piles of snow blocking the entrances to Eisenhower are . . ."

"No, not the news about the streets, I mean, that's very good news. No, I was talking about all the news reports about people wanting to help the foundation."

"It's incredible, don't you think?" Franklin asked.

"We'll see" was Jo's response. Once again she'd returned to one of her favorite Zen stories. She repeatedly used the "We'll see" story when it came to trying to predict the future. Her story that morning went like this: "A young man, after saving his money, purchased a horse he truly loved. When told about this fact and asked the question 'Isn't that great?' the Zen master said, 'We'll see.' Not long after he'd purchased his prized horse, the young man was thrown while riding it and broke his leg. The Zen master was asked, 'Isn't that awful?' The Zen master replied, 'We'll see.' A week later, a war broke out, and the young man found himself unable to be drafted into the Army due to his injury. Once again, the Zen master was asked, 'Isn't he lucky to have broken his leg?' The master once again replied, 'We'll see.'"

Franklin was used to Jo's "We'll see" response, and he knew the wisdom of it. It's not a good idea to be attached to any particular interpretation of a situation. Instead, it's important to simply take "what is" and let it be "what is." The foundation clearly had tremendous momentum happening right now what with the potential offers of help, but without a commitment to doing things differently, it might be easy for the foundation, and Franklin, to return to old, bad behaviors. Jo, in her direct manner, was in effect "calling out" Franklin to see if he was truly committed to doing things differently.

"Okay, okay. I get it," replied Franklin. "I've been questioning myself, too, about whether or not I'm really ready to do things differently. We've had some pretty significant insights hit us over the past 12 hours or so, but there's so much to do."

"Freddie, I believe in you. Always have, always will, even though sometimes I think it's up to me to bring you back to Earth." Jo's tone was direct, yet compassionate.

"I love you. Always have, always will," Franklin replied. "Anyway," he said after a moment, "we'll definitely be out of here as soon as possible. I'm wanting to get everyone back to the office so we can roll up our sleeves and get to work.

Franklin repeated Jo's words to himself, "We'll see," reminded himself to remain open to new possibilities, and rejoined the team, who were continuing to pore over Rebecca's Facebook entries offering assistance to the foundation.

# Taking a Stand

Friday: About 3:00 P.M. MST

*(Falcon Foundation Boardroom)*

Week 1

| SUN | MON | TUE | WED | THU | FRI | SAT |
|-----|-----|-----|-----|-----|-----|-----|
|     |     |     |     |     | 3:00 P.M. MST |     |

The hotel manager had called an "all clear" at about noon. She told everyone the parking lot was "mostly free of snow" and that the major roads in and around Loveland were passable, albeit with only one lane in each direction in most areas. She gave an extemporaneous speech filled with heartfelt gratitude for her staff, the guests, and especially for the members of the Falcon Foundation. She'd broken down into tears of fatigue, joy, and thankfulness as the staff and guests had given her a long and enthusiastic ovation, which had transformed into a massive "reception line." Dozens of people hugged the manager, and then each other, as the realization dawned that everyone could begin heading out of the hotel. The hugging and crying continued for several minutes, almost as if no one really wanted to leave.

Ernesto was reminded again of his own experience in Iceland. Those who survived had become completely absorbed into their new reality. Then, upon being rescued, he remembered having some initial feelings of being a bit angry at the interruption. He was relieved, certainly, but also somewhat miffed that his "new reality" was being impinged upon by his "old reality." His feelings at the hotel were similar. He'd enjoyed his experience of serving others so thoroughly at the La Quinta hotel that knowing it was time to leave invoked in him a sense of loss.

However, Terrence was quick to remind them that they had a major challenge still facing them. Using the renewed sense of purpose that had reinvigorated all of them, Terrence mobilized the Falcon team, having them organize their stuff, load the vehicles, and head back to their offices. They'd already showered and changed into fresh clothing long before the manager had called them together to say goodbye, so the process of getting back to the foundation was relatively quick and painless. They marveled at the work done by the Public Works Department; they'd managed to literally move mountains. As they drove back to their offices, the piles of snow along Eisenhower and Cleveland dwarfed their vehicles. There must have been 10 or 12 feet of snow piled up throughout the city. Impressive.

Once at the offices, Franklin suggested they each take a couple of hours to reconnect with their families, handle any administrative stuff that had piled up during their stay at the hotel, and maybe just sit at their desks with their feet in the air for a while. He wanted them to get together at 3 P.M. but wanted them rested and focused beforehand. The break was welcomed.

"I hope we're not imposing on your vacation plans, at least not too much," Franklin said as he looked at Rebecca and Jack Miller, who had joined the executive team as they reconvened in the boardroom at 3 P.M.

Rebecca said, "Oh, no, no, no. It's my honor to have been asked!" Her cheeks turned crimson, and she quickly broke eye contact.

"I'm always up for an adventure," said Jack Miller, smiling broadly. "I don't know who said it, but someone said 'if you're praying for an uneventful trip, you've missed the point of the trip.'"

"My sentiments exactly," said Nicole. "I knew joining the Falcon Foundation would be a wild ride." More smiles around the table.

"And," started Franklin, "the ride is about to get even wilder, I think."

"Indeed," Ernesto said quickly, "but from where we were on Thursday to where we are this afternoon, it's hard to believe it's been only a little more than 24 hours."

Heads nodded in unison as Jennifer began, "But one of the most important changes in my mind in that time was our decision to attack things together. Before Ernesto got here, and the snowstorm and the hotel and everything, I was feeling as if we were going in several directions. Now, I feel like we're going forward together. I'm just not sure where 'there' is."

They all agreed with both aspects of Jennifer's statement. It was obvious that they had grown together in many important and meaningful ways and that they had tremendous passion about wanting to move forward as a team. However, there were so many potential options they'd uncovered through their own insights and the input flowing from around the world that the prospect of settling on a common direction for the future seemed challenging.

"One thing is for certain." Betty's statement was emphatic. "We will not go back to doing things the way we used to, right?" It was a command, not a question, and she stared, eyes narrowed, directly at Franklin as she stated it. During the past couple of days, Betty had come out of her shell and had decided to break down her self-imposed barriers, which caused her to sit on the sidelines. She was willing to stare Franklin down all afternoon if necessary.

"Betty, you've just said something that I know I've been thinking," said Franklin, a slight grin on his face. "My biggest fear right now is that we'll take all the suggestions for help, the financial assistance that's been offered—my goodness, it must be close to $15 million by now—and learn nothing from the experience and continue to do things the same old way. I have to believe that one of the biggest reasons we received such a considerable outpouring of help has to do with the fact that we asked for help to be open to new possibilities, not to be validated in our old approaches and given a handout to continue that way."

"Right!" Betty nearly shouted her agreement. Her newfound courage was contagious, and the rest of group was being infected by it. She'd taken a stand and was willing to put herself on the line to hold the others accountable as well. It was inspiring to all of them.

"That said," Franklin continued, clearly showing his pride in Betty's brimming confidence, "we have much about which to feel good. Our mission of offering educational opportunities to deserving children, and at the same time assistance to their families, is still a valid one, I believe. Do any of you disagree about that?"

He looked from face to face looking for disagreement. When Franklin made eye contact with Ernesto, he decided to speak. "No, Mr. Falcon, I don't believe any of us would disagree with that as being the central mission of the Falcon Foundation. However, maybe our view has been too limited, too restrictive, too inwardly focused. I'm going to take a risk here and say something that might offend you, but I think the old ways we're talking about don't have much to do with serving deserving families. Instead, the old ways I'd like to be sure we don't return to are all about doing things ourselves, not involving others in our vision for the future, and being extremely private in the ways we make decisions, and such. We became myopic, and that's certain death over time."

A week ago his statements would have been unthinkable in this room; after all, it wasn't that long ago that Franklin Falcon held iron-fisted control over the organization—its mission, its decision-making, its finances, and its leadership. But the insights they'd gained in the past several hours had the chance to permanently, irreversibly change the culture of the foundation.

That is, until Franklin might disagree with something. That was everyone's unspoken concern at the moment: Was Franklin "really" committed to doing things differently?

A tipping point had been reached. What Franklin said or, more importantly, did in the next minute or two would have far-reaching ramifications on what the foundation would, or could, become. They sat quietly, waiting for him to respond to Ernesto's assertion.

"Ernesto, once again, I thank you." Franklin's eyes brightened. "While I'm sort of new at the idea of involving others in the future direction of the foundation, I'm convinced it's the right thing to do. As I said here on Thursday, I've been taking myself too seriously in everything, and it's time to focus on the situation as being serious, and not myself. Don't get me wrong; I'm still passionate about serving deserving families, but how we serve them may be in for some substantive changes."

Ernesto didn't realize he was literally holding his breath. It wasn't until he was nearly starved for air that he allowed his subconscious mind to take over breathing once again. Restarting his breath must have made more noise than he'd thought, as everyone turned to look at him.

"Thank you, Mr. Falcon," he stated. "We have an amazing future ahead of us, and I believe it's time for us to start sorting through all the options and choices so that we can chart the best possible strategies, plans, and actions for the short term. After all, good ideas that aren't implemented are just wasted."

"Darn right." Betty's arms were crossed, and her eyes were determined.

# INSIGHT

## Friday: About 3:15 P.M. MST

### (Boardroom)

Week 1

| SUN | MON | TUE | WED | THU | FRI | SAT |
|-----|-----|-----|-----|-----|-----|-----|
|     |     |     |     |     | 3:15 P.M. MST |     |

"Mr. Falcon," said Elaine, "I know I'm not an expert in data analysis and technical stuff like that, but I do know people. I've been looking through all the Facebook entries, the emails, the text messages, really everything that's been sent our way, and I've been thinking there are some very important concepts in there that might not pop out if we just use analytical tools."

The team's curiosity was piqued.

"Go on," said Franklin simply.

"Okay. So maybe part of the reason we got ourselves into trouble was that we hadn't been seeing how the needs of those we might be able to serve have been changing. We've pretty much focused most of our efforts on selecting acceptable candidate children of immigrant families while the kids are in late elementary or early middle school and then nurturing them, and their families, through the process until college graduation. But in reading between the lines of some of the communication we've received, I see some unexpected connections.

"Most importantly, the attitude toward immigration overall here in the United States has changed in the past few years. As our economy slumped and as the job market dried up, along with the significant debate within Congress about immigration overall, well, the general feeling toward immigrants has deteriorated, it seems."

You could see the gears trying to mesh in Franklin's mind. He was hanging on to what Elaine was saying, but it was clear he wasn't following her completely.

Terrence added, "I'd agree with that, Elaine. I'm not sure the discussions related to immigration have resulted in much light, just a lot of heat, if you get my meaning."

They understood. Friction creates heat, but rarely does it result in enlightenment.

Elaine continued, "So, maybe the general feeling toward immigrants and the general population's desire to help them have changed. Therefore, in a 'negative energy' sort of way, our efforts have been stymied by a shift in attitude. Maybe one of the things we could look at doing is to help reshape the discussion about immigration overall, to give it a more positive tone."

Franklin's family had immigrated to the US during a time when large-scale immigration from Eastern Europe was almost impossible. Back then, Americans were afraid of being overrun by refugees from countries that would eventually find themselves behind the iron curtain. Today, immigration was also viewed by many as negative, as a threat to those already in the US—more pressure on social services, education, jobs, traffic, you name it. Elaine's words were insightful; maybe they needed to view potential solutions from a totally different perspective.

"You're on to something there, Elaine," Franklin suggested. "But . . ."

Elaine cut him off. "Sorry, Mr. Falcon, but there's something else I've thought of as well. I want to get it out before it pops out of my mind." He nodded and smiled.

"Another dynamic related to our future might be that we don't wait until a family actually immigrates to the United States before we offer assistance. After all, the central theme, or core value, for us has to do with education, right? So maybe we extend our vision to include all children who are in need of education, regardless of where they might be. Afghanistan, Haiti, Thailand, needy areas of our own country as well as England and Australia, etc., etc. Maybe the Falcon Foundation for Families looks at all families. Maybe part of our historical problem is that we've been looked at as being elitist snobs, focusing only on those fortunate enough to make it to the US and deserving enough for us to serve them."

All sound left the room. If the tipping point they'd passed a few minutes ago was profound at that point, this one was monumental.

Elaine had managed to put the central issues on the table, the things none of them really wanted to admit. While the Falcon Foundation had done some remarkable things for many, many families, the vast majority of families were left "out of the tent." The foundation's insular, internal view of things was the cause of the substantial problems they were facing now. That's why Greg's assertion that all they needed was more money was completely wrong. More money would have kept fuel in their tanks, but the inevitability of their fundamental flaws would have caught up with them eventually. It was time for them to address these things and to make new, better decisions.

"I'll have to admit I'm having a little difficulty not taking your comments too personally, Elaine," Franklin said quietly, but not in an accusatory tone. "The 'two voices' have returned." He was referring to the conversation they'd had on Thursday about Mrs. Liu's phone call that really got the ball rolling in the first place.

"One voice is telling me that you're wrong about all of this, that the safe way is the best way. I've listened to that voice for much of my life, and its influence on me and my decisions have been well-documented, I think. The other voice is saying that you're absolutely right. The correct thing for us to do is to look at fixing the bigger system so that children who are in need are able to receive a quality education regardless of where they might live. As I stop and reflect right now, both voices are speaking, but I'm recommitting myself to the notion that the safe decision is not the right decision here. It is time to jump out of our hole and move forward with a new sense of purpose."

He stopped for a moment, adjusted his tie—reflecting for a moment on his need to put on a fresh shirt and tie upon returning to the office—before asking all of them, "What do you think?"

Rebecca surprised them all by speaking first, "Mr. Falcon, I'm not sure I'm objective here, being a school teacher and all, but I think Elaine's views are very insightful. I hadn't thought about things this way before. Your foundation has such a positive reputation in the world, but it's almost as if it's unreachable. Our kids in Australia would love to be able to be served by your foundation, but to them, it's just a dream."

Jack Miller added, "And that dream doesn't stop only for kids who are still in other countries. I know of some neighborhoods in the greater San Antonio area where there are kids who would benefit from a hand up in their education and whose families are struggling to feel powerful and successful in raising their kids. Not to suggest that the Falcon Foundation can do everything for everyone. I know that's an unreasonable suggestion, but maybe, just maybe, there might be a different approach to serve more kids in more places while at the same time helping the foundation be sustainable and successful. It's one of those situations we encounter all the time in DI. Maybe we can combine two seemingly different ideas into one new better idea. I don't know. I'm just thinking out loud here."

Terrence was clearly conflicted. His role within the foundation was key to what was now being described as the "old way," and the fact he himself had benefited by being one of Franklin's kids, well, he, like Franklin, was having difficulty not taking things over-personally. But listening to Rebecca and Jack speak had made an immediate impression on Terrence.

"Mr. Falcon, I'm *beginning* to see things differently myself," started Terrence. "I may not be objective here either, as I have my picture right there on the wall [he pointed above and behind Franklin], and given the fact my job here is all about selecting and nurturing Falcon Families. However, after listening to Elaine express her views, and then hearing what Rebecca and Jack have just said, I'm thinking we're on the right track for expanding our vision while at the same time exploring ways to keep the foundation viable from a financial perspective. It's just going to require some new, yet-to-be-discovered ideas. But I'm up for that!" Terrence's enthusiasm surprised everyone, including Terrence.

Nicole was next to speak.

"Terrence stole my idea," she deadpanned.

Franklin actually snorted he laughed so hard. The tension that had been building since the first major tipping point of the meeting evaporated, and the camaraderie they'd built during their overnight experience returned.

Betty simply raised her hands, cocked her head to the side, and gave a look that said, "My views remain. We need to do something different!" There clearly was no need for her to speak.

Only Jennifer remained. She'd been drawing, making notes, doodles it seemed, while the others were speaking. But in reality, she'd been planning. One of the things she'd done extensively in her history with Falcon was to plan meetings: large-scale meetings, where groups came together to establish vision and to build strategy. She'd been framing the basics of an idea when it became obvious that she was the last to offer her viewpoint to the group.

All eyes shifted to Jennifer.

"I think it's pretty simple," her tone of voice was matter-of-fact. They were intrigued. "It's time to get others involved—in substantive, meaningful ways—to help us sort out our options. And," she continued, "if we do it right, we'll be able to accomplish Jack's suggestion of taking two seemingly opposing needs—to serve more families in more ways and to ensure the long-term viability of the foundation—and glue them together in a powerful, positive, and potentially radically different way. I'm thrilled about it!"

Jennifer smiled in an "I've got a secret" kind of way and shrugged her shoulders as she returned to her doodling.

"What?" shouted Elaine, barely able to contain her curiosity. They snickered at Elaine but were equally intrigued with Jennifer's statement.

Jennifer's smile broadened, and she looked at them, one by one. "It's easy," she repeated. "All we need to do is get a large group of folks together, as many as possible face-to-face and the rest through virtual means, to work with us in deepening and widening our insights and then to offer specific implementation ideas. I'd suggest a few hundred would be the right number, and we should do this as soon as possible. I'm thinking tomorrow would be perfect."

Their expressions varied from "She's completely insane" to "Okay, that's a great idea, but how in the world would we pull that off?" to "Hmm . . . hundreds of people involved in the process? How would we manage everything to get real input?" Jennifer was enjoying her time in the spotlight, not as a way to make herself feel important, but in seeing the way the group was reacting to a strange, seemingly impossible thing to do. They were seeking solutions, not trying to poke holes, and that by itself was big.

"Jennifer, let me see if I understand," Ernesto began. "You're suggesting we put together a meeting and invite hundreds of folks to attend—tomorrow?"

"Yes," was her one-word reply.

# WICKED WITCH FROM THE EAST

### Friday: About 9:15 P.M. MST

*(Grand Junction, Colorado)*

Week 1

| SUN | MON | TUE | WED | THU | FRI | SAT |
|-----|-----|-----|-----|-----|-----|-----|
|     |     |     |     |     | 9:15 P.M. MST |     |

Marissa and her team had arrived at Grand Junction's airport, located about 300 miles west of Loveland, after connecting through Dallas. It was the best travel option they could find at such short notice, and Marissa just grunted when she was told each of their four tickets cost more than $1,200. She just wanted to get as close to Franklin as soon as possible, and cost was irrelevant. In addition, she was so consumed by her desire to confront him in person that she'd failed to notice that Grand Junction's weather was completely different from the blizzard on the Front Range. As they were standing by their black Chevrolet Tahoe in the President's Circle at Hertz, it was still nearly 65 degrees. She was sweating.

The Tahoe barely swallowed their gear; in fact, Marissa and her staff had various bags and cases strewn throughout the SUV just to make it all fit. The only person who was truly comfortable was Marissa herself, as she'd insisted that nothing impose on her space in the driver's seat. Once they'd "sardine-canned" themselves into the SUV, they knew they'd be in for a long drive.

In ideal weather, it was normally about a four-hour drive to Loveland. However, their trip would take them into the heart of the Denver area, and they had no idea how long it might take to reach Loveland from there. Initial traffic reports had described the roads as "passable," but as the city awakened from its frozen paralysis, no one could predict how many people would be trying to move simultaneously. It could be nasty.

However, Marissa wasn't interested in how her staff was feeling, nor was she particularly interested in traffic reports. She would make it to Loveland, one way or the other, and would find a way to bring Franklin Falcon down. She was driven by, and was driving with, her rage. Other drivers along I-70 in the mountains of Colorado had better beware. Marissa Grant was on her way.

# Stage Four:
# Make It Real

"You can't make footprints in the sands of time
if you're sitting on your butt.

And no one wants to make butt prints
in the sands of time."

—*Bob Moawad*

# Accidental Celebrity

### Friday: About 9:30 P.M. CST

*(Eden Prairie, Minnesota)*

Week 1

| SUN | MON | TUE | WED | THU | FRI | SAT |
|-----|-----|-----|-----|-----|-----|-----|
|     |     |     |     |     | 9:30 P.M. CST |     |

If Angela had 200 years, she wasn't sure she could answer all the Facebook friend requests, respond to all the text messages and emails, and ever have a prayer of reading everything that people were sending her way. She felt completely overwhelmed; she'd gotten four more requests for "news interviews" just this afternoon. Part of her was wishing everything could go back to the way it was on Wednesday, but that part was losing the battle. She had no interest in returning to the feelings of worry and concern where she didn't know what might be happening with the foundation. However, she did long to be just another high school kid in a small town.

When Mr. Falcon himself had called earlier this evening and asked Angela and her mom to come to Fort Collins tomorrow—to be part of a worldwide event designed to help the foundation make some decisions—Angela's first thought was to come up with an excuse. She really hated being the center of attention and had never expected to become an overnight celebrity of sorts. She was just doing what she'd been raised to do, to help those whom she cared about when times were difficult. Mr. Falcon had asked for help and Angela had responded.

But she was also raised to finish what she started. As such, she knew, as uncomfortable as it might be, she needed to go to Colorado. She would work through her fears and would do what she could to continue helping.

That's what her parents had taught her.

# Making the Impossible Possible

Friday: About 9:15 p.m. MST

*(Falcon Foundation Offices)*

Week 1

| SUN | MON | TUE | WED | THU | FRI | SAT |
|---|---|---|---|---|---|---|
|  |  |  |  |  | 9:15 P.M. MST |  |

Franklin was flabbergasted. From what was a seemingly crazy suggestion from Jennifer about six hours ago—to hold a giant face-to-face meeting in less than 12 hours' time—to now, they'd actually put in place a plan to make her idea a reality. The whole thing started once they realized that Jennifer was serious and that she truly believed they could pull it off. They moved away from their normal "That's not possible" stance to a new viewpoint of "Well, we don't know what we don't know; let's take the first step!" And that first step toward making the meeting happen was when Ernesto asked the simple question, "Who would come?"

Who indeed. After he asked the question, they worked as a group and identified about 100 names that were obvious choices. They wanted a mix of current Falcon Families like Angela's, some families who were in the process of being selected, and some additional alumni families, like Terrence's and Ernesto's. They also wanted to bring in certain members of colleges and universities: some in the admissions area, some regents, some deans, presidents, and so on. They also talked about some influential politicians, philanthropists, etc., etc. The list grew quickly.

Then Rebecca asked the big question, "But what about international participation?" Her question just about pulled the whole idea off track. International participation? How would they accomplish that?

"Easy," again was Jennifer's one-word answer. Mock frustration abounded, but she followed up with more details as she suggested they use video and tele-conferencing. They could also use Twitter to keep others involved. It would require some creativity and some excellent technical assistance, but Jennifer again was undeterred in believing something could be done to make it happen.

So, starting at about 3:30 P.M., they divided their responsibilities and began framing a detailed plan. Betty offered to take charge of finding a suitable meeting space. Franklin and Terrence took responsibility for the invitations and quickly went about adding hundreds more names to the list. Nicole took responsibility for all the logistics related to the meeting, Ernesto offered his assistance to Nicole to be her gopher, Elaine was responsible for rounding up volunteers, and Jennifer offered herself as the financial manager as well as overall project manager. By 4 P.M. they were so busy working to make the meeting a reality that any initial misgivings were long forgotten.

Jennifer called a status meeting at 5 P.M., and they began by giving short reports about what they'd accomplished in the last couple of hours, what was next to do, and any issues that might need some creative thought to resolve.

"Angela and her mother's flight arrives tomorrow morning at DIA at 8:10 A.M.," Betty said. "I've arranged for a limo to meet them."

Terrence then followed up by saying he and Franklin had received confirmed RSVPs from hundreds of people. They had asked the original 100 individuals if they'd be willing to participate, initially hoping a few dozen might say yes. However, when the yeses had grown beyond 500 within the first hour, Franklin and Terrence realized they'd grossly underestimated the response they'd receive. They reported about half of the attendees were planning to use technology so they could attend in a virtual manner. Even more amazing was the fact that about 200 were planning to make the journey to Colorado to attend in person. All of this happened in just 90 minutes. What might happen next?

As a result of their early success in getting RSVPs (they weren't sure how large the list of actual attendees might be, but it was going to be far larger than 200!), Betty concluded that no meeting space in the Loveland area was large enough to hold their meeting. As such, she expanded her search to the greater Northern Colorado area. She had a terrific personal relationship with the president of Colorado State University in Fort Collins, about 25-30 minutes north of the foundation's offices. Once Betty contacted her friend, it seemed as if gasoline was placed on the fire: The intensity surrounding the meeting logistics just exploded!

Adding the fact that Franklin was regarded as one of the most, if not the most, successful graduates ever to come from CSU, well, the president said CSU would be thrilled to host the meeting and would do whatever they could to make it happen. Yes, yes, yes, the details about insurance, contracts, security, etc., could be dealt with Betty was told, and CSU's president committed the use of Moby Arena, the 11,000-seat facility used for basketball, volleyball, and other sports. It had the required combination of size and technological capability, and best of all, it was not committed to any other event right then. She agreed to have the school's entire technical support team available to help, and she gave Betty contacts to all the student associations after suggesting they might be a great source of volunteers. Finally, the president committed to asking as many members of CSU's staff and faculty as possible for their assistance.

Betty hung up the phone and immediately got with Elaine to talk about the president's offer related to volunteers. Elaine suggested maybe they should contact the student associations at the Universities of Colorado, Northern Colorado, and Wyoming to see if they might be interested in helping also. Within the hour, Elaine's list of committed volunteers grew to about 150, with many offering to drop everything and head over to the foundation's offices immediately. It was going to be a long night, but they might just be able to get things coordinated before the meeting was to start at about 11 A.M. Elaine thought, "This is crazy, but fun crazy!"

Jennifer, Betty, and Nicole were balancing the seemingly ten million details about food, markers, easels, drinks, transportation, sleeping rooms . . . Events like this normally took months to plan and execute. They had given themselves about 18 hours. But once the fire had been lit, there was no stopping them.

Their confidence was high. Tomorrow was going to be a special day. Very special indeed.

# A Channel

## Saturday: About 9:45 A.M. MST

### (Falcon Home)

Week 1

| SUN | MON | TUE | WED | THU | FRI | SAT |
|-----|-----|-----|-----|-----|-----|-----|
|     |     |     |     |     |     | 9:45 A.M. MST |

"Maggie!" Franklin playfully chided the big white dog. While her fur did a wonderful job in keeping her warm in the harshest cold, white dog hair and the slate gray suit he'd chosen to wear clearly weren't mixing well. He wasn't the least bit angry, and in fact, he stooped to scratch her behind the ears. She responded with a sloppy kiss.

The shower had done him a world of good. Franklin's instincts had told him that he needed to head home, if even for a short time, as he needed some time to himself. Jo had stayed behind at Moby; she'd been completely absorbed into helping Jennifer and Nicole. The details were being handled, but like the Whac-a-Mole game, more heads kept popping out of the holes. Jo, along with the executive team, was "swinging her mallet" to bop the "heads" back into the holes with the best of them, and they were making good progress with everything.

It was like a gigantic dance at the arena, with Jennifer choreographing it all, Betty playing the music for everyone, and the dancers moving with passion and precision. It was amazing to watch, but something was telling Franklin to separate himself from it, to "step out" of himself, to be fully present—to trust his intuition, to follow his instincts, and to trust the process that was going to unfold today.

He needed some time to recover and to reset.

He regarded Maggie once again. "I'm not sure when we'll be home today, Maggie. It's a big day."

She wagged her tail enthusiastically.

"I need for you to take care of things around here for me, okay?

She inched forward.

Franklin scratched her some more and thought to himself, "I may be asked to step back in some ways, step up in other ways, but more than anything, I need to be open to what's going to happen. The old Franklin Falcon would be all about controlling the outcome, but I need to trust what's happening. Trust Ernesto. Trust Jennifer. Trust those who are willing to devote themselves to the success of this meeting."

Maggie smiled, Franklin was sure of it, and he was reminded that dogs represent one of the best, if not the best, examples of unconditional love and trust. Maggie believed in Franklin completely. Her smile told him everything about what he needed to do next.

Franklin headed to the car, drove back to Fort Collins, and reminded himself of just how lucky and blessed he was. Magic was happening.

# A New Reality

## Saturday: About 11:00 A.M. MST

*(Moby Arena Home Locker Room, Colorado State University, Fort Collins)*

**Week 1**

| SUN | MON | TUE | WED | THU | FRI | SAT |
|-----|-----|-----|-----|-----|-----|-----|
|     |     |     |     |     |     | 11:00 A.M. MST |

They were all nervous and elated simultaneously. This was the most amazing event of any kind that any of them had coordinated, especially considering the incredibly short time frames, the weather-related challenges, the technological gremlins, and such. But they knew they were doing something special.

Franklin was trying to calm the pounding in his chest when Ernesto came into the home locker room.

"Mr. Falcon, I think everything's ready to go." Ernesto waited. Franklin regarded him, knowing he was right. Franklin stood slowly, smiled weakly, straightened his tie, ran his fingers through his hair, brushed off his pants for the fifteenth time, and then walked toward Ernesto.

"Ernesto, I'm not sure what . . ." Franklin stopped and looked down, his hands moving to his pockets. Ernesto put his hand on Franklin's shoulder.

"Mr. Falcon," Ernesto said, guessing at what Franklin was going to say. "I'm not sure what's about to happen out there either, but whatever it is, it's the result of thousands of people—their positive energy, their prayers, their ideas, their genuine interest in helping. Something magical is going to happen, I just know it."

Their eyes met for a moment, with Franklin's softening a bit as he reflected on how much had been done in just a few days.

"I know," Franklin said simply. "I'm just—so—humbled by the whole thing. I've made so many mistakes recently . . ." his voice trailed off.

"I'm . . . not . . ." he started again, then stopped.

"Mr. Falcon, the world wants to help. It's almost as if the universe is completely in alignment with us, with you. Let's go. They want to see you." Ernesto reached out his hand to him, looking to guide him toward the door. Franklin brightened as he stood to his full height. A luminous quality surrounded him, his confidence building with each step. By the time they reached the platform, he was nearly floating, bouncing on the waves of positive energy flowing throughout Moby Arena. Ernesto was captivated.

It had taken some hard work and some old-fashioned "bailing wire and bubble gum" to make it happen, but the "Town Hall" meeting for the Falcon Foundation was about to begin. The university had dedicated its advanced telecommunications services, including its fiber optic network and satellite capabilities, so that the community of interest represented "in the room" included Falcon kids in 20 different countries, 45 states, and more than 300 cities. Rumors were swirling that a few heads of state were participating in some places and that more than just a few Hollywood celebrities and sports stars were online as well.

In addition, over the past 17 hours, an army of volunteers from the surrounding communities, members of the Falcon Foundation, and students, faculty, and staff from CSU had transformed Moby Arena into a giant workroom. It had been taken over by a maze of wires, a flotilla of round tables and chairs, a forest of flipcharts and easels, and a cornucopia of sticky pads, colored markers, and other workshop-related stuff.

Beyond the estimated 1,000 participants across the world, about 500 people were physically in the building sitting around the 50+ tables. Those lucky enough to be attending in person had braved the blizzard-related travel difficulties. Some had flown to Denver once DIA had resumed operations; others had flown to Grand Junction, Eagle, Hayden, and other mountain airports in Colorado and then driven to Fort Collins. Others simply got in their cars, trucks, or SUVs and had driven in some cases hundreds of miles overnight just to be here.

Marissa Grant and her production team from *The Grant Report* had left Grand Junction at about 9:30 P.M. the night before. The drive through the mountains had been uneventful, and they'd made it to Idaho Springs (normally about 45 minutes from Denver) in short order. However, once they hit the Front Range, the effects of the March blizzard were everywhere. With the heavy traffic, the drive to Denver from Idaho Springs had stretched to three hours, meaning they arrived in the western suburbs of Denver at about 4 A.M. Even Marissa's fire had its limits, and she was forced to grab a quick nap in their SUV.

She'd relented to the fact that sometimes sleep was absolutely required, even if it was for small periods of time. So, armed with two hours of sleep and a Caffè Mocha from Starbucks, they were back on the road. Then, what would normally have been about a 90-minute drive from Golden to Fort Collins doubled to nearly three hours, meaning they finally rolled into the parking lot at Moby Arena a little before 9:00 A.M. Marissa and her team had been among the first to arrive. The members of the foundation were troubled to see Marissa but not totally surprised. They'd expected Marissa to overcome whatever hurdles necessary to come to Colorado. She was smelling a scandal, and that was like blood in the water to a shark like her.

While *The Grant Report* may have been an early arrival, they were far from being the only news organization in Fort Collins. News magazines, newspapers, local affiliates of the major TV networks, bloggers, and independent news organizations from across the world had come to cover everything from gavel to gavel. Marissa was glaring at the members of the foundation executive team from her seat in the press corps, burning laser-like holes through whomever was unlucky enough to pass through her line of sight. The crews nearest to Marissa and her group, those from CNN, the BBC, and Telemundo, had tried to set up a physical boundary between themselves and *The Grant Report* team. It was as if Marissa's toxic energy was contagious and would infect them if they got too close.

Student volunteers from Colorado State University, the University of Northern Colorado in Greeley, and the University of Colorado at Boulder had been organized by Elaine into a well-coordinated army of helpers. They'd started arriving at Moby Arena at about 9 P.M. the night before, and most of them had worked straight through the night. The room was literally buzzing with energy, and the massive display screens were switching from one remote location to another: Los Angeles, Mexico City, Toronto,

Halifax, Nassau, Buenos Aires, Sydney, Rome, Hong Kong. Faces followed more faces, which followed more faces.

And then it was time. The president of Colorado State University came forward and stood at the podium.

"Ladies and gentlemen, I am pleased to welcome you to Moby Arena on the campus of Colorado State University." She nodded at the applause.

"We are here today, both in person and across cyberspace, as a result of an unprecedented flurry of activity across the world. We've been asked to be here by Mr. Franklin Falcon, founder of the Falcon Foundation for Families." Just then, Franklin came walking across the stage, waving awkwardly to those in the vast arena.

More applause and cheering . . . and as everyone jumped to their feet, they started chanting, "Fal-con . . . Fal-con . . . Fal-con . . ." The 500 or so participants, and the 500 or so volunteers, staff, faculty, and others involved in supporting the meeting made far more sound than seemed possible. The 1,000+ voices filled the arena.

Franklin looked genuinely embarrassed and put his hands out in front of him, as if he could push everyone back into their seats and cause them to quiet down. CSU's president, rather than trying to rid Mr. Falcon of his growing discomfort, did exactly the opposite. She walked to Franklin, put her arm around his shoulder, embraced him in front of the crowd, and enticed the crowd to get louder with her free arm, clearly intending to further agitate and excite the crowd.

Strangely juxtaposed within the passionate outburst were the members of the news media. They sat quietly, keyboards alight with pithy thoughts and observations. The words "warm welcome" were keyed over and over as the journalists struggled to keep their coverage objective. The powerful emotions associated with the meeting were eroding the detachment of all but the most jaded journalists.

The crowd began settling down, and the president returned to the podium with Franklin in tow and addressed everyone once more. "Those in our arena have traveled in some difficult circumstances to be here. Mother Nature put on quite a show the past few days." More cheering erupted. This time they were shouting for themselves, to acknowledge their collective efforts and sacrifices.

"I wouldn't have missed it," snarled Marissa just a little too loudly. Those near her moved even farther away.

Then the president said, "And those who are joining us through more virtual means: video conferencing, teleconferencing, Facebook updates, blog posts, Twitter feeds, MySpace updates, YouTube posts, etc., etc." Hands waved and smiles erupted on the video screens. "Thank you for being here as well. For some of you, it's the middle of the night, or will be soon enough, as we do our work throughout the day here in Colorado. We owe so much to so many who have made this event happen, especially on such short notice. Countless students, faculty, and staff from CSU, from CU, from UNC, from Wyoming—I'm not sure where all else."

A smattering of spontaneous voices shouted out the names of other schools, and clapping and shouting pocketed the arena while the president continued. "And other volunteers have dedicated themselves, and we've been truly blessed with the amazing creativity and results from our network engineers, the caterers, event planners, custodial staff, executives, moms, dads, and many, many others. Thank you!" Her voice rang out, and the chorus of cheers intensified and reverberated.

"But," she paused and looked from face to face, "we are here to work today. We have much to do, so I'm urging you all to be ready to dig in, to contribute, to offer your energy, your commitment, and your wisdom. Clearly, the Falcon Foundation for Families has been an iconic organization, providing help to thousands of immigrant families over the past four decades. Some of you may have been a Falcon Family [again, isolated cheering], but it's our turn to help today." She barely got the word "today" out before a standing ovation ensued, followed by more chanting, "Fal-con . . . Fal-con . . . Fal-con . . ."

It was the president's turn to look embarrassed. While she had intended to share some positive opening remarks, it was as if she'd mixed "nitro" and "glycerin" together. Moby Arena was rocking! She looked at Franklin, raised her eyebrows in an "I didn't expect this" kind of manner, shrugged her shoulders, and smiled broadly. He returned her smile.

# The Launch

Saturday: Exactly 11:22 A.M. MST

*(Moby Arena Press Section)*

Week I

| SUN | MON | TUE | WED | THU | FRI | SAT |
|-----|-----|-----|-----|-----|-----|-----|
|     |     |     |     |     |     | 11:22 A.M. MST |

"Launch it."

The directive came from Marissa, delivered via text message to one of her staff members who was in the network control section. His laptop had access to an ultra high-speed Internet connection, and Marissa wanted him to post her "hate" video by running the script they'd carefully prepared early that morning. At the press of a button, the script sent the video to all the major news agencies across the world, posted the video to several sections on YouTube and other video server sites, updated dozens of Facebook and MySpace pages, and fired off hundreds of text messages, emails, and Twitter entries designed to reach community leaders, university and college presidents, Falcon Families, bloggers, reporters, and other market influencers. In about 10 seconds' time, her video entitled "Falcon Foundation Extorting the Public: STOP THE DONATIONS NOW!" was available to millions across cyberspace.

Marissa's Blackberry confirmed the launch within moments as she simultaneously received dozens of update messages containing the subject line she'd crafted. Her lip curled in satisfaction, and she thought to herself, "It's almost over." Her eyes glinted, her expression evil, and those nearest to her winced unconsciously.

# Transformation

## Saturday: About 11:22 A.M. MST

### *(Moby Arena Main Stage)*

Week 1

| SUN | MON | TUE | WED | THU | FRI | SAT |
|-----|-----|-----|-----|-----|-----|-----|
|     |     |     |     |     |     | 11:22 A.M. MST |

"Ladies and gentlemen, students, faculty, staff, members of the media, honored guests, both here and connected via technology, it is my privilege to introduce to you the man behind the vision, a person who has devoted himself tirelessly and selflessly to supporting others, a man whose service to humanity has few equals, the founder and leader of the Falcon Foundation for Families, Franklin Falcon."

Franklin stood, quietly bowed to the audience, raised his hands together in front of him as an attempt to subdue the crowd's loving enthusiasm, and nodded subtly. Tears welled in his eyes as he sought out Jo, who was standing off stage. Their eyes met, and he motioned to her to join him. She refused. She was not fond of being in the spotlight and was not eager to come on stage. Sensing that she wouldn't come on her own, he walked to her, took her hands in his, and slowly, gently led her on stage with him. She sheepishly stood beside him, and they basked in the adoration from the crowd. Seconds turned into minutes when Franklin's attempts to quiet the crowd were fully ignored. "Fal-con . . . Fal-con . . . Fal-con . . ."

Finally, the crowd's storm blew itself out, and they quieted enough for Franklin to speak.

"Thank you so much. Thank you."

"I love you, Mr. Falcon!!" came a shout from the floor. The crowd laughed as Franklin said, "I love you, too!" His mood was softening; the concern and fear he'd felt off stage were melting. He visibly relaxed, and continued, "You honor me, and you give me far too much credit. There are many, many involved in the work of the Falcon Foundation, and truth be told, Jo here is the true inspiration behind it all."

Amid more applause, she covered her face with her hands, shaking her head back and forth, and then gave Franklin an expression of mock anger.

"You see," Franklin continued when he was able, "Jo told me years ago that we should never forget our heritage, our upbringing, and our struggle to make a life here in this great country. She was right, but I must admit, I have forgotten some other things over the years, and I've personally caused great harm to the Falcon Foundation and to those who depend upon us."

Murmurs began. Marissa's post was popping up here and there, and the tone Franklin had taken with his last remark seemed to add some measure of credibility to Marissa's poisonous video posting to those who were watching it.

Franklin's attention was drawn to the slight shift in the energy in the room as he continued, "Some of you may question the circumstances leading up to holding this conference today, but I need to take full personal accountability for the mess we have found ourselves in."

Just then, Jennifer walked urgently to the podium, interrupted Franklin, and whispered in his ear, "Mr. Falcon. We have a . . . situation . . . that's come to light."

"One moment, please," he said into the microphone, and he turned to face Jennifer.

Jennifer covered the microphone.

"Mr. Falcon, within the last five minutes or so, someone—we believe it's Marissa Grant—launched an inflammatory and patently false video painting you as a con artist. The video claims you have orchestrated this false crisis, a scam if you will, as a means to extort money and support."

"How is that possible?" Franklin asked, just loud enough to be overheard on the microphone.

The crowd's muttering intensified. Marissa's heart quickened.

"We don't know," continued Jennifer in a hushed tone, her hand wrapping more tightly around the microphone, "but I've seen enough of the video to know that with its clever editing, well, it's believable."

Franklin stared at Jennifer and slowly shook his head. His voice of reason was trying to gain a foothold as it screamed, "Franklin, stop this nonsense. It's time to fight back!"

Jennifer steeled herself. Franklin had always taken reason seriously.

Instead, he paused, closed his eyes, and soundlessly recited a short prayer. Upon finishing, he took a deep breath, turned and winked at Jennifer, and retook the microphone from her.

"Ladies, gentlemen, please, please . . . may I have your attention?" His voice was calm, yet firm. The audience quieted slowly.

"I've just been told that within the past several minutes a video has made its way across the Internet, with the single intention of bringing doubt into your minds about the real purpose behind this meeting."

More grumbling.

"I understand that some of you feel you are owed an explanation," said Franklin directly, "but I have not seen the video myself, and I expect that many of you in the audience haven't seen it either. Now I don't know what's involved in what I'm asking, but I'm hoping someone in technical support could show the video on the screens."

He motioned in the general direction of the technical support crew. After a few moments of flashing and some garbled sound, Marissa's video began playing. It was clearly of high production quality. No credit was given directly to either Marissa Grant or *The Grant Report*, but the editing and production style were an exact match for their approach. The opening scene included a "devious-looking" Franklin Falcon, an expression that he reserved for when he was playing games with Maggie, along with a subtitle growing across the screen, "HE MUST BE STOPPED!!" Obviously, the image was captured secretly when Franklin and Maggie had been playing at the park, at their cabin, or in their yard.

The seven-minute video continued, with clips coming from Falcon Family interviews clearly taken out of context, with "new" versions of sentences describing the actions of Franklin Falcon as anything but honorable. It was a masterful hatchet job, including expert use of video manipulation techniques, and the audience was transfixed.

The mood in the arena was growing unsettled; after all, the attendees had braved the elements and endured personal sacrifices just to be part of this meeting. The video came to a close with a call to action: *"Franklin Falcon is*

*a sham—and it's time the truth was known. Stop him. Stop him now. Today."*
A few shouts could be heard expressing feelings "not of love" for Franklin.

Marissa was jubilant.

"Please look at me. Please, I need to speak to you for a moment. Just a moment. I'll answer your questions, and I'll . . ." Amid the conversations, the questioning, and the impromptu discussions about the validity and motive for the video, a few in attendance began shushing others. "Shhhh!" rang out across the arena. Quiet returned.

"Thank you. Thank you. Please . . ." He stopped. His body language was completely open, his face serene, and he made eye contact with as many as he could. "I can understand how that video would raise some questions," he said, "and cause some of you to question what's happening here."

A single voice rang out, "Why?" More shushing.

"Why?" repeated Franklin. "All I can offer to you is that the content of that video was carefully and deliberately stitched together to paint me in the worst possible light. However, a specific image included in that video clearly gives away the person who produced it—an angry, troubled, and vindictive person who has never forgiven me or the foundation for revoking our support for her and her family when she was just a young teenager."

Silent anticipation replaced confusion within the crowd.

His gaze shifted as he continued, "I can only imagine how difficult this must be for you . . ."

Marissa's feelings of triumph evaporated as Franklin turned to face her.

He looked directly at her as he said, "Marissa. Yes, Marissa." Hundreds of heads turned in unison toward her as he continued, "I'm so sorry, Marissa. It was such a difficult decision to make in your situation, but we had to choose. In fact, *your* choice forced us to do something we've rarely done in the history of the foundation." His face showed the pain he'd felt some 20 years ago as he relived the decision process they'd made. The crowd was silent.

"Marissa, it was clear you had cheated on your application essay to the foundation, and the basis upon which we had originally selected you and your family to be part of the Falcon Family was founded on a falsehood. I'd hoped you had found a way to grow beyond your feelings of humiliation and anger, but as evidenced by the video you sent out this morning, you have obviously been holding on to tremendous rage and feelings of revenge.

I am truly sorry, but the hard work, commitment, and integrity shown by all the other Falcon Families took priority over your wish for us to look the other way on your application."

Cameras were now showing Marissa's expression of pure hatred, almost animal-like as she showed her teeth, panting, sweating, seething. The world witnessed her meltdown—live. The void of life around her had grown to more than 15 feet as all of her staff had left her standing alone, and all the others in the press section were now focusing on her as "the story."

Marissa had severely miscalculated. She was normally fully in control of the outcomes in her life, a survival mechanism she'd taken on once the foundation had removed its support for her family, and she'd vowed never to be out of control ever again. She was not prepared, however, for the power of unconditional love and forgiveness. While the world had shifted its attention to Marissa, Franklin had silently left the podium and was making his way toward her.

After a few moments, Franklin appeared on camera next to Marissa and made his way to her side. He paused as one might pause in front of a cornered wolf. Not showing any fear whatsoever, he did the unthinkable. He opened his arms, smiled ever so slightly, moved to her, and attempted to embrace her.

"Don't!" she spat, and stepped back hurriedly, putting her hands out in defense, the spotlights detailing her discomfort.

"Marissa . . ." started Franklin, as he lowered his hands slightly. "Please." His words were still being amplified as he had brought the microphone with him.

A flicker in her eyes, but her resolve returned. Her mouth began to form a response, but it stuck in her throat. She looked quickly from side to side, orienting herself. Then in one swift motion, she marched to the table where she'd been sitting, forced her computer into its case, grabbed her purse and coat, and escaped to the nearest exit.

The arena was frozen. Even the normally chatty TV types were silent.

Then, the clapping began slowly. One person, then 10, then 50, and finally the entire arena was clapping. Clapping turned to cheering, and cheering transformed to adoration. The crowd had witnessed Franklin vanquishing Marissa, but Franklin felt no victory. He was conflicted. He knew that having Marissa gone was a positive and much-needed outcome, but he hurt for her. He raised his hands to quiet the crowd once again.

"No, no. Don't do this. It breaks my heart to see Marissa with so much hatred and rage in her heart. She needs our compassion, not our scorn."

Turning his head slowly, he scanned the faces near him. Heads nodded their agreement; grim smiles met his determined gaze. The moment continued.

Then, with nothing but the electronic hum of the equipment in the background, Franklin spoke to the shadows, "I'm sorry, Marissa. I truly am. I hope someday you'll find it in your heart to forgive."

He meant it.

# Backstage

Saturday: About 11:30 a.m. MST

*(Moby Arena Locker Room)*

Week 1

| SUN | MON | TUE | WED | THU | FRI | SAT |
|-----|-----|-----|-----|-----|-----|-----|
|     |     |     |     |     |     | *11:30 a.m. MST* |

"Mom, I'm not sure I'm ready." Angela's confidence was waning. She'd poked her head into the arena and was momentarily panicked by the size of the crowd. Her mind began cycling again: "I can do this, I can do this, I can do this . . ."

"Angela, I'm so proud of you." Mrs. Liu was holding Angela's hands and sitting directly across from her. Normally the one who had more difficulty in maintaining her sense of calm, Liu Ping was uncharacteristically relaxed this morning. She, too, had been asked by Mr. Falcon to speak to the crowd today, but instead of worrying and being nervous, she'd found time to pray. She prayed for the ability to do what she needed to do, to say the right words. Her prayer had given her strength.

Angela misinterpreted her mother's words. "I know, Mom. But I don't really deserve all the attention I'm getting." Angela had been besieged by reporters over the past couple of days. While Rebecca had become the "collection" point for the feedback with ideas for supporting the foundation, Angela had reached near cult status as being the "one." She was thought of as the one who had started the phenomenon related to the Falcon Foundation in the first place. Angela thought her mother was proud of her for being so popular right now.

"Oh, Angela, I'm not proud of you because you're getting all the attention you're getting; I find that a bit strange actually. No, I'm proud of you because of who you are becoming. The reason behind all the attention you're getting right now is the fact that you are a loving, committed person who was more interested in helping others than in helping yourself. What you did is a result of who you are. I am so proud to be your mother." Her voice fell to a whisper.

Tears welled in both of their eyes, and they embraced. They shared a long, loving, soul-to-soul moment.

"Ten minutes, ladies!" came the enthusiastic voice of one of the volunteers.

Brushing aside the wetness on her cheeks, Angela replied, "Okay! Thank you."

Angela's mom took Angela's hands once again and looked directly into her daughter's eyes. She paused and then said, "I don't know exactly why we've been asked to be here, nor did I know what might happen when I called Mr. Falcon on Thursday. But what I do know is this: Something special is going on right now, and I thank God that we have the chance to be part of it."

"Me too," was all Angela could manage. The lump in her throat was the size of the arena itself. She reached for her mother and hugged the woman she admired and loved most in the world.

# What's Right, Not Who's Right

## Saturday: About 11:30 A.M. MST

### (Moby Arena Main Stage)

Week I

| SUN | MON | TUE | WED | THU | FRI | SAT |
|-----|-----|-----|-----|-----|-----|-----|
|     |     |     |     |     |     | 11:30 A.M. MST |

Franklin had made his way back to the stage, returned the microphone to its cradle, and was now standing at the podium.

"Ladies, gentlemen . . . the past few minutes have been very difficult for me." The arena slowly returned its attention to him. "Yet it's time for us to look ahead." His smile grew.

"No question the past two or three days have been amazing. Literally on Wednesday of this week, I felt as if the foundation's future was anything but certain. I was concerned about that, mostly because I had made so many poor decisions recently. But through a genuine desire to look at things differently, getting clear about our intention to look at new options and possibilities, and some unexplainable, okay, serendipitous, events, hard work, and courage, we have the chance today to make some amazing things happen." He paused and soaked in the positive energy in the arena.

"But before I bring up the executive director of our foundation, Jennifer Boyle, a person to whom I am personally indebted in so many ways, I would like to introduce to you the two women who provided the spark to get everything moving. I'd like you to meet Angela Liu and her mother Liu Ping!" Franklin waved to Angela and her mom and encouraged them to come on stage. They walked quickly to the podium, Angela looking quite nervous and Mrs. Liu the opposite. Thunderous recognition accompanied their walk, and Angela thought she might hyperventilate.

"I've talked with Angela and Ping several times over the past few days, and they're as amazed as all of us about what has happened. And I wanted them to be here this morning to see the results of what they started." His hands reached out to the arena, to the video screens, to those standing off stage, to the news media, to everyone, as he continued. "Because it all started with a simple phone call. Mrs. Liu, would you mind telling everyone why you called me?"

Liu Ping stood behind the podium, closed her eyes for a moment, mouthed a short prayer, and began, "First, Mr. Falcon, Angela and I are honored to be your guests here this morning. As you know, life in our home has been difficult, and we are so grateful for your vision, your help, your belief in us. My husband, Tao, has been fighting cancer, and I've had to stop working to care for him. It's been hard, and the cats have gotten tired of listening to me. Actually, I've found some comfort in cooking. You know, I've been working on a nice puttanesca sauce; the secret is to start with the burner at low heat, and . . ."

"Mom!" Angela whispered loudly as she gave her mother the "get on with it" face that she'd perfected over the years.

"Oh, sorry," Mrs. Liu confided. "I have trouble sometimes keeping my thoughts organized." The crowd laughed with her.

"Where was I . . . oh, yes, Angela [she motioned to her daughter] is so looking forward to coming back to Colorado this fall and studying at the School of Mines. We owe so much to you and to the foundation for your financial support, support for our health insurance needs, and for helping Angela get a wonderful education at a great school." She took a deep breath and gripped the podium with both hands before continuing.

Liu Ping then spent a few minutes describing the conversation she had with Franklin and the fact that he'd asked for her help. She recounted the story of telling Angela about the situation, the fact she'd gotten her prayer group together, and just how important she felt when Mr. Falcon had asked her to help. Upon finishing her story, Liu Ping was embarrassed by receiving a spontaneous standing ovation of her own. The crowd was clearly back into a positive state of mind.

"Thank you, Mrs. Liu. I must say, your conversation with me got me to listen to a voice that I hadn't paid much attention to for many, many years. One might say it was the voice of the divine. Thank you for having the courage to take action and to call me. Who knows where we'd be if you hadn't? Oh, and one more thing. Thank you *very* much for telling Angela about our telephone conversation." Franklin motioned to Angela to come forward to the podium; she'd been slowly inching her way off stage as her mother was speaking.

Angela stiffly made her way back to the podium. "Angela, I realize you've gotten some unwanted attention in the past couple of days, and I don't want to do anything to add to your discomfort. But I think everyone would be interested in hearing about what started this incredible movement. What exactly did you do?" His tone was calm, his manner gentle.

Angela stood at the microphone, stared at the crowd, blinked into the spotlights, and tried to forget the fact that her face, her voice, everything about her was being broadcast across the world. Her mom took her hand, squeezed it, and whispered in her ear, "Go ahead. It's okay." Angela looked at her mom, smiled slowly, turned back to the microphone, and began.

"It really wasn't any big deal. I just asked a few friends if they'd be willing to help you, Mr. Falcon. It just felt like the right thing to do; after all, you've helped so many other people and have never asked for anything in return. I know how important you've been to me and my family, so I wanted to do something to help you. I had no idea it would turn out to be . . . ," she paused, looked all around her, and continued, ". . . this big!"

The largest ovation of the day erupted. The crowd was cheering for Angela, for Franklin, for Mrs. Liu, for themselves, for the fact they'd all come together, and for hope for the future.

"Thank you, Angela; thank you, Mrs. Liu. I hope you'll be able to stick around for the rest of the day, if I may be so bold as to ask, to help us some more." The ladies nodded shyly, standing arm-in-arm, facing the crowd.

"Okay. On to the business of our meeting," Franklin began. "We have received literally millions of messages related to helping us, and I'm a bit embarrassed to report pledges for some $15 million in donations as well. The opportunity is now to leap beyond our old ways of thinking and the resulting limitations we've placed on our ability to succeed. We have some important work we'd like to ask you to do so that we might serve the needs of families throughout the world in transforming and powerful ways. We've developed a few potential ideas, and we'd like your perspectives on them. Before we get you started, however, let me introduce you to all the members of the executive team of the Falcon Foundation for Families along with two honored guests."

Franklin paused, turned around, and invited the entire executive team as well as Rebecca Anderson and Jack Miller to join him front and center on the stage. He announced their names, told the crowd what their roles were, and then ended each introduction with the same thing: "I'm especially proud to be part of a team with 'him' or 'her'" (as the case may be).

Franklin then shared how much he appreciated Rebecca and Jack's contributions at the hotel. He told the crowd that he wanted them both to be here this morning to witness the outcomes of their conversations in Room 212.

"I'm especially proud to have met you both and to have had the chance to share with you." Rebecca bowed demurely as Jack waved to the cheering crowd.

"Finally, I'd like to introduce the executive director of the foundation, Jennifer Boyle. Jennifer has worked with me for decades, and I have come to rely upon her completely. She's an amazingly capable professional and a good friend. I am especially proud to be part of a team with her, and I know you'll feel the same way by the time we're done working today. Jennifer?"

Franklin waited for Jennifer to walk up beside him. She stood, bearing a look of pride mixed with fatigue and a sense that she was more than ready to get started. She smiled confidently, took the microphone stand, adjusted it, and addressed the crowd who was cheering for her as well.

"Thank you, Mr. Falcon. Actually, I'd really like to start calling you "Franklin." Is that okay?" She stopped and smiled at him. The crowd whistled its agreement. Franklin was taken aback briefly but then nodded approvingly. The memory of Marty Wright came flooding back to both of them. Marty called Franklin "Franklin," but few others did.

Relishing the moment, Jennifer paused just a little longer before continuing. "Franklin, thank you for your leadership and for your passion all these years. But more than anything, thank you for your courage the past few days. I can only imagine how difficult these past 72 hours have been for you. Please know I admire and respect you more than anyone I know." It was Franklin's turn to blush. More whistling and cheering from the crowd rained down.

"Okay, ladies and gentlemen, are you ready to get to work?"

"Yes!" came the reply. Jennifer smiled, waited a moment for the room to settle down, and then continued.

"Okay, then. We've got volunteers in the arena right now who are passing out several sheets of paper to each table, and for those of you joining us online or via video or teleconference, we've just posted the sheets to our website for this meeting. These sheets of paper have a list of ideas—really categories of ideas—that represent the big insights we've developed in the past couple of days about potential options for the foundation's future. In a few minutes, we're going to ask you to dig in and evaluate these ideas, connect them if that makes sense, improve them in any possible way, add new ideas as they come to you, and finally present back to us at the end of the day."

Papers rustled, and the activity level in the room shifted from what was happening on the main stage to what was to happen at each table. Volunteer facilitators had positioned themselves at each table, and several had taken up "virtual facilitator" roles for those online as well. Elaine and Jennifer had prepared the facilitators earlier this morning to be able to assist each table in successfully completing the exercises Jennifer had designed.

"There should be enough papers for everyone to have their own copy; if not, we can get more copies made, or you could share with your neighbor. Let's take a moment so I can familiarize you with what's in front of you."

As Jennifer spoke, it became clear that the future mission of the Falcon Foundation for Families had the potential to be forever different. Fundamentally, they were still focused on education and in helping others help themselves, but the feedback from "the world" had told them that their view needed to expand and to be far more inclusive. The participants in the workshop were clearly in agreement and were chomping at the bit to get started.

"We have two basic chunks of things we're asking you to do. The first chunk has to do with evaluating the ideas we've just presented, and the second chunk has to do with helping us with implementation. After all, I think it was Thomas Edison who said, 'The value in ideas is in the implementing of them.' Great ideas that are never implemented are irrelevant. Anyway, I'll check back with you from time to time up here on the main stage, but for the rest of the day, you'll be doing most of the work where you are."

She stopped for a moment, letting the groups orient themselves.

"Okay, all of our facilitators are ready to go, so let's begin!"

The facilitators kicked off the activities at each table and across cyberspace, and the participants began their work for the day. One of the primary things the facilitators would be using throughout the day was Marty's concept of appreciation. They reminded the tables 1) to see the value in, and 2) to increase the value of, each other and the work they were doing. The mission at hand was to accelerate the greatness of what the foundation stood for while at the same time looking for new ways and places to develop additional capabilities and opportunities. In addition, the attendees were asked to focus on "solution finding" and not "problem solving." Each of these messages to the attendees was aimed to result in positive, growing, innovative, and powerful outcomes.

Appreciation was running rampant! The arena literally was humming with activity.

# And—Then What?

Saturday: About 12:00 P.M. MST

*(Moby Arena Backstage)*

Week 1

| SUN | MON | TUE | WED | THU | FRI | SAT |
|-----|-----|-----|-----|-----|-----|-----|
|     |     |     |     |     |     | 12:00 P.M. MST |

"Jennifer, your preparation has been wonderful." Ernesto spoke to her immediately after she'd gotten everyone working. "It's not an easy thing to have hundreds of people working together, and I can't wait to see what sort of wisdom they come up with about the insights we developed. It's just fantastic!" Ernesto found it difficult to contain his enthusiasm.

"Thanks, Ernesto," Jennifer offered. "I'm confident they'll come up with some compelling, powerful, motivating ideas for us. So compelling, in fact, I expect their ideas will be 'resistance-proof' as much as possible."

"I don't follow you," he said.

Elaine jumped in, "I think I know what she means. When a vision is compelling and powerful enough, it will withstand the challenges from any resistance that might be applied against it. In other words, the bigger and more powerful the vision, the less likely it is to be pulled off track."

"Exactly!" agreed Jennifer. "However, and this is a big however, getting the vision completed is really the easy part. The tough part of the job is for us to do something with it. Actions complete planning, as the old saying goes."

Ernesto had never heard that old saying, but he nodded his agreement.

Elaine continued, "And one of the more important things that's happening right now is that we have hundreds, maybe thousands, of individuals who are coming together, unifying really, in their views, their passion, and their motivations to work as a group, both right now and into the future, on helping the foundation move forward. These people have committed themselves big time to what they're doing, and they are trusting us to do something real with the output of their efforts. We can't let them down."

Elaine hustled off somewhere. The caterers were working to feed the crowd, and some decisions were needed at the loading dock. Jennifer smiled at Ernesto, squeezed his arm, and joined the throng on the floor. She was clearly in her element when it came to workshops like this.

Ernesto stood there with his thoughts, and a memory came to him. He had a client who once said to him, "We're good at planning; we're also good at doing; we're just not very good at doing what we plan to do." The foundation couldn't afford—literally—to not execute the plans being developed in the arena and across cyberspace. While the workshop would end today, they as a leadership team really had to ask themselves the question, "And then what?" They needed answers to that question. Ernesto went off to find Franklin to ask him what he was thinking about the next steps. They'd been so completely focused on getting the workshop together that they really hadn't asked themselves the "And then what" question yet.

It was time.

# Innovative Change

### Saturday: About 10:00 P.M. MST

*(Moby Arena Main Stage)*

Week 1

| SUN | MON | TUE | WED | THU | FRI | SAT |
|-----|-----|-----|-----|-----|-----|-----|
|     |     |     |     |     |     | 10:00 P.M. MST |

The day's activities were coming to a close, and everyone was waiting for the collective wisdom of the workshop to be revealed. While the workshop attendees had busied themselves with storytelling, napping, and card playing, Jennifer and her entourage of facilitators had spent the past two hours or so collecting, collating, assembling, and preparing the output from the day. Some 1,500 people across the world had dedicated the entire day (some the day and night before as well!) to this task and had built tremendously high expectations as a result of their work.

While the caterers had packed up their serving dishes and portable ovens some time ago, the buses to take the attendees to their hotels, to open dormitories, and to various other places of rest were still sitting at the arena. Empty. No one had left the arena.

Instead, while waiting for Jennifer to return to the main stage, the attendees had spontaneously self-organized into groups. Some groups were interested in remaining active in fund-raising for the foundation. Others were looking at ways to increase international activities, while others were motivated to drive for systemic changes to the world's approaches to education so that children everywhere were able to attend safe, relevant, challenging, and high-quality schools. Laughter rang out constantly, and hugging was incessant.

Just then, the lights came up on the main stage, and Jennifer returned, trailed by the dozens of facilitators and the members of the foundation executive team. She thought to herself, "If I didn't know better, I'd wonder about this group!" Their appearances were totally deceiving, as they looked to be a rag-tag assembly. But they were smiling and bouncing across the stage. Even a couple of cartwheels and back handsprings were on display. The arena instantly responded with joyous applause, giant smiles, and that strange, bark-like noise "Woo-woo-woo!" heard at sporting events, TV shows, and other places people gather.

Jennifer waved her hands and asked for everyone to quiet down. It took awhile, but finally she got her wish.

"What a day, huh?" Jennifer grinned as she asked. More cheering, whistling, and shouts of "I love you, Jennifer!" Everyone laughed.

Jennifer smirked, "I love you, too, because I tell you what: You've done some amazing work today. Thanks for giving us some time to collate and assemble everything. I think we've been through about 200 flip-chart pads and who knows how many sticky notes in the last hour or so. Wow!"

More "woo-woo-wooing."

"Anyway," she said while smiling proudly," as much fun as it has been today, and as hard as we have all worked, we did have a purpose for our activities, and that purpose has been fulfilled. We took thousands and thousands of individual ideas, condensed them—negotiated, integrated, improved, negotiated some more, improved some more—and finally boiled the whole thing down to what we're showing you now."

The facilitators had left the stage and returned to their tables—some dancing, some skipping, others just walking slowly, but all with huge, toothy smiles. They brought more papers; again, one for everyone.

"What we're passing out right now we're also showing on the main screens, and we've uploaded it to our website so everyone across the world can see it, too."

She reflected for a moment on the contributions coming from those outside of Moby. Certainly it was unusual to have such participation in this way, but the results exceeded her expectations.

"For those of you online, we could not have done this work without you. It's harder because we can't be there with you, but consider this a massive group hug coming from Fort Collins to you."

Again, more applause broke out, and those in the arena started doing some weird, expressive gestures, simulating hugs to virtual folks across the earth. It was an amazing moment, and the news media by now had given up on trying to simply cover the story; they were extending their arms, too, in gestures of affection to those not in the arena.

"So, Mr. Falcon, er, I mean Franklin," she grinned at him, "it seems we've been blessed with some amazing, powerful, and compelling ideas about what the foundation needs to do in the future. Clearly, much work lies ahead of us to implement these ideas, but the wisdom of everyone here, and across the world, is reflected in what we're sharing with you now."

The arena was electric, and goose bumps were commonplace.

"Ladies and gentlemen, here are your ideas." Jennifer spent the next several minutes sharing the specifics of the workshop results (*for a complete set of the workshop results, including the suggested actions the attendees developed, go to the Epilogue on page 233*).

Everyone read along with Jennifer:

VISION:

The Falcon Foundation for Families:

- Is selflessly grounded in equal educational opportunities for all children
- Courageously drives systemic, permanent culture and societal change for children who lack educational advocacy
- Serves families and children with direct financial and life-related assistance as often as possible
- Is committed to continuous refinement of its programs and operations through innovative, collaborative solution finding

GOALS:

1. *ADDRESS THE ROOT CAUSE*: Become and remain active in addressing the root causes of social injustices related to education, where some "have" and some don't.

2. *DON'T OVER-REACH*: Ensure we are doing the best job possible serving those we can with the resources we have available while at the same time stretching ourselves to never stop expanding both.

3. *MODEL CULTURAL DIVERSITY*: Actively engage in purposeful dialog and culturally changing situations to spread appreciation for the diversity in our cultures throughout the world; we are a divine tapestry.

4. *ENLIST AND EMPOWER OTHERS*: Develop and nurture on-the-ground groups throughout the world who look for places where new educational opportunities for children would have profound benefits.

5. *BALANCE OPPORTUNITY AND ACCOUNTABILITY*: Continue stressing the balance between equality in opportunity and the need for strong personal accountability related to the decisions and actions we make.

6. *BOND AND SERVE TOGETHER*: Provide relevant and motivating opportunities for individuals, groups, and organizations to connect with each other and to support each other as they support our abilities to deliver significant and ongoing financial, volunteer, spiritual, educational, and emotional support to families throughout the world.

As Jennifer was speaking, Franklin moved next to her and was beaming. He was impressed beyond words.

The imposing amount of work, the incredible lack of sleep, the pressure of the past several weeks had etched some new lines in his face and added to his already substantial inventory of steel-colored hair. But as he might have told you himself, he welcomed the wrinkles, additional gray hairs, etc., because he was witnessing something profound. His own transformation had occurred simultaneously with the foundation's. What was happening "to" him was also happening "through" him. Ernesto would certainly have described it as a "tangled hierarchy"—the chicken and the egg problem. The foundation's full transformation was based upon Franklin's transformation, but Franklin wouldn't have transformed fully without the transformation in the foundation. What came first? Ernesto loved those questions.

Jennifer completed her description of the workshop results accompanied by more applause, cheering, and feelings of genuine pride and satisfaction. The group was clearly pleased with what they'd accomplished. Soaking for just a moment in the sounds of success, Jennifer turned the platform back to Franklin, who had just a few final words.

"Ladies and gentlemen, I am overwhelmed. And," he said loudly, overriding the regenerating applause, "I realize the value of the gift you've given us today. You've given us the benefit of your time, your passion, and your wisdom, and for that I'm truly appreciative. Thank you."

There was nothing he could do at that point to stop the building power of the passion that was flowing back to him. The waves of emotion grew and crashed over and over as the group expressed itself.

Finally he was able to make himself heard once again.

"You are amazing! Where is this energy coming from?" He smiled, realizing just how energized he was; in spite of his fatigue, he felt buoyed. "Anyway, once again, thank you. Thank you especially to CSU, to all the students, the network types, the teachers, the staff, all the volunteers. My heart overflows with my gratitude. But rather than being an ending— certainly we all will have the chance to leave Moby Arena in a short time—I for one will be quite different as a result of this experience. No, this is not an ending; it is a beginning. A fresh start, an opportunity to make new choices and create new results." He paused, loosened his tie, finally took off his jacket, and leaned on the podium. His eyes narrowed and his jaw firmed as he said, "And you have my personal commitment that we will take your gift and use it well. Thank you."

# Courage to Act

## Sunday: About 2:00 P.M. MST

### *(La Quinta Inn Lobby)*

Week 2

| SUN | MON | TUE | WED | THU | FRI | SAT |
|---|---|---|---|---|---|---|
| 2:00 P.M. MST | | | | | | |

Franklin and Jo had turned out the light, kissed each other goodnight, and said "Sleep well" to Maggie by 1 A.M., but the final buses that took the last of the attendees away from Moby Arena didn't actually leave until nearly 3 A.M. Everyone was in a celebratory mood and was looking to "party" for a while. It wasn't until about midnight that everything settled down, and the quiet activity of tearing down and cleaning up began in earnest.

While it took a few hours to return Moby Arena to its pre-workshop condition, the volunteers did their work basking in the glow of the successful outcome they'd witnessed. Rarely was it possible to witness pure energy flowing, creating, enveloping, and transforming. They'd been part of it and would forever be changed because of it.

Just after Franklin's commitment to everyone about using their gift well, the executive team had met briefly and decided they all needed some rest before getting together again. Specifically, they'd decided that a 2 P.M. meeting on Sunday back at the hotel would be a good idea. Elaine had suggested going back to the hotel, and she expressed her desire to bring along some gifts for the staff. They had all enthusiastically agreed, and surprisingly, Franklin offered to take the lead with the gifts.

Most of them had arrived long before 2 P.M. and were involved in friendly conversations with members of the hotel staff. They were sharing stories about the workshop the day before and recounting their experiences with the hotel staff. Franklin arrived at about 1:50 P.M., bringing several wrapped boxes with him.

"Mr. Falcon, how wonderful it is to see you again!" The clerk's excitement was obvious. "Let me tell my manager that you're here."

"Thank you," replied Franklin, and he addressed the team again. "I've brought some special pictures for our friends here at the hotel," he said, winking at them while aligning the stack of packages he'd set on the counter.

The manager came around the corner and nearly flew over the counter to embrace Franklin. She about hugged the "stuffing" out of him. "Mr. Falcon! I'm so glad you came back!"

"Oh, it's my pleasure. Thank you for allowing us to use your conference room this afternoon. We felt it would be appropriate to come back here and finish the work we started last Thursday. But before we get to that, let me get to these," he said, waving his hand toward the pile of packages.

"I thought you might like to have these. One of the guests with us the other night was taking pictures, showing each hotel staff member working hard to serve those like us who were stranded. She sent me the pictures, and I thought they were wonderful. I've had the pictures framed, one for each staff member. I hope it will help connect them forever with the power of that evening. It was remarkable."

The manager's eyes welled with tears, and she hugged Franklin again. "That's wonderful" was all she could muster. "I'll be sure to let them know. Thank you. Thank you so much."

More hugging. It seemed like they'd hugged each other 100 times in the previous few days, but no one was complaining. Now it was time to get to their meeting. They moved from the reception area to the small conference room in the conference center so that they could finish up the work from the workshop the night before. They didn't plan to work through all the details just yet; there were too many of those. Instead, they wanted to decide what each of them should commit to doing next. They'd have several days—okay, weeks—of specific work to do, but they needed to be organized as they moved into the next few days. They didn't want anything to fall through the cracks.

At the start of their meeting, Jennifer told them that they'd received pledges for more than $50 million, an amount that provided enough immediate breathing room for them to handle their short-term financial obligations. They'd also heard from some of their lenders, who were willing to be somewhat flexible in the next 60-90 days. With some more good luck, good planning, and good decision-making, it was looking like their imminent financial crisis had been averted.

Franklin told them that he'd heard from Greg that morning. Even with all the positive changes happening at the foundation, Greg was still firm in his decision to not return to the foundation. He was considering moving back to Northern Ireland for a few years and reconnecting with family back there. His grandparents were quite old, and he wanted to spend some time with them before they died. He thanked Franklin for everything and wished them well.

It was then time for Ernesto to share his decision.

"First of all," he started, "thank you for accepting me as part of this amazing group right from the start. You've dealt with my nerd-like ideas, my descriptions of the weird world of quantum physics, and everything else. I've had an amazing week. But my next few weeks will be even more amazing, I hope. I was talking with Mr. Falcon earlier today—sorry, I just can't bring myself to call you "Franklin." Maybe some day . . ." Everyone smiled at him. "I said yes."

A pause. Franklin and Jennifer smiled. Ernesto smiled. They each smiled and looked at each other, their grins becoming goofier by the moment.

"What?" implored Elaine.

"Well, you'll have a new employee shortly. I've agreed to Mr. Falcon's request that I join the foundation's executive team—for real—and work with you to bring more international focus to what we do. I can't wait to get started!"

"Congratulations! How exciting! That's just great!" The words of encouragement and affirmation came from everyone. Ernesto was enveloped in good feelings. He felt even more confident that his decision was the right one.

"But that's not the only big announcement." Franklin was still grinning. "There's one more I'd like you to know about." He glanced at Jennifer. She glanced back and mouthed the words to him, "Should I?"

"Yes, why don't you tell them?" Franklin suggested.

"Okay, well, again in talking with Mr. Falcon," she stopped. "You know, I cannot call you "Franklin" either; I just can't." They laughed with her.

"Anyway, this morning Mr. Falcon told me that he was ready to make a change in his role at the foundation."

They all shot looks at Franklin, but he still had that stupid, boyish smile.

"He asked me, and I also said yes." More waiting. More grinning.

Terrence had had enough. "What, for goodness sake?" His good-natured impatience brought his stadium voice out again.

Franklin cut in, "I asked Jennifer to take over the foundation's day-to-day leadership in all respects. While I know I'm still in great shape and have plenty of energy and passion for what I do, I'd like to spend more of my time with Jo, and Maggie, our kids, our grandkids, and just traveling around this amazing planet, meeting others, sharing, offering hope and support, and learning how we might be able to be even more effective in our work."

He paused. "And I have come to realize that I need to get out of your way. I've stifled you at times. Lord knows I can be a slave to routine!"

"Nah," joked Betty. They all laughed out loud.

Franklin hugged her.

"I know I have some huge shoes to fill," said Jennifer, looking at Franklin, "but in reality, it will be easy." There she was again, saying things would be easy. The last time she said that it turned into a monstrous task of planning and running the workshop.

"Easy to you has a different meaning altogether," joked Nicole.

"Yeah, maybe so. But the real reason I think this will be easy is because I have the privilege of sharing the task with all of you."

"Easy? Well, let me check back with you in a few weeks and see what you think then," said Franklin. "But I agree with you. It has been my pleasure and honor serving with all of you, too. I'm not disappearing, but you'll see much less of me. And I'll be moving myself out of the middle when it comes to actions, planning, strategies, etc. Don't worry; I'll still be weighing in here and there, but I'm looking forward to serving with you in a new way."

As they looked at each other, it was clear that they would need some time to fully understand what Franklin had just said, but they'd figure it out. In the meantime, there were about 7 million details coming from the workshop that needed their attention.

"Okay, gang. Back to work! We're going to need all of our ideas, our passion, and commitment in the next several days." It was Jennifer's first official message as the new president.

They dug in. For the next three hours, they made decisions about how to spend the funds they'd been pledged, how they'd follow up with their kids, how they'd communicate with educational, business, and governmental leaders, and how they'd continue the process of fleshing out the details of their new strategy. The time literally flew by, and they accomplished a substantial amount of work in a very short period of time.

They were a team. They were focused. They knew their individual roles. They knew the mission. They had the courage to act on the right things and to let the rest fall away. They were committed to ongoing innovation.

They were rolling.

# Fish and Bread

## Monday: About 1:00 P.M. MST

### *(Gate B42, Denver International Airport)*

Week 2

| SUN | MON | TUE | WED | THU | FRI | SAT |
|-----|-----|-----|-----|-----|-----|-----|
|     | 1:00 P.M. MST |     |     |     |     |     |

Rebecca's whirlwind trip to the States was nearing an end. Her flight to LAX would be boarding in just a few minutes, and she looked forward to getting home. She'd arrive at her house sometime around 6 P.M. tomorrow. Just that thought caused her a flicker of worry about acclimatizing all over again as her body clock was finally in synch with the sun here in the mountain time zone.

However, Rebecca's attention was drawn to the post she was finishing. She'd just this morning set up a Facebook page specifically for "Fans of the Falcon Foundation" as a measure to help her regain her private identity on her own page. She'd accumulated thousands of "Falcon-related" friend requests over the past few days, and she had begun to redirect them to the new Facebook page for the foundation.

In just a few paragraphs, she'd summarized the events of the past few days: the request for help by Franklin, the unbelievable outpouring of support, the workshop at CSU, and everything that had happened since, including the pledges (now $57 million and growing), Ernesto's decision to join the foundation, and Jennifer's new role as president. Rebecca also shared her own story—at the hotel, at Moby Arena, and how lucky and blessed she felt to be part of it all.

She ended her post with this:

"I remember a story from my childhood. When I first heard it, I thought it was about a miracle where food magically came from nowhere. As I've gotten older, though, I believe it's really a story about the miracle of giving.

"It goes like this.

"Jesus and his disciples were about to address a large crowd, and it was nearing the time for dinner. It was too late in the day for the crowd to go out and find their own food, and the disciples were fearful that the crowd would expect to be fed. The disciples had only a few fish and loaves of bread among them and didn't know what to do. Jesus told them to have no fear, that the provisions they'd brought with them would indeed feed the crowd. At first the disciples resisted, but they then came to trust his words.

"They began sharing joyfully and freely with others, and what happened next was amazing. As the crowd witnessed the disciples truly believing that they had more than enough and saw the act of *selfless* giving they were demonstrating, the same feelings spread through the hearts of the crowd. The miracle that day was that when offered the chance to share selflessly with others, the crowd did exactly that. Baskets opened, food poured forward from everyone, and by the time all had been fed, the disciples collected several extra baskets of food overflowing with excess.

"I've witnessed exactly the same thing in Colorado the past few days. May the joyful and selfless giving continue, not only in monetary means, but in service to others, in choosing positive energy over negative energy, in empowering others and removing barriers to their success, and in finding ways to bring equal opportunities to all.

"Thank you, Mr. Falcon. Thank you to everyone."

She pressed Enter to upload the message, closed her laptop, gently rubbed her eyes, and stretched.

"Goodbye, Colorado. I'm leaving part of my heart with you," she said to herself as the boarding announcement came over the loudspeaker.

# More Than Expected

### Tuesday: About 1:00 P.M. CST

*(Liu Home, Eden Prairie, Minnesota)*

Week 2

| SUN | MON | TUE | WED | THU | FRI | SAT |
|-----|-----|-----|-----|-----|-----|-----|
|     |     | *1:00 P.M.* *CST* |     |     |     |     |

The remnants of the Federal Express package littered the kitchen table. Liu Ping sat at the table, with a pile of tissues resting near her right elbow. She'd been crying for some time now, even before she'd made the call to Angela. She got Angela's voicemail and then put two and two together: Angela was still in class. Ping was finding it difficult to sit still. Angela should be the first to know.

Finally, Ping's phone rang.

"Mom!" Angela was breathless. "I only listened to a little of your message. Is what you said really true?"

Upon hearing Angela's voice, Ping broke down and sobbed. Angela's impatience only grew.

"Mom! Are you there? Are you okay?"

Slowly Ping recovered her ability to speak and said, "Yes, Angela. It's true. Not only has your scholarship been fully funded, an anonymous donor in The Netherlands has offered something remarkable for your dad." Ping choked up again. Her words came out slowly, deliberately, and at a much higher pitch than normal.

"Mom, it's okay. What is it?"

"They've offered to fly him—all of us, actually—to Germany, where they're working on some remarkable new treatments for people with the kind of cancer your dad has. The success rate is good, but obviously there's no guarantee. The same person has also created a trust fund for you and me, to take care of us. Once . . ." Ping stopped speaking altogether. Her body was wracking and heaving at this point; months' worth of stress had finally come loose.

"Mom, I'll be home in a few minutes. I love you."

With that, Angela closed her locker, told her friends to let her seventh period teacher know what was going on, and headed home.

# DAY ONE

## Wednesday: About 9:00 A.M. CST

### *(Chicago)*

Week 2

| SUN | MON | TUE | WED | THU | FRI | SAT |
|-----|-----|-----|-----|-----|-----|-----|
|     |     |     | 9:00 A.M. CST |     |     |     |

Even the sun seemed to agree with Ernesto's decision to join the foundation's executive team. Chicago had endured weeks of gloom, but today the lakefront beaches were crowded with the office and cube dwellers playing hooky so they could get their dose of vitamin D. Their bosses didn't mind; they were part of the exodus.

Giving notice about his decision to become a full-time member of the foundation consisted of about seven or eight phone calls to his clients. His workload had actually diminished a fair bit due to some projects being canceled and others being delayed, so it looked like he'd need only a couple of months to fully complete his consulting work as he transitioned to support the foundation's international aspirations. Each of the conversations with his clients included sincere messages of thanks, wishes of good luck in the future, and offers to assist the foundation's activities. Ernesto was humbled on each level.

Additionally, he had several speaking engagements scheduled during the next six or eight months, and he planned to weave in the story of the Falcon Foundation in his presentations. The story of Falcon's quantum jump was evidence that the stuff he and his peers studied actually had some application outside the laboratory. The "white coat types" were always looking for a way to describe to "real" people the ways in which quantum physics plays a role in their everyday lives. He'd already begun the process of updating his speeches.

Ernesto's life was certainly in a state of significant transition, but the pieces were falling into place. Eventually he wanted to move to Loveland, but he wouldn't be home very much anyway for the foreseeable future.

His phone buzzed.

It was Jennifer; they'd arranged to talk that morning.

After exchanging some news about the happenings of the foundation, and reflections again on the success of the weekend, Ernesto said, "Before we get into planning my first few trips, I guess it's time for us to talk salary. I have some clear expectations related to compensation."

"Oh, yes, Ernesto. We didn't talk about that at all over the weekend, but I've had some preliminary conversations with Mr. Falcon about executive compensation packages. I have some ideas . . ."

He stopped her. "Jennifer, I'll accept nothing above $1 a year."

A short pause.

"Well, hmm . . . I'm not sure that's in the budget for the next year, but I'll see if we can swing it. We're down a CFO position right now but hope to hire someone in the next 30 days. I'll have to get their counsel to see if your expectations are in line with our cost structure."

"I can wait."

They laughed.

"Ernesto, again, I'm so pleased to have the chance to continue working with you. I think we'll do some great things together!"

"If you can deal with my not infrequent need to be a total dork, we'll do fine."

"Dorks are some of my best friends. But as to what you'll be doing, specifically, can we talk about that now?"

"Definitely. I've already been thinking about where we might best leverage ourselves internationally!"

Day two was going to be even better than day one. He just knew it.

# RETURNING TO A NEW PLACE

## Thursday: About 9:00 A.M. MST

### *(Falcon Headquarters)*

Week 2

| SUN | MON | TUE | WED | THU | FRI | SAT |
|-----|-----|-----|-----|-----|-----|-----|
|     |     |     |     | 9:00 A.M. MST |     |     |

Jo embraced Jennifer just before heading to Franklin's office. It was a warm, loving hug. Jennifer was about to convene her first executive staff meeting as the new president of the foundation.

They separated.

"Jo, I'm a little light-headed. Mr. Falcon is showing such confidence in me. I just want to live up to his expectations of me," Jennifer confided.

"Freddie's not falling off the planet," Jo chuckled. "But, I am planning to be a bit selfish with his time for the next couple of weeks. He'll resist me, of course."

Jennifer grinned. The prospect of keeping Franklin separated from the day-to-day activities would take some effort, on Jo's and Jennifer's behalf.

"I'll 'let' him answer some emails, participate in some conference calls, maybe even come in for a meeting or two. I'm sure there are some strategic decisions for him from time to time. But . . . I'm telling him I expect him to finally perfect his 'fountain of youth' smoothie that he's been working on for so many years." Jo's eyes twinkled. "Jennifer, you'll do great." Jo's words embraced Jennifer as they headed in opposite directions down the hall.

"Freddie, we should be going." Jo was gently prodding Franklin as he sat at his desk. Even though the days were growing longer, the sun would be setting by 6:15. If they were to get some skiing in without using flashlights, they needed to leave soon. While he and Jo had originally planned to go on vacation to Maui with their sons, daughters-in-law, and grandchildren, they'd decided it could wait. Franklin and Jo knew their family would have a great time on their own in Hawaii, and they also knew that Franklin being "too" far away from the foundation wasn't the best idea right now.

"I know. One more minute," Franklin said.

He had one more note to write. Even though he had made great progress in being open to new possibilities during the past week, he still clung to a few formalities. One was writing personal thank you notes. He'd finished dozens of them—to his executive team, to Ernesto, to Rebecca and Jack, to the hotel staff, to the president of CSU, the heads of the student associations, politicians, business leaders, sports stars, celebrities. The list was long and distinguished.

But he'd saved this note for the end, and he wanted to take a few minutes more to make sure he got the sentiments right. He'd written and rewritten this last note about three times and finally was pleased with the outcome. Rereading it once more, he said out loud, "Dear Angela." He finished reading silently.

Reflecting for just a moment on the fact that just about a week ago he was considering how to write a note of a very different kind to Angela Liu, he found himself quite pleased with this version of his thank you note. He signed his name, placed the note in the envelope, sealed the envelope, and stood slowly.

It was then he allowed himself to reflect on his decision to hand the day-to-day leadership of the foundation over to Jennifer. He knew that it was the right thing to do, but pangs of nostalgia washed over him. He absent-mindedly started shuffling some papers on his desk as his eyes moistened and the lump in his throat grew. He was so proud, so fulfilled, so amazed . . .

And he was so ready to spend the next couple of weeks with Jo. He smiled, small and tentative at first, and then big, wide, and toothy.

He said to Jo, "What if . . ." But before he could finish his sentence, Jo walked to him, hugged him tightly, and smiled herself.

"Freddie, all will be well. I'm sure of it."

# The Model

"If you can't describe what you're doing as a process,
you don't know what you're doing."

—*W. Edward Deming*

# The 50,000 Foot View

As I promised in the introduction, this section of the book will give you an overview of the JUMP! Innovative Change Model, which fueled the behind-the-scenes process I used to tell the Falcon Foundation story. I'll use some references from the story to reinforce the concepts of the model, so for those of you who skipped the "right-brained" story to read the "left-brained" model, these passages won't make any sense to you (unless, of course, you are clairvoyant, but then you would know what's in the fable already and could predict what I'm about to say. What came first, the fable or the clairvoyant?). Anyway, for the non-clairvoyants reading this section before the fable, I'll let you know specifically when I'm connecting something from the Falcon Foundation story to the JUMP! model. That said, I do encourage you to read the story about the Falcon Foundation at some point!

Additionally, I'll use simple pictures, graphics, process maps, and such to illustrate aspects of the JUMP! Innovative Change Model. However, don't look for everything associated with the JUMP! model here. Instead, information such as case studies, templates, comprehensive process maps, short videos, facilitator's guides, etc., are available for you at the JUMP! website.

*(For more detailed information about JUMP! and to download your own set of tools, please visit the JUMP! website at www.OurJUMP.com. We'll be*

*updating the toolbox on an ongoing basis, and we're particularly interested in hearing your success stories involving your own use of the JUMP! Tools.)*

With that as background, let's move on with the description of the JUMP! Innovative Change Model. The graphic below describes each of the four innovative change stages in JUMP!, along with the four steps included in each stage. For simplicity's sake, I show all four stages—with all four steps within all four stages—following one right after the other.

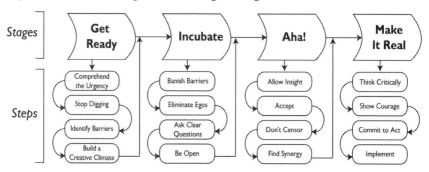

Obviously, the entire Falcon Foundation story is an example of the JUMP! model. However, mini-versions of the JUMP! model occur throughout the story. One such example involves the process by which Franklin "transformed" during his phone call with Mrs. Liu. Before taking her phone call (and interrupting the staff meeting), he'd prepared himself to start looking at things differently when he asked Betty to clear his calendar so he and Jo could go to the cabin on Monday morning.

His conversations with Jo at the cabin on Monday and Tuesday more fully prepared him to be open to new ideas, and he let his subconscious incubate. Then, once he was confronted by Mrs. Liu's question, "What can I do to help?" his preparation and incubation lead to his Aha! moment of asking her to pray that the executive team would be open to new possibilities. However, it wasn't until he actually *asked* her during their Thursday afternoon call that the Make It Real stage occurred. As such, he demonstrated the courage to act on the Aha! moment he experienced during his conversation with her.

# The 25,000 Foot View: What It Feels Like

The flowchart I shared in the previous section shows the JUMP! model moving in a linear, step-by-step, stage-by-stage manner. However, it's the rare project, organizational transformation, or personal journey that starts at the beginning and then flows all the way through the JUMP! model, touching each step only once and being in each stage only once. Normally, different steps within a single stage are repeated—in some cases, entire stages are revisited—before you make it to the finish line. Thus, each step can be iterative in that each step can involve its own Get Ready, Incubate, Aha! moment(s) and Make It Real mini-process.

Further, it is typical for the JUMP! model to iterate many, many times in the overall duration of a project, during an organizational change initiative, or even during the design and construction of a bathroom remodeling project. Do-it-yourselfers know exactly what I mean. I'm sure there's some formula to tell you that for every hour the home repair project takes, you'll wind up driving to the hardware store at least once. So, for an eight-hour sink repair project, you'll be visiting George in the plumbing section eight times.

Again, there are certain times and places when you'll find yourself using the linear JUMP! model (where you move through all steps in all stages). However, for a more accurate view of JUMP! (where JUMP! is an iterative, organic process), I show three different spiral-based views of the process.

Therefore, the linear, step-by-step model I shared previously looks more like this in reality (an iterative, circular view):

*Spiral One: Classic Fibonacci*

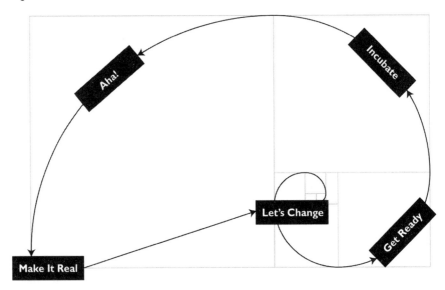

*(NOTE: I implicitly show the steps within the stages here. Additionally, the very center of the spiral, before the Let's Change section, represents the background machinations, discussions, events, challenges, issues, etc., that served to develop the impetus to change in the first place.)*

No doubt this first spiral representation of the JUMP! model is similar to the linear "all steps in each stage" view. I've shown it that way on purpose to help you make the transition from a straight-line, linear mode of thinking to more of a circular, iterative mode of thinking. As such, in this first spiral, I have you move along the entire spiral, from the beginning to the end, and return to the Let's Change area to begin the next phase in your project, organizational transformation, or personal journey.

Moreover, I chose the Fibonacci Spiral on purpose. The golden mean contained in this spiral (where each number in the series represents the sum of the previous two: 1, 2, 3, 5, 8, 13, 21, 34, etc.) shows up in nature on a regular basis; a nautilus shell is one example. You'll also see it in the ratio between the size of your hand and your forearm, the length of the different bones in your fingers, the placement of spots on certain species of moths, the size of the rings on Saturn compared to the planet, the structure of leaves, flowers, and trees, the design of the human face, and so on. It's everywhere in nature—because it represents a highly efficient design.

For my purposes within the JUMP! model, the golden mean represents the acceleration in your energy when you use it. The energy in each stage feels as though it grows at a rate proportionate to the Fibonacci Spiral. Consequently, by the time you reach the Make It Real stage, you are literally sitting on a space rocket's worth of positive energy. You are moving forward, farther, faster—being propelled by the energy you've been building along the way. It's *powerful!*

## Spiral Two: A More "Real" View

Now, to get closer to reality with the JUMP! model, the second spiral (below) represents a situation where a person or group using the JUMP! model spends little time in the incubation stage (because they've gotten *so good* at it, they might only need to experience one step in that stage), but then they go through nearly all the steps in the other stages.

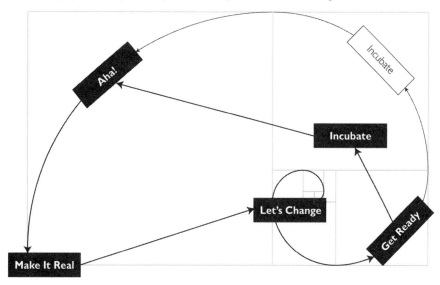

All permutations are possible in the graphic shown above (e.g., spending little time in the first and third stages and then following all steps in the second and fourth stages, or spending a great deal of time in the first three stages and little in the fourth, etc.). This spiral is just one example.

## Spiral Three: The Fastest Path

The final spiral (below) represents the "fastest path" approach to using the JUMP! model, where you might need to follow only one or two steps in each stage. This fastest path becomes the norm with individuals, groups, and organizations who have significant experience and are well-skilled with the JUMP! model. When this happens, amazing results happen very quickly. You are truly moving forward, farther, faster on a regular, consistent basis.

It's magic.

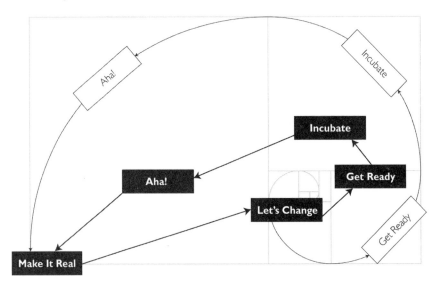

# THE 15,000 FOOT VIEW: STEP DESCRIPTIONS

Thus far, I've described the big picture related to the JUMP! model, but I haven't yet detailed the specifics of each step within each stage. This section (the 15,000 foot view) will give you a more detailed description of each step, one at a time, in each stage. The section following this one (the 5,000 foot view) will show you process maps, where you can see the flow from one step to another, and one stage to another, in a far deeper level of detail. Feel free to flip back and forth between the 15,000 and 5,000 foot views if you'd like.

However, before I get into the step descriptions, let me introduce the concept of Stage Zero.

### Stage Zero: Impetus

There's a stage that precedes the entire JUMP! model. Call it Stage Zero, or the Impetus Stage, or the Need-to-Change Stage. Stage Zero may involve only seconds (the plane has just crashed; we need to get out NOW!), or minutes (I'm about to run out of gas; I'd better pull over at the next gas station I see.), or hours, days, weeks, months, or years (What? I'm considered morbidly obese? I have developed Type 2 diabetes? Maybe it's time to change my diet.). Unfortunately, the impetus for change is usually based upon a response to a crisis, either real or imagined, and one that is either about to occur or has already occurred. Rarely do individuals or organizations change for positive, proactive reasons.

The teacher to whom I refer in the fable (Ernesto's high school science teacher) is the only real character in the Falcon Foundation story (okay, other than Maggie; Maggie is actually our family dog, Cinnamon. She does think of herself as a person!). Mr. Strickland was one of my teachers at John F. Kennedy High School in Denver, Colorado. In my junior-year physics class, he gave me the secret to making forward progress: "Take a step. Any step." I didn't appreciate the wisdom behind his statement then. But I do now. Even if the facts aren't fully clear, even if support for potential change isn't aligned, even if funding is missing, take a step—even a small step—in a different, new direction.

Therefore, to activate the JUMP! Innovative Change Model, do something different. Don't think about doing it, don't plan to do it—*do* it. In the case of Ernesto, he made the decision to travel to Colorado to meet with Mr. Falcon. He bought a plane ticket, went to the airport, flew to DIA, and drove to Loveland. He did it. He didn't try to do it. We don't know exactly how long Ernesto processed his feelings before he took action; that's not an important detail. What's important is that he chose to do something different. He took a step in a new direction.

Dropping a little in "altitude" here, let's take a deeper look at each of the four stages and each of the steps within each stage.

## Stage One: Get Ready

In my experience, about 99 percent of the organizations, groups, and individuals with whom I work struggle to Get Ready effectively. Why? There are many reasons, but it usually starts with difficulty in overcoming the status quo bias. Without a compelling, unifying reason to change, people will remain anchored to what they know. The old saying "The devil I know is better than the devil I don't know" comes to mind. However, the greatest failure related to change isn't choosing the wrong path forward; it's choosing NO path forward.

**1.1** *Step One:* Comprehend the Urgency

Both the intensity of the urgency and how widely shared the urgency is are important components as you prepare to JUMP!. Intense, shared urgency brings focus, determination, and power to the situation. Then, by adding positive energy to the shared intensity, the power of the urgency multiplies. However, insidious negative forces (like micromanagers, over-zealous auditors, unneeded regulation, mindless bureaucrats, etc.) can chip away at even the most intense, shared urgency over time. After all, complying with entities like auditors, federal government regulators, or tax authorities is a poor motivator for greatness. Therefore, keeping the positive energy associated with your urgency requires long-term commitment.

**1.2** *Step Two:* Stop Digging

The advice to "stop digging if you find yourself in a hole" may seem incredibly obvious, but it amazes me how many individuals, groups, and organizations continue to make things worse, even after they've discovered they're in a hole of some kind. Logic disappears and emotions rule. An example of stopping to dig the hole would be to act upon the noise your car makes when you start it on a cold morning instead of ignoring it. If there's a loud, metallic, screeching noise coming from the engine, it means something is wrong. Ignoring it won't make the noise go away; instead, the situation is likely to get worse and more expensive to fix.

**1.3** *Step Three:* Identify Barriers

There's a saying I like: "Change is inevitable, but progress is optional." Progress implies forward movement of some kind, and too often organizations have set up impenetrable barriers to forward movement. Identifying too strongly with the past, relying too heavily on tradition, sticking too closely to long-held beliefs—whatever the barrier, it needs to be called out and named. However, resist the tendency to want to "fix" the barriers here. That activity comes later. Just name the barriers right now.

**1.4** *Step Four:* Build a Creative Climate

I wish I had some form of magic wand I could use to create a climate for creativity. Unfortunately, I don't. Instead, getting the climate right for innovation, for incubation, takes time and intention. It doesn't often happen quickly, nor does it happen through chance. Instead, it requires commitment and diligence.

Stopping the process of digging a hole is a great beginning in establishing a climate for innovation. However, there's another hidden trap waiting for you. Your climate needs to survive the "cleaning the basement, attic, or garage" dynamic. What do I mean? Describe what it looks like when you're in the middle of cleaning any one of these clutter traps. Does it look better or worse than when you started?

If you're like most people, once you've begun to take down the boxes from the shelves, to pull away the piles of stuff from the walls, to move, shift, push, or pull all the things you've accumulated, you begin to seriously question your decision to begin in the first place. Why? Everything looks worse than when you started. Sometimes much worse, and when that happens, the closet finger-waggers jump out everywhere. You know these folks: They're the ones just ready to say "I told you so." This attitude can destroy your ability to innovate and can bring the status quo bias rushing back into the room amazingly fast.

### 2  Stage Two: Incubate

It almost sounds oxymoronic to say that "the most important activity of Stage Two is not to do anything. Instead, remain open to new ideas, and do not force judgment, prejudice, preconceptions, or any other form of censorship."

Incubation isn't about causing the result. It's about ensuring that the right elements in the environment—attitude, energy, focus, etc.—are present so that the outcome is ensured.

In other words, incubation is a process of nurturing, of trusting, of expecting, and waiting. It's not a process of continued list making (pros on the left, cons on the right), spreadsheet manipulating, or resume writing. Often when we fully engage our conscious mind in doing something repetitive (like washing dishes, as Franklin was doing at the hotel), our subconscious mind is set free to explore, to reflect, to begin the process of making unexpected connections, each an important part of the Aha! experience contained in Stage Three of JUMP!.

**2.1** *Step One:* Banish Barriers

As I've shared previously, the incubation stage is primarily a subconscious activity where we percolate, process, and think in the background. It is critical to keep the incubation process moving along in as uncontaminated a way as possible. As such, it is vital that you continue to handle barriers to progress throughout the incubation stage. Remember, the status quo bias (the *hairiest* barrier) can be insidious in that it can creep back in at any point in time. Be on your guard.

**2.2** *Step Two:* Eliminate Egos

For some, the whole JUMP! model fails right here. Encountering someone who "must be right" is frustrating, and we *really* don't want to spend much time with people like that. You know what I mean: Who wants to be around a fulltime know-it-all? On the other hand, we love being with people who are clearly committed to working hard by fully leveraging their skills, talents, energy, etc., as an integral part of the team.

Additionally, simply getting the egos out of the way can be difficult enough, but keeping them out of the way requires diligence, commitment, and focus. New members of the team need to know that egos aren't welcome here, and everyone's behavior needs regular check-ups to ensure you are committed to what's right, not who's right.

**2.3** *Step Three:* Ask Clear Questions

Instead of saying, "Be careful what you ask for, because that's what you're likely to get," I much prefer saying, "Be *clear* what you ask for." However, the usual approach to asking questions involves finding the *first* right question instead of the *best* right question. Take the time to develop great questions, and you'll increase the likelihood that you will find amazing answers. Why? Because the universe acts a bit like a genie in a bottle when we ask questions: "Your wish is my command." Make sure you've taken the needed time to uncover the best questions.

**2.4** *Step Four:* Be Open

The unknown is my friend. Repeat after me, *"The unknown is my friend."*

Change is a neutral word; it has neither a negative nor a positive connotation. It isn't until we apply an emotion to change that it is given any meaning. Unfortunately, most people have been conditioned to believe that change is inherently negative because they've been subjected to negative experiences more frequently than positive experiences in change activities. It's not because change itself is negative. Be open to new ideas and new possibilities, and your relationship with the status quo will move forward.

## 3 Stage Three: Aha!

Encouraging Aha! moments to happen requires us to surrender to what *wants* to happen, not to focus on what we're trying *to make* happen. Surrender is a tough word to get our heads around. After all, admitting to anyone that you are incapable of making a decision, or solving a problem, or finding an answer to a question is a sign of weakness. We are conditioned to be decisive problem-solvers who have clear and unambiguous strategies for our work teams, our businesses, and our lives. When we aren't all those things, people think we're somehow less than we should be, and an internal struggle ensues.

However, when surrender comes, it's amazing how the universe rushes in to provide us with an opportunity to be "in the zone." And, I'd be surprised if there's anyone (by the time they've reached adulthood) who hasn't experienced an Aha! moment at some point in his or her life.

## 3.1 Step One: Allow Insight

There are two bodies of water in the Middle East: the Dead Sea and the Sea of Galilee (also known as Lake Tiberias). Both bodies of water are served by the Jordan River, but that's about where the similarities end. Because the Sea of Galilee has an outlet, the water flows and life flourishes. The lake is healthy. Conversely, the Dead Sea has no outlet. The water stagnates and becomes brackish instead. By analogy, insight must flow so that the JUMP! model can succeed. Whenever insight is arbitrated, filtered, controlled, or otherwise blocked, innovative change is hampered or stopped, and you are *far more* likely to wind up with more of the same old things.

**3.2** *Step Two:* Accept

Have you ever heard anyone say "I just can't figure out what to do next!"? That's a clear sign that they are not "accepting" because there's no "figuring it out" here. Instead, this step (accepting), in this stage (Aha!), is about accepting what wants to happen, not trying to set a plan for what you want to have happen. There's plenty of time for planning later (in the Implement step in the Make It Real stage). Don't start planning here, or looking at pros and cons, or doing research, or establishing measures yet. Accept what wants to happen. Accept that what is, is.

**3.3** *Step Three:* Don't Censor

There's a word I really don't like—mentor. Webster's dictionary definition of the word is okay with me: *a trusted counselor or guide.* That's just fine. However, the popular definition of the word is what troubles me: *Do what I do, the way I do it, and you'll wind up being successful because you'll be like me.* "Mentoring" has taken on a cookie-cutter feeling; we've ended the process of discovery when we mix each individual's unique experience with the learning and new skills that come from others. Consequently, today's mentors seem to be attached to a particular outcome: "I'm me. I'll mentor you to become 'mini-me.'" I see this happen *all the time* in organizations where tenure or seniority is valued over creativity and innovation. It's unfortunate, because mentoring (using the popular definition) is cementing in the same old results by simply creating clones or duplicates.

I prefer the term "coach." Outstanding coaches are attached to outcomes (love of the game, knowledge of strategy, success at a position, success as a team) but not to any particular outcome for any particular player or person. Excellent coaches are interested in the success of the individual, not in making mini-me's anywhere. Therefore, mentoring is about censoring, and coaching is about allowing. Are you mentoring or coaching?

**3.4** *Step Four:* Find Synergy

This final step in the Aha! stage has to do with making unexpected connections. In other words, look at the Aha! in new ways: deepening, widening, stretching, inflating, shrinking, reversing, inverting, etc. In addition, look at connecting your Aha!'s with other Aha!'s in new and unique ways. "What if we did this forward and that backward?" or "What if this was done before that was done?" or "What if we had 20 times more of these and 25 percent of those?" Finding synergies, unexpected combinations, unique connections, etc., is possible if the other three steps in this stage are present. If you are allowing, accepting, and not censoring, it's amazing how synergies begin to show up.

## **4** *Stage Four: Make It Real*

We've arrived at the fourth stage—Make It Real. By this point, the JUMP! model has assisted you with creating some amazing, insightful, creative, and powerful Aha!'s. However, the process involved in generating ideas (Stages One, Two, and Three) is very different from the process involved in implementing ideas (Stage Four). Turning good ideas into action requires critical evaluation, decisiveness, courage, and a commitment to see things through to completion.

## **4.1** *Step One:* Think Critically

Once the "magic" of creating Aha! moments has occurred, it's vital to begin the process of evaluating your new ideas. Critical evaluation is objective, comprehensive, and multi-dimensional. However, a word of caution: Your old friend the status quo is ready, willing, and highly motivated to return because it loves the same old things. Therefore, remaining open to a new better future is vital as you evaluate your Aha!'s. If you return to your conditioned responses, your historic views—where the status quo creeps back into your evaluation process—you might just find yourself wasting the effort you put forth in Stages One, Two, and Three. Remind yourself of this, remind those who are part of the Make It Happen stage (including the evaluation team), and then remind the others (managers, executives, directors, stakeholders, family members, etc.) to whom you present the outcomes of Stage Four.

## **4.2** *Step Two:* Show Courage

Step Two is about making decisions, not doing more evaluation or research. You've already done both of those by the time you get here. As such, when you look up the word "decide" in the dictionary, it is *not* defined this way: *Keep all of your options open.* Instead, the word decide is defined as *putting all other options aside.* In other words, making a decision does not involve sticking your toe in the water and just trying it out. This process involves the courage to choose to implement the best solution, idea, Aha! moment, etc., and to let the rest fall away.

###  *Step Three:* Commit to Act

The previous step was about making decisions. This step is about taking action. After all, even the *greatest* ideas, if not manifested, are useless. In other words, if you are not going to commit to take action, you might as well not go through the effort of creating Aha!'s in the first place. Just remain in close contact with the status quo, because that's what you'll have. Commitment here is beyond just the decision to act. It involves ensuring that the right conditions exist for a successful implementation. A commitment includes unified leadership as well as the necessary time, money, and other resources to ensure success. If you don't have the right conditions for success, you are allowing failure to be an option. And failure can't be a choice if you're serious about JUMP!.

###  *Step Four:* Implement

JUMP! doesn't go into all the aspects of actually implementing new ideas. Maybe I'll write the sequel to JUMP! and call it "DO!." I don't know, but there's a great deal associated with excellence in implementation that I'm not covering in JUMP!. However, I do look at a couple of characteristics in the implementation step that are critical to success: 1) agility, and 2) learning to improve.

Agility shows up when we make good decisions even in the face of ambiguity, when we get comfortable with uncertainty, and when we value our intuition over the "cookbook." (Again, exceptions here would be some aspects of certainty-based organizations like the Department of Defense or nuclear power plants.) Agile organizations value human interaction over processes and procedures, and they keep formal contracts, written agreements, etc., "in the drawer," because their mentality is more about doing whatever it takes and not simply complying with clauses and preambles.

The second characteristic, learning to improve, has to do with committing yourself, your group, or your organization to learn from all situations (positive or negative) with the intention of using the lessons to help you improve, not punish. Each activity offers the prospect of learning, but it's the rare person, group, or organization that captures the learning as it happens, and even fewer still take that learning and do something with it to improve. Instead, we can all tell stories about micromanagers who look over our shoulders, who criticize everything we do, and who are looking to pounce on our mistakes. That's the direct opposite of JUMP!.

# THE 5,000 FOOT VIEW: PROCESS MAPS

I need to return to Ed Deming's statement that I shared in the introduction and on the cover page of this section: *"If you can't describe what you're doing as a process, you don't know what you're doing."* I'm a firm believer that pictures are vital to understanding, and as such I use process maps to describe the flow among steps in a particular stage, as well as the details associated with each step. Here's a sample process map:

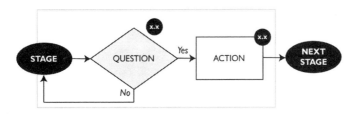

- Each step within each stage in the process map is a black circle with a number (1.1, 1.2, 1.3, 1.4, etc.).

- Questions are light gray diamond shapes.

- Actions are white rectangles.

- JUMP! points (where you move from one process map to another) are black ovals.

To orient you to the entire JUMP! model, I show below all four of its process maps. Don't worry if you're not able to follow them in detail on this one page. Some of our minds love reading flowcharts and process maps without descriptions, but not all of us. For those who prefer some description with the flow charts, I'll describe each of these process maps more fully in the next section, and I'll use more words, too!

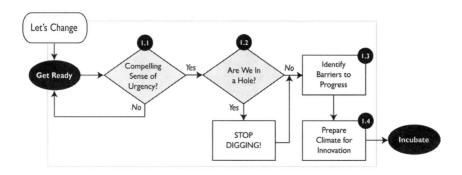

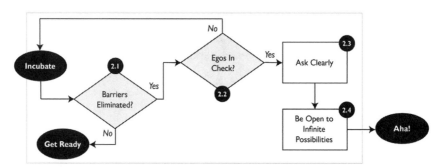

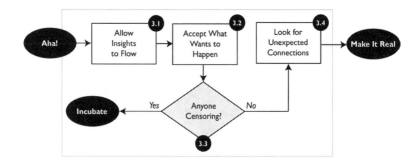

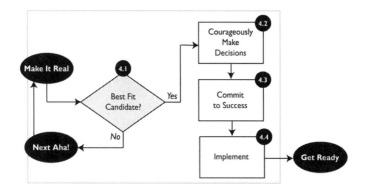

# The 1,000 Foot View: Tools / Techniques

Okay, here we go with the guts of the model. You'll first see the process map for each stage, and then I'll break down the description for that stage into four sections, one for each step. Then the description for each step will have three components: 1) a brief description of the step, 2) a brief overview of the tools and techniques I use in that specific step, and 3) examples from the Falcon Foundation story related to that step. Again, for more information —and to download your own copies of the templates, tools, etc., I reference here, please visit the JUMP! website: www.OurJUMP.com.

*Stage One: Get Ready*

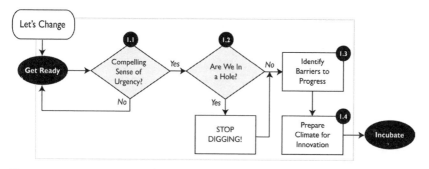

🔵**1.1** *(Stage One: Get Ready)* Step 1: Comprehend the Urgency

Description: *Without urgency, momentum falters. And positive energy is a far more powerful force for instigating and maintaining momentum than negative energy is.*

Yes? *Continue to Step Two*

No? *Return to the beginning of Stage One, Get Ready*

Tools / Techniques:

Shared, intense, and positive urgency is critical for creating momentum to achieve the best results from the JUMP! model. Consequently, I'm a real fan of using scenario-based planning to build this kind of momentum. Scenario-based planning is the process of using storytelling as a part of building plans for the future. Typically in scenario-based planning, we spend time examining three scenarios: the worst case, the best case, and the most preferred case.

Why look at the worst case? Because it releases the negative energy. You look at it, identify it, name it—and then laugh nervously about it. But by naming it and saying "This really isn't going to happen, and even if it did, we'd still survive," the worst case fails to have any power over you. Next, I have people look at the best-case scenario. I ask them to look way beyond their limitations to where everything goes well. The right people show up (or go away), you have all the funding, resources, time, etc., you need. *Everything* goes well. Now, having everything in the best-case scenario happen is probably unlikely (although I've seen some amazing things!), but just looking at the best-case scenario gets the energy flowing in a positive, aligned, and powerful way.

Finally, after looking at (and releasing) the worst-case scenario, and after dreaming while examining the best-case scenario, I ask people to build their most preferred–case scenario. In other words, what do you prefer to happen? Usually, at this stage, the group is passionate, aligned, and looking well beyond the limitations they originally may have had.

Examples from the Falcon Foundation story:

I used several different ways to convey and heighten the sense of urgency for the Falcon Foundation to change: potential damage to Franklin Falcon's personal reputation if the foundation defaulted on payments (that by itself wasn't strong enough; they'd known about that situation for weeks); the impending doom associated with Marissa Grant's visit (again, Franklin and the executive team seemed ready to deflect any potential damage coming from *The Grant Report* interview); Greg's continued browbeating of the executive team (that didn't work either); and Greg's attempts at shaming Elaine and Nicole (in particular) for their lack of progress in getting things done. None of these worked very well. Why? Because they each used some form of negative energy.

Instead, what ultimately caused Franklin to *finally* get moving was the combined actions of just two people, Ernesto and Mrs. Liu. Both of them ultimately broke out of the trap of simply worrying about the situation and did something positive. They took action, action motivated from a desire to help, to make things better. Their positive, pure (no hidden agendas) energy was a catalyst in increasing the foundation leadership's urgency to do something different.

### 1.2  *(Stage One: Get Ready)* STEP 2: STOP DIGGING

DESCRIPTION: *If you have a problem, stop making it worse.*

YES? *(Are We in a Hole?) Stop Digging, and Then Move to Step Three*

NO? *Move Directly to Step Three*

TOOLS / TECHNIQUES:

The tool I use here really relates to the approach I take in my facilitation. I like the metaphor of the elephant in the room. Why? Because elephants are big, hairy, smelly (at least to me) creatures who take up a lot of space and are hard to ignore. However, I encounter elephants in the room *all the time* that people are fully into denial about. Usually, elephants represent something that's continuing to worsen, like attitudes, funding, product quality, etc.

In talking about elephants, I'm pretty direct. Okay, very direct. But I tell my clients that I'm "compassionately detached." In other words, I tell them, "I feel your pain, but I have to tell you about it anyway." I have to be clear here: To be an effective facilitator, you need to remain separated and objective from those whom you are facilitating (Just try—I dare you—to facilitate your teenaged children! I've tried on more than one occasion, and I *always* go down in flames. It's not a pretty sight.), and you need to say what needs to be said in a purposeful, positive-energy, compassionate way.

So—talk about the elephants in the room. Name them. List them. Do something about them. Just stop them from being ignored any further.

EXAMPLES FROM THE FALCON FOUNDATION STORY:

Consider the outcome of Ernesto's snowmobiling accident. A few members of his party kept thinking that rescue was "one more hill away" as they staggered off in a dream world. Ultimately, those who died in the accident were those who were unwilling to "stop digging" and come to grips with the fact that their circumstances were very different, and it was time to adapt and overcome. Now. Survivors (whatever the circumstance) are identified by their willingness to adapt and by the actions they take in adapting quickly to their new circumstances.

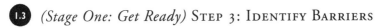 *(Stage One: Get Ready)* STEP 3: IDENTIFY BARRIERS

DESCRIPTION: *Understand your barriers to progress.*

TOOLS / TECHNIQUES:

The tool I use to build awareness of barriers to progress is called a "force field analysis." Now don't confuse this with something out of *Star Trek* or *Star Wars*! The forces to which I refer are those that are holding you, your group, or your organization in a state of equilibrium (see the template below). There are driving forces that are perfectly offset by restraining forces.

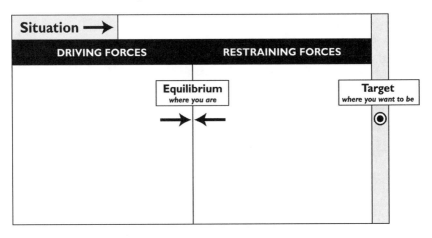

I use this template as a tool to help identify what's holding you back from reaching your targets. It could be that a driving force isn't strong enough or that a resisting force is too powerful. In either case, it's highly useful to use the force field analysis tool to objectively "name" your barriers to progress.

EXAMPLES FROM THE FALCON FOUNDATION STORY:

Franklin called one of his barriers "the voice of reason." He told us this voice is the one that was consistently trying to pull him back into his comfort zone, to keep the pressures of their financial crisis secret, and to continue attempting to solve the problems himself. It wasn't until Franklin actively "named" this voice that he made himself aware of the power it held over him. He then was able to see that barrier and ultimately have the chance to do something about it. The Falcon Foundation story contains many references to characters encountering and naming their barriers: Terrence's upbringing, which made him feel obligated to serve everyone; Elaine's reticence to commit again to "do whatever it took" to move an organization forward; and Greg's utter inability to see anything but a historical approach to solving their funding crisis. Naming the barrier is the first step in moving through it.

###  *(Stage One: Get Ready)* STEP 4: BUILD A CREATIVE CLIMATE

DESCRIPTION: *Creativity and innovation are accelerated in the right climate.*

TOOLS / TECHNIQUES:

Each situation is different, no question, but there is one thing I need to make very clear about establishing a great atmosphere conducive to innovation. The first ingredient to get right is a high level of trust. Groups that have high trust are naturally interested in the best overall success of the group, are open with each other, and operate in an environment where new ideas are welcomed. They play together, are vulnerable with each other, and genuinely enjoy spending time together. They also are undeterred by the "mess in the middle" when change is underway (the cleaning the basement analogy I used earlier). Certainly there are other aspects related to creating a climate for creativity beyond developing trust (inclusiveness, playfulness, experimentation, risk-taking, challenge, etc.), but I'll just focus on trust here. It's that important.

Trust is earned, not demanded, and you know when you are in its presence and when you are not. It can take years to build it but only one bad decision or one indiscretion to tear it apart. Therefore, the only way trust can be built is through transparency. Building or rebuilding trust— if it is damaged or non-existent—rests squarely on the shoulders of the leaders. Leaders must model the behaviors they want from others, and as such, leaders must demonstrate and give away trust if they expect to get it in return. Micromanagement? Little or no trust. Operating like the hub to all the spokes in every decision? Little or no trust.

The technique I use to build trust is based upon a marketing model of awareness, understanding, and preference. First, I help the organization (or group or individual) become fully aware of the trust-related challenges they have. I usually interview the individuals one-on-one beforehand, and I identify where gaps in trust exist. Next, I help the group understand the ramifications associated with continuing to operate with lower-than-desirable trust levels (pointing out risks to their success, etc.). I then help them build a preferred plan to start to build and continue to build trust. When trust is present, creativity is possible. Without trust, the opportunities for innovation and creativity are few.

### EXAMPLES FROM THE FALCON FOUNDATION STORY:

The first place where we saw the climate for creativity shift for the Falcon Foundation was when Franklin himself stepped out of the rigid, inflexible mode of operating that had become part of the culture. He spontaneously went to the cabin with Jo, he called an impromptu meeting with the executive team and Ernesto, and he admitted his personal failings with openness and transparency. Additionally, he showed his trust in Ernesto when he asked for Ernesto's assistance in the executive team meeting and in Jennifer when he named her as president of the foundation. He clearly demonstrated trust in both circumstances.

Further, getting the leadership team out of the boardroom and into the hotel was another example of creating a climate for creativity. Call me strange here, but I believe places store memories. As such, for most of the leadership team, the Falcon boardroom primarily held memories of rigidity, inflexibility, time constraints, and control. It was a low-energy location. Just getting the team to the hotel for the evening—all by itself—represented a step in creating the right climate.

Finally, the leadership team needed to recapture its sense of serving together—working together and being a force for good together. They'd forgotten about that as they turned their work into nothing more than meeting obligations. Consequently, they rebuilt not only their personal relationships together by serving together at the hotel (cooking, delivering meals, doing dishes, etc.), they recaptured the trust they had for each other.

## Stage Two : Incubate

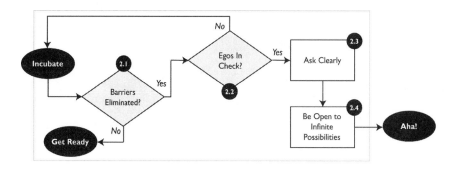

**2.1** *(Stage Two: Incubate)* STEP 1: BANISH BARRIERS

DESCRIPTION: *Have we named our barriers and worked to eliminate them or at least to mitigate their effects?*

YES? *Continue to Step Two*

NO? *Return to Stage One, Get Ready*

TOOLS / TECHNIQUES:

An organization's culture (or a person's belief system) is often full of things they treat as facts, but in reality, they're just decisions they made in the past that continue to influence decisions in the future. Call these "Conditioned Responses." Think of Dr. Pavlov and his dogs for a classic example; a ringing bell would cause the dogs to salivate in anticipation of being fed. However, not all conditioned responses create the anticipation of reward. Instead, in my work I see how conditioned responses related to change cause people to suffer in advance. The past plays such a strong role in people's perceptions of the future that sometimes they predict the future as if they were clairvoyant. But they aren't. People stop before they start because they're suffering negative consequences in advance. Isn't that dynamic weird when you look at it that way? I think of this Mark Twain quote at times like this: "I have been through some terrible things in my life, some of which actually happened." Suffering in advance looked at rationally makes no sense, but we do it all the time.

Therefore, I'm always looking for key phrases or words in conversations, written communication, and body language that tell me that barriers are still present. If I hear (or see) any of the following things, I tell the folks I'm working with that they are still in Stage One and not ready for Stage Two.

- If it's not broken, don't fix it.

- We've always done it this way.

- Let's form a committee (council, task force, tiger team) to look at it and then report back later.

- We'll need to get approvals before we can move forward.

- Who's got time for that?

- What would they (insert the group) think if we did that?

- You can't teach new tricks to an old dog.

Even the ancient Greeks knew the danger of being stuck—after all, about 2,500 years ago Heraclitus said, "*The only thing permanent is change.*"

EXAMPLES FROM THE FALCON FOUNDATION STORY:

One of the most powerful barriers to progress is the notion that uncertainty is negative. Uncertainty is a neutral term in that it just describes a period when the future is unknown. The future could be fantastic! However, in my experience, most people perceive uncertainty negatively. Think back to the Zen story Jo shared with Franklin about the road ahead. Is your road ahead easy, hard, neither hard nor easy, or both easy and hard? Your choice—but quite often, our unconscious barriers, our programmed, conditioned responses are the things driving us. If that's true, you haven't prepared yourself yet for Stage Two.

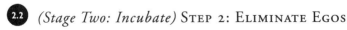 *(Stage Two: Incubate)* STEP 2: ELIMINATE EGOS

DESCRIPTION: *Take the situation seriously, but not yourself.*

YES? *Continue to Step Three*

NO? *Return to the beginning of Stage Two, Incubate*

Tools / Techniques:

In every workshop I lead, I start with a series of agreements together by which I will facilitate the activities. Notice, I intentionally call them "agreements together," not ground rules. The term "agreements together" invokes positive images (both words are positive), while the more common term, "ground rules," creates images that are negative, maybe even punitive. Words matter. Choosing the right words is a powerful component in ensuring the best possible outcomes using JUMP!.

Okay, back to the agreements together I use. One of the agreements is this: *We'll focus on what's right, not who's right.* In other words, take the situation seriously, but not yourself. As such, I disallow speech-making and positioning that is designed to prove that one person is right about something at the expense of someone else. No win/lose situations allowed. Instead, I force the workshop participants to look at the situation as being primary—to describe "what" needs to be done. We'll get to assigning some accountabilities for the doing part of the project later. However, insecure types tend to be more interested in appearing to be important than in being interested in doing important things.

Examples from the Falcon Foundation story:

Greg is the poster child (okay, he's a bit of an exaggerated stereotype—on purpose) for someone who must be right about things. He's so focused on what he thinks is the right answer that he's not listening to the feedback around him, nor is he open to change. Ultimately, to him, it's *his way or no way.* He's stuck. In addition, reflect on the example I used with Elaine's former employer. The organization she was part of was failing, but those in "leadership" were more focused on ensuring that their own part of the organization was fine (or worse yet, that their own butts were covered). Ultimately, the organization failed and took down everyone with it. I see this dynamic happen again and again.

Conversely, I used Angela Liu, Liu Ping, Rebecca Anderson, and Jack Miller (and others) in the story as examples of people who had nothing but the best interests of the Falcon Foundation in mind. They simply did what they did for the pure joy of doing it. Clearly these characters were central to the story, and the fact they were taking the situation seriously, but not themselves, was a necessary component to moving the whole story forward.

**2.3** *(Stage Two: Incubate)* STEP 3: ASK CLEAR QUESTIONS

DESCRIPTION: *"Be clear about what you want, because that's what you'll get."*

TOOLS / TECHNIQUES:

I have adapted the Appreciative Inquiry (AI) theory as a tool to help me develop great questions. *(David Cooperrider, Suresh Srivastva, Frank Barrett, John Carter, and others developed the AI theory in the 1970s at Case Western Reserve University in Cleveland, Ohio. A Google search on Appreciative Inquiry will result in a vast array of resources on the topic.)*

Certainly I'm not going to give you all the details associated with AI here, but I'd like to give you a taste of the theory as I've adapted it to developing questions. However, before I do that, use the graphic below to help you understand what AI is not.

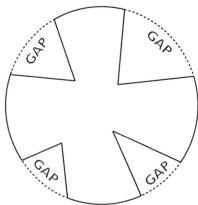

This graphic shows the approach used in most change-related activities. The theory here is this: A completed circle represents a perfect organization, team, life situation, etc. Therefore, *identifying and filling the gaps* must be the goal. Consequently, the question you'll hear most often during activities like these is this: "What problems are you having?" Then, once you have your problems identified (gaps), you can focus on fixing what's broken, repairing what's decaying, and righting what's wrong (filling the gaps). Most people I encounter love this approach because it's so comfortable, so normal, so expected. However, just closing your gaps—without addressing the causes for the gaps to be there in the first place—is a bit like using spackle to patch a wall that has black mold growing behind it. The wall looks okay on the surface, but the root causes haven't been addressed, and the mold is still growing.

AI uses a 180-degree different approach. Instead of focusing on closing the gaps, AI first involves finding (or recapturing) the core essence, the greatness, the "secret sauce" of an organization, a group, or an individual. AI uses a series of questions, and involves a large population, to drive the organization toward its most preferred future. When you're involved in the AI process, you'll hear this question, "What is working well around here?" The graphic below depicts (in a highly simplified form) the AI theory in action. For illustrative purposes, I depict the secret sauce using the star in the middle.

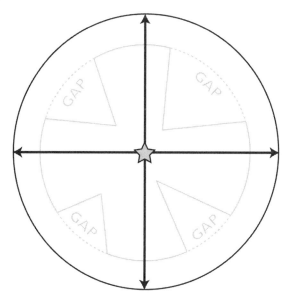

AI focuses on these three things: 1) searching for solutions that already exist, 2) amplifying what's working well, and 3) using positive energy to appreciate the situation (find the value in, and increase the value of). What happens next? The greatness expands (as shown by the arrows and the larger overall circle), and nearly all of the gaps close naturally. Why? One major reason is this: You're not using negative energy in "problem solving." Instead, you are using positive energy in "solution finding." As a result, the resistance you typically find in change-related activities is mitigated, buy-in happens quickly and grows rapidly, and the overall experience looks like *magic*. It's wonderful.

One caveat: AI is not usually 100 percent effective in closing all gaps. As such, you may need to employ more traditional means to close some gaps. Sometimes you still need to look at remediating or removing certain employees through formal, HR-related activities. Further, some gaps may require changes in behavior or strategy that need more formalized activities. Therefore, I use AI to assist me in getting great questions to come to the surface *and* as a means to help accelerate positive energy. I don't rely upon it solely to help with closing all gaps in a particular situation.

Some starter questions in AI might include:

1) What strengths do we have that we can leverage?

2) What options are available to us?

3) What else might we be able to do?

4) Where are our sources of pride?

5) What is working well around here?

EXAMPLES FROM THE FALCON FOUNDATION STORY:

The Falcon Foundation had spent months spinning its wheels trying to solve its short-term cash flow problems. However, their efforts were unsuccessful largely because they hadn't addressed the root causes behind the sudden disappearance of funding, i.e., they hadn't yet asked the right questions. In fact, it wasn't until the morning at the hotel, when the executive team had been percolating all night on their dilemma, that the really great questions came forward. It was then that they began asking about the general feelings toward immigration, the perceptions of elitism from some people related to the foundation's activities, and the possibility of serving kids outside of the US. Those were the *important* questions for the team to ask, and they became the basis of the work done by the attendees at the Moby Arena workshop.

 *(Stage Two: Incubate)* STEP 4: BE OPEN

DESCRIPTION: *Revel in the world of infinite possibilities. Don't collapse your probability waves prematurely.*

TOOLS / TECHNIQUES:

Divergence is key to remaining open to new possibilities, and I capitalize on the work done in best-case, scenario-based planning to assist my clients here (the work started in Stage One, Step One—Comprehend the Urgency). Creating a powerful best-case scenario means you need to think comprehensively, look well beyond the traditional boundaries you may have placed upon yourself, your team, or your organization, and dream just a little (okay, more than just a little). It also requires a multi-disciplinary view of things: planning, funding, customer service, spiritual growth, etc., etc. Outstanding best-case scenarios are compelling, they don't settle for "good enough" anywhere, and they have nothing in them from the worst-case scenario. Anything is possible in the best-case scenario. Anything. Change is a positive force here.

Don't settle, don't converge, don't eliminate possibilities prematurely. Dream, and dream big. Keep pushing the envelope everywhere, and you'll remain open to new possibilities.

EXAMPLES FROM THE FALCON FOUNDATION STORY:

Obviously I knew how Franklin would respond to Mrs. Liu's question, "What can I do for you?" I used this mechanism to start the process of the Falcon Foundation, and of Franklin personally, being open to the infinite possibilities available to all of us, all the time. As Franklin Falcon discovered, simply being open to new possibilities can be truly transformational all by itself. He'd spent much of his life in a controlling posture, and when the financial results of his foundation started faltering, he found it difficult to step forward and look at the world differently.

Let's go back to Greg. He couldn't make the transition at all, and because he refused to look at new possibilities, he eventually departed. Greg even referred to the JUMP! Innovative Change Model as voodoo. However, had Franklin not forced the issue of looking at things differently, Greg's negative, stifling, and inflexible perspective most likely would have continued to contribute to the foundation's difficulties. Therefore, Greg's departure was one of the most important aspects of preparation for the foundation's leadership team to be open to new ideas. It was as if a giant stump had been removed from the field, allowing the ground to be tilled and softened.

*Stage Three: Aha!*

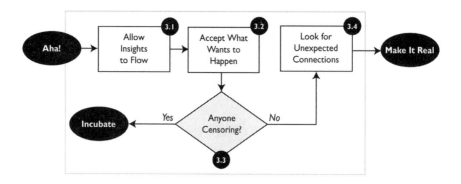

### 3.1 *(Stage Three: Aha!)* STEP 1: ALLOW INSIGHT

DESCRIPTION: *Be interested in outcomes, just not any particular outcome.*

TOOLS / TECHNIQUES:

I use a feedback exercise to help my clients understand how we tend to strive for specific outcomes on a regular basis. The exercise involves two people, and here's how to set it up:

- Choose a partner.

- Sit facing each other, and move your chairs so that your knees are almost touching.

- Decide who will be A and who will be B.

*I then give specific direction to both A and B.*

- A—You are to talk about the thing you like most of all, your passion (as long as it's something you can do in front of your grandparents), for about a minute or two.

- B—You are to remain in eye contact the whole time, but you cannot give any feedback. No facial expressions, no head nodding, no talking—just a passive, blank expression on your face. Period.

About this time there's a bunch of grumbling and nervous laughter, but it ends within a few moments. I then say, "Go," and the exercise begins. I love to watch this exercise because some of the As get so frustrated with their partners that they reach across and shake the Bs' shoulders. Other As start yelling or just give up. On the other hand, some Bs just can't "hold it" for long, and they crack. Other Bs are so good at it, I'm convinced they could probably keep their poker face on for days.

Then I stop time and wait. The resulting release of the tension in the room is full of laughing, loud conversation, and general chaos. It's great. Once the moment passes, I ask for reflections. Some comments I get regularly are "As an A, I found myself questioning the value of what I like to do!" or "As a B, I had to just stop paying attention; I really wanted to know more, but I wasn't able to ask." And generally, I find both As and Bs think their own role is more difficult.

I use this exercise to help people break free from their need for approval, their reliance on outside feedback, and their desire to be right about things. In other words, don't be stuck looking for any particular feedback. As such, be attached to outcomes (results) but not to any particular outcome (the status quo, or what you've always asked for in a particular situation).

EXAMPLES FROM THE FALCON FOUNDATION STORY:

The transformation for Franklin and his foundation begins in "Ernest" (pun intended) once the group has reconnected to their vision with Ernesto's help. It became time for them to adapt and allow rather than make more lists, do more pro and con analysis, create more market research, etc. Ernesto helped them to stop forcing outcomes or to rely too heavily on historical approaches. Ernesto shared with them that there's a natural flow to things.

That's why I included the reference to the movie *Finding Nemo* in the Falcon Foundation story. *Finding Nemo* is about a single father of a disabled clownfish son (Nemo), who while struggling to prove he's capable, not disabled, runs afoul of his father's advice and becomes ensnared in a tropical fish collector's net. The story unfolds as Nemo's father, Marlin, survives one trial after another in the quest to track down his wayward son. One particularly powerful part of the movie involves a group of sea turtles (who are gnarly dudes that speak in a dialect that would be very comfortable in Southern California). These turtles are traveling (their end destination is not known) and are fully "in the zone" as they do so. They are using the current known as the East Australian Current to travel toward Sydney, the city named on a piece of evidence found by Marlin. It's the best clue he has as to where his son may be.

Rather than trying to fight against the current in any way, the turtles relish their journey and feel completely confident and power-filled as they make their way. They have no worries, even when a "little one" somehow finds himself kicked out of the current and is now out of the zone. Rather than panic, or whine, or complain, or wish for circumstances to be different, the little turtle's father, Crush, simply says, *"Kill the motor, Dude* (referring to Marlin's building panic). *Let's see what Squirt does flying solo."* Sure enough, the zone is fully accepting of the little turtle's (whose name is Squirt) rapid return, and in short order he is laughing and playing once again with the other young turtles.

Marlin has the chance to learn something significant from the turtles: Allow and adapt. Adapt and allow. The lesson is this: Instead of controlling things very tightly with his son, maybe there's a better approach. Find the flow, and then trust. Marlin learned that his controlling influence is what ultimately led Nemo to rebel in the first place. The same thing happened with Franklin Falcon: His micromanagement style failed to deliver results in saving the foundation from financial ruin. Rather than ensuring outcomes by being the decision-maker about things, Franklin stifled the ability of his executive team and his foundation to succeed. In both situations, once Nemo's father and Franklin surrendered to what wants to happen, an amazing turnaround followed.

When we find ourselves fully engaged in what wants to happen (similar to Heraclitus's ancient observation: *"You cannot step twice into the same river; for other waters are continually flowing in."*), we are not resisting, pushing against, or making pro/con lists about what to do next. We are not trying to force outcomes. Instead, Aha! moments flow *to* us, like water in a river.

## 3.2 *(Stage Three: Aha!)* STEP 2: ACCEPT

DESCRIPTION: *Non-locality.*

TOOLS / TECHNIQUES:

I use a technique in my workshops whereby I'll have three or four groups simultaneously working to come up with ideas related to the exact same thing. Some of you may think this exercise would be a waste of time or of limited efficiency, and on the surface, it appears that way; after all, dividing and conquering has been a tried and true process for achieving efficiency for years (and yes, there are times when it's highly useful, but not here). Now, for those attached to the divide and conquer concept, or the "I don't believe it unless I see it" types, or the "there's no such thing as non-locality" skeptics (and you know who you are), JUMP! doesn't apply to you. Your need for efficiency and proof is so powerful that you just aren't wired for innovative change. But if you've read this far, you're probably not one of those folks!

Anyway, I use the quantum principle of non-locality, or the situation where an action can be seen happening simultaneously in two different locations, to drive accepting behaviors. Non-locality defies traditional physics in that the *same thing* is happening in *two different places* at the *same time*. Again, envision a school of fish that instantaneously (from the one in the front to the one in the back) shifts its direction to avoid a predator. They move in absolute unison. And if they waited for the message to make its way to the poor fish in back using traditional means of communicating, the predator would be feasting on the stragglers at the rear of the school.

Enough of the biology lesson. Where's the value in non-locality in a workshop setting? The primary benefit is this: Shared experience creates shared acceptance. Once the groups realize that the same thing (generally, of course) is happening throughout the room, the energy level accelerates and becomes fuel to drive more insights. Arbitration disappears, filtering ends, and blockages to progress are dropped. Thus, to achieve the best results, this step requires you to disconnect from your need for certainty and for proof of what's happening. Trust, don't filter.

EXAMPLES FROM THE FALCON FOUNDATION STORY:

Non-locality in the Falcon Foundation story shows up in what occurs throughout cyberspace as a result of Angela Liu's actions. She sends a selfless plea for help to all of her friends, and within just a few hours, a news reporter in Amsterdam is reporting on how the Internet has been overwhelmed with messages about helping the Falcon Foundation. Certainly you could ignore this result or pass it off as "impossible." But then you'd stop the JUMP! process, too. Both Franklin (when he met Rebecca and heard about her school's interest in helping) and Jennifer (when she met the Miller family at the hotel as she was serving food) were amazed to hear the non-local results associated with Angela's message.

### 3.3 *(Stage Three: Aha!)* STEP 3: DON'T CENSOR

DESCRIPTION: *What is, is.*

YES? *(Censorship missing?) Continue to Step Four*

NO? *Return to Stage Two, Incubate*

TOOLS / TECHNIQUES:

At the start of my work with individuals, groups, or organizations, I establish the fact that censorship of ideas is intolerable. New ideas must at least be tolerated, even if they're not openly welcomed, to make the JUMP! model work. *(As a side note, just tolerating new ideas isn't a strong platform, but it is a step above outright censorship! I like to strive for eagerness in seeing/hearing/receiving new ideas—that's the long-term goal.)*

However, eliminating censorship is a difficult thing because there are two kinds, overt and covert. Overt censorship is easy to spot: When someone uses their positional authority (I'm a director and you're not. You're a peon.) to drive an outcome or when someone invokes one of the statements I used back in Stage Two (Incubate), Step One (Banish Barriers): Let's form a committee. Covert censorship is more difficult to spot, and no surprise, it's more important to address. Covert censorship shows up in body language or in bad behaviors. Some examples:

- Eye rolling
- Head shaking
- Squinted eyes with furrowed brows
- Arm crossing
- Multi-tasking (can't put down that Blackberry)
- Showing up late
- Leaving early
- Hanging back
- Drifting in and out of sleep

This list is not all-inclusive, but I'm always on guard and watch for behaviors on it. And, as the pain-in-the-backside facilitator, I mention it when I see it. I don't put people on trial for their bad behavior or distracting body language, but I point out the fact that there are some detractors in the group, and I ask the group what they want to do about it: Allow it? Address it? What happens here is that covert censorship becomes overt as *everyone* (in addition to me) becomes aware and begins looking for it. The detractors have been flushed into the open. As such, the group begins to establish norms related to censorship. I find that the group itself will begin calling out those who are censoring things and will look actively to address the situation and eliminate censorship.

EXAMPLES FROM THE FALCON FOUNDATION STORY:

One more time, I used Greg's character to show bad behavior. Greg was not shy about rolling his eyes, making disparaging comments, shooting hostile glances, etc. He was clearly in opposition to what was happening, and his body language was destructive. However, as Franklin became more enlightened and became more interested in seeing the big picture, Greg's influence over the larger group diminished. As Franklin quit allowing Greg to pout, the rest of the team was empowered to challenge Greg as well.

Further, I had one ghost character in the book—Marty Wright. While he didn't say it in the book, I can imagine him saying the words "What is, is." I used him as a steadying force, a moral rudder. I can imagine he'd be the type of person who wouldn't tolerate bad behavior, but he'd have something philosophical to say about it. He wouldn't degenerate into bad behavior of his own. I used his character to remind Jennifer (in particular) that taking the high road is the preferred road.

 *(Stage Three: Aha!)* STEP 4: FIND SYNERGY

DESCRIPTION: *Look beyond the obvious and make unexpected connections.*

TOOLS / TECHNIQUES:

I use a process of refinement in my workshops to help create synergies. Here's how it works. First, I am absolutely convinced small groups are vitally important in getting things started (even if I'm working with hundreds of people in a workshop, I still break the group down into "table teams" of seven or eight). I then ask each table team to create some ideas using a variety of techniques (look at the JUMP! Tools website for some specific examples). Then, just when the table team is feeling particularly smug about the quality of their ideas (I may even hint at some vague notion of competitiveness as they're preparing.), I ask for the ideas from one table team to be rotated to another, throughout the room.

I then give the following instruction: "You have just received the collective wisdom from your neighboring table team. I'd like for you to take a moment to familiarize yourself with what they've created, and then," I pause and look around somewhat deviously before continuing, "you are fully empowered to do anything you'd like to what they've created. You can add to it, scratch things out completely, refine or improve it in any way you want."

The reaction here is fascinating. Basically I can describe it this way: "Oh, crap." The smugness disappears, genuine fear grows in some places, and the competitive juices overflow for some.

I then have the table teams rotate the content (from one table to another) several times before I finally have it return to the group who created it originally. Once the originating table team gets its "creation" back—full of scribbles, feedback, additions, changes, etc.— transformation happens. The wisdom of the group has truly developed synergy. Unexpected connections are everywhere. I *love* this process; it's amazing to watch. People go from skepticism to synergy in short order.

EXAMPLES FROM THE FALCON FOUNDATION STORY:

The desire to find synergies was in large part the impetus behind the workshop at Moby Arena. Certainly, the executive team could have (as many do) simply been satisfied with the Aha!'s they'd created as a result of sleeping on it at the hotel. They came up with some good ideas concerning immigration and how the economy might affect societal views about it, the fact that the foundation might be seen as elitist because it serves only a select few, and the opportunities to serve the needs of kids around the world before they came to America.

The executive team could have taken those ideas back and worked them, and they may have created some success. However, by leveraging the combined energy, wisdom, passion, and power of hundreds of others, the overall results from the Moby Arena were extraordinary. Making unexpected connections results in highly innovative and powerful synergies.

## *Stage Four: Make It Real*

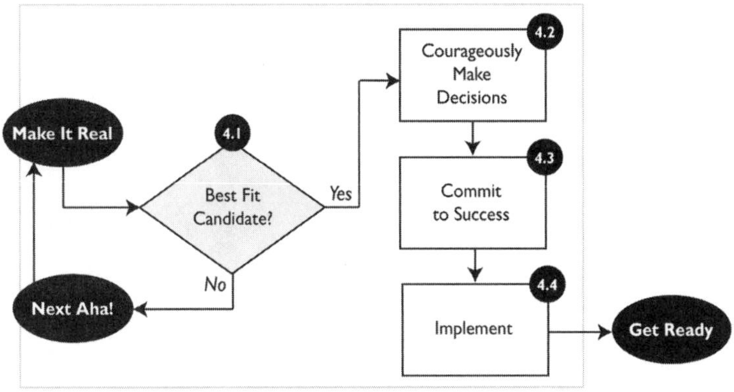


### 4.1 *(Stage 4: Make It Real)* STEP 1: THINK CRITICALLY

DESCRIPTION: *Evaluate your Aha!'s and select the ones that are most appropriate.*

YES? *(Best Fit?) Continue to Step Two*

NO? *Select Next Aha! and Reevaluate for Best Fit. If No More Aha!'s, Quit*

TOOLS / TECHNIQUES:

I use a tool to assist in evaluating the best fit for a particular idea. It's called the BLUE Tool (B.enefits, L.imitations, U.niqueness, E.valuation), and I include a sample template below.

| IDEA → | | |
|---|---|---|
| **BENEFITS** | **LIMITATIONS** | **UNIQUENESS** |
| | | |

First, take an idea and write it at the top. Then brainstorm the benefits offered by this particular idea, create a list of the idea's limitations, and then list the unique features of the idea. Examples of benefits usually have to do with improving culture, attitudes, financial return on investment, etc. Limitations can fall all over the board, but I often hear things like "management won't go for it" or "it's too radical" or things like that. Again, comments like these are very "un-JUMP!-like," and when I hear them, I point out that the group needs to rethink how well it has done with the Get Ready stage. Then there's the Uniqueness column. I always have people ask me to define it, and here's what I say: "Uniqueness has to do with any special qualities associated with this idea, something that brings unusual, uncommon, or unexpected benefits by using this idea." That usually gets the group moving forward! Here's how the BLUE Tool might be used:

- Individuals can use it by themselves (if they are working on something just for themselves, or if they are working as an individual who is part of a small group).
- Small groups (like table teams) can fill out one form together as a group.
- When I'm working with large groups (more than one table team), I have each table team fill out one BLUE form.
- I collect all the ideas by asking a representative from each table team, one at a time, to read "new thoughts" they have from each of the columns.
- I write the ideas on a flip chart at the front of the room.
- That way, the input coming from each of the small groups is captured by the larger group, and everyone has a chance to see the general commonality of the input and the occasional comments made by some table teams that are highly insightful.

The BLUE Tool is useful in mitigating strong personalities (who may be championing their own idea, even if it isn't the best fit), the "we've always done it that way" biases, and other limiting factors. It can help you critically evaluate your Aha!'s in a comprehensive way.

EXAMPLES FROM THE FALCON FOUNDATION STORY:

While I didn't call it out specifically in the story, one of the activities the participants did during the workshop at Moby Arena involved using the BLUE Tool to evaluate the ideas coming from the executive team.

**(*Stage 4: Make It Real*) Step 2: Show Courage**

Description: *Decide.*

Tools / Techniques:

Deciding on the best thing to do requires leadership. Unfortunately, many individuals and organizations want to have a process lead them to the right decision. A process is not a proxy for leadership: Processes support leadership; they don't supply it. Consequently, I assist my clients in enabling courageous decision-making by using my platform as the facilitator to "call the question." Remember, by the time you get to Stage Four (Make It Real), Step Two (Show Courage), you've already generated a great idea (Aha!), and you've chosen it as a best fit option for the future. Further evaluation is not needed here. Action is needed here.

Consequently, I ask this question: *"Are you up for this?"*

If the answer is no, then we need to move backward through the JUMP! model, maybe all the way back to Stage One. Or, maybe we need to find a different leader or leadership team, those who will act courageously.

Examples from the Falcon Foundation story:

The Falcon Foundation story is full of courageous decision-making. One of the first examples was when Franklin decided to listen to the other voice in his head while on the phone with Mrs. Liu. His voice of reason was trying to pull him back into the status quo, but he showed the courage to be transparent with Mrs. Liu. Had he not done that, I wouldn't have had a very good story to tell, would I? The story would have ended right there, and the Falcon Foundation's death sentence may have been written as well.

How many stories in your life have ended because the leader (who might have been you!) wasn't "up for it" and wasn't ready, willing, or able to show courageous decision-making? I bet it happens far more frequently than you think. Each of these situations represents a missed opportunity, and that's tragic all by itself.

**(*Stage 4: Make It Real*) Step 3: Commit to Act**

Description: *Courage without action is noble but pointless.*

Tools / Techniques:

I use the "compliance to commitment" continuum I show below to help explain what commitment looks like. Compliance is at the left, and it is characterized by these statements: "You can't fire me for doing what's in my job description" or "I'm doing what it says here; if the instructions aren't clear, that's not my fault." Compliance is all about doing the least to get by. On the other hand, commitment is characterized by doing whatever it takes. You'll hear things like this when the environment is strong on commitment: "I know I don't own the company, but I choose to act like it's mine." Unfortunately, too many situations allow compliance, and too few encourage commitment.

## Compliance                                    Commitment

Driving commitment is a straightforward thing. I ask for it. How? At the end of my time working with a client, during a particular workshop, organizational assessment, training, etc., I always make sure the actions and accountabilities from our work together have been addressed. First, I ensure there's enough time to drive commitment; I don't rush the meeting to the end and run out of time. In fact, I'll consciously forego something else on the agenda just to be sure I have enough time.

I drive commitment in a public and direct way by doing the following:

- Reciting the list I've been creating of the decisions they've made, the dates they've established, and the individuals who they have assigned as accountable.

- If they haven't done a good job being specific here, I'll call that out and force them to be specific. What? When? Who?

- I then give them time to cement in their commitment together—to agree to be held accountable to each other.

- I leave plenty of time for looking each other in the eye, asking each other for any disagreement, reciting the reasons behind their decisions in the first place, etc.

- I wait for genuine agreement to flow. *Then* it's time to adjourn.

I expect integrity here, and it can get very uncomfortable very quickly if they only want to make feeble agreements, or if they intend to go back to their offices and do things the same old way. If that's what they want, I make them say it. Few do that in words, but sometimes they do it non-verbally. I call that out, too. The effort and time spent to develop powerful Aha!'s leading to significant actions is far too important to treat disrespectfully. I make sure *everyone's clear* about what they intend to do and why. I *love* this part of my job!

It's too bad that many meetings (clearly none with me as facilitator!) do not end with real accountability and genuine agreements together. Instead, if dates and assignments are mentioned, it's either in a cursory, "fly-by" kind of way, or it's done in a heavy-handed, directed manner. Neither of these methods works very well.

EXAMPLES FROM THE FALCON FOUNDATION STORY:

Franklin used my technique of driving accountability and integrity when he told the executive team that their participation at the hotel was optional, not mandatory. He asked them for their perspective, and he wanted to have real participation, not obligatory or begrudging head-nodding. In the story, everyone agreed to go to the hotel, and once there, they all participated fully. Franklin knew it was vital to have commitment, not compliance.

 *(Stage 4: Make It Real)* STEP 4: IMPLEMENT

DESCRIPTION: *Give yourself the best chance possible to be successful.*

TOOLS / TECHNIQUES:

Again, I could write an entire shelf of books on the subject of successful implementation, but I choose to focus on two elements here: 1) agility and 2) learning to improve. First, agility is a critical element in long-term success. As such, I use the following table when I enter into a discussion related to agility:

## Agile Organizations Value:

| | | |
|---:|:---:|:---|
| Individuals and Interactions | *over* | Processes and Tools |
| Instinct and Intuition | *over* | Comprehensive Documentation |
| Client Collaboration | *over* | Contract Negotiation |
| Adapting to Change | *over* | Following "the" Plan |

The chart on the previous page always elicits interesting dialog. I'm not asking anyone to ignore what's in the list on the right; each of these things is important. However, agile organizations and individuals place more importance (relatively speaking) on the items on the left when confronted with a decision. In other words, agile organizations will seek out face-to-face communication with individuals when necessary instead of relying upon the email message they are supposed to send based upon the process they're using. Agile organizations will value gut feel over the cookbook (e.g., someone actually says that a particular step or activity just doesn't feel right and takes steps to find out more about it). Rigid organizations will blindly follow the steps. Period. Agility helps you with considering the "why" behind your choices. The world continues to grow more uncertain and more complex all the time, and agility helps you deliver higher levels of success.

This concept reminds me of the theory of Negative Capability that John Keats expressed in his letter to George and Thomas Keats dated Sunday, 28 December 1817:

*". . . I mean Negative Capability, that is when man is capable of being in uncertainties, Mysteries, doubts without any irritable reaching after fact & reason."*

*Learning to Improve*

When it comes to learning to improve, I'll use a coaching example. I've coached a lot of competitive athletics over the years (baseball, football, basketball), and I've learned something valuable about learning to improve. It's called the "coaching sandwich," where direction is sandwiched between positive statements. It is based on the notion that you can never shame a person into loving the game or yell them into playing with real passion. However, there are times when direction is needed, and learning can help with improvement. At times like these, the coaching sandwich is appropriate:

1) Recognize something positive.

2) Give direction.

3) Provide encouragement.

Here's how you could use the coaching sandwich in the context of a basketball game where, say, the point guard caused a turnover in a particular situation (your understanding of basketball isn't critical; just substitute any sport or activity):

- Call time-out, or wait for the next stoppage in play (but no more than a few minutes after the event has occurred).

- Call the player over to you, and put your hands on the player's shoulders.

- Make eye contact and say, "I really like your hustle out there" (recognize something positive). Wait a moment.

- Then say, "But, it works better if you ball fake to the left before passing to the right. Without doing that, the other team guessed where the pass was going, and we got a turnover" (give direction). Smile.

- Finally say, "I know you can do it. Now get back in there and show me" (provide encouragement).

- Put the player back in the game as soon as possible. Wink at them.

I find the coaching sandwich isn't used often enough, particularly in work-related settings. Instead, direction shows up in the form of an impersonal email or an offhand remark. As such, learning doesn't happen, and little improvement occurs because the person reacts with defensiveness, shame, irritation, anger, or some other negative emotion.

EXAMPLES FROM THE FALCON FOUNDATION STORY:

The concepts of agility and learning to improve are sprinkled throughout the Falcon Foundation story. However, a specific example of agility was when Jennifer used the word "easy" when describing the process of putting together a substantial public event, overnight, in the middle of a snowstorm, at a university, and involving dozens of virtual locations scattered across the world. Had she followed the "cookbook" associated with planning and executing an event like that, it would have never happened. Instead, Betty's personal relationship with CSU's president got the ball rolling, and those charged with planning the event used their intuition, valued their personal interactions, used a collaborative approach with each other, and adapted to the situations as they presented themselves.

Nowhere in the story was learning used to punish. Even when the crowd at Moby was cheering Franklin for vanquishing Marissa, he brought them back to a grounded position by saying he felt compassion for her. Clearly, learning to improve was central to Franklin's "hero's journey" throughout the story. At the beginning of the book, he found himself lost, frustrated, and afraid. His old approaches were not working, and he believed the foundation stood a strong chance of failing. Throughout his experiences in the story, he had chances to learn—from Jo, from Ernesto, from Jennifer, from Betty, from Rebecca, from Jack, etc., and he consistently used the lessons as opportunities to improve. At the end of the story, we find him back at his desk, a changed man. He traded control for trust, self-reliance for transparency, and failure for success.

# Epilogue

"The best way to find yourself
is to lose yourself in the service of others."

—*Mahatma Gandhi*

# Moby Arena Outcomes

While the Falcon Foundation fable is a work of fiction, if the workshop at Moby Arena had *actually* occurred, more details would have emerged. However, rather than bogging down the story to go through all of those details in the middle of the fable, I decided instead to include them here. I've done that for two reasons: 1) to support those of you, like me, who like to see the specifics—the proof of the design, if you will; and 2) by sharing the details with you this way, I'm also able to explain more about my approach to developing vision, goals, and objectives.

If you felt satisfied with the highlights that Jennifer shared back on page 167, or you're not interested in reading about my approach to developing vision, goals, and objectives, you can stay satisfied and skip this section if you'd like. In either case, before you dig into the details from the Moby Arena workshop, or if you're "done" reading at this point, I'd like to share with you my favorite Bible verse. It has to do with implementing—the Make It Real stage—the great ideas you'll generate as a result of using the JUMP! Innovative Change Model.

Matthew 5:14-16 *You are the light of the world. A city built on a hill cannot be hidden. No one after lighting a lamp puts it under the bushel basket, but on the lamp stand, and it gives light to all in the house. In the same way, let your light shine before others, so that they may see your good works and give glory to God.*

Go forward. Let your light shine.

*Definitions*

Okay, before you read the details of what everyone would have come up with during the workshop at Moby Arena, I have found it's vital to provide some clarity and consistency related to terminology. There are about 7 billion different ways to interpret something (one opinion for each soul on Earth!), so let me share with you my definitions of the words Vision, Goals, and Objectives. We need to do that because those definitions are what Jennifer had the Moby workshop attendees use to develop what you're about to read.

Vision:

An organization's vision represents an aspiration, something big and compelling. Your vision needs to be large enough and powerful enough to overcome whatever resistance is thrown at it. One of the best examples of this was when President Kennedy shared these words in a speech he presented at Rice University, September 12, 1962:

*"We choose to go to the moon. We choose to go to the moon in this decade and do the other things, not because they are easy, but because they are hard, because that goal will serve to organize and measure the best of our energies and skills, because that challenge is one that we are willing to accept, one we are unwilling to postpone, and one which we intend to win, and the others, too."*

Now, for the nit-picking types, yes, JFK used the word "goal" in his sentence; he also used the word "challenge" almost as a synonym for goal. It's confusing to me. If I had had the chance to write his speech, I would have used the word "vision" instead. However, he didn't consult me, as I was not quite four at the time!

Goals:

Goals are outcome-based statements that are never finished. They may span several years, and they are designed to help you understand what needs to be done to deliver your vision. It's a good idea to have only four, five, or maybe six goals at a time. If you have more than that, it will be difficult to succeed in delivering them, and people will start to get that creeping "Yeah, sure" skepticism.

OBJECTIVES:

Objectives describe the how associated with delivering the goals. Keep the number of objectives to about three for each goal. Again, any more than that, and implementation becomes questionable. It just isn't possible to do everything. Choosing the right objectives to support the right goals is critical.

Okay, enough of the definitions and ramblings. Here's the document that Jennifer and the volunteer facilitators passed out on Saturday evening at Moby Arena.

## FALCON FOUNDATION FOR FAMILIES
## MOBY ARENA WORKSHOP OUTCOMES

*Vision:*

*The Falcon Foundation for Families:*

- Is selflessly grounded in equal educational opportunities for all children

- Courageously drives systemic, permanent culture and societal change for children who lack educational advocacy

- Serves families and children with direct financial and life-related assistance as often as possible

- Is committed to continuous refinement of its programs and operations through innovative, collaborative solution finding

*Goals / Objectives:*

GOAL ONE: *Address the Root Cause*

*Become and remain active in addressing the root causes of social injustices related to education, where some "have" and some don't.*

OBJECTIVES:

1. Develop awareness and understanding throughout the world related to the foundational benefits to each country of having well-educated citizens.

2.  Wherever and whenever injustices exist in educational opportunities, provide resources and leadership to assist in transforming problems into opportunities.

3.  Use positive examples of where equal opportunities in education have resulted in significant societal and cultural benefits.

GOAL TWO: *Don't Overreach*

*Ensure we are doing the best job possible serving those we can with the resources we have available while at the same time stretching ourselves to never stop expanding both.*

OBJECTIVES:

1.  Involve a broad-based group in openly and transparently managing the finances of the foundation.

2.  Transform our approach to funding the foundation by capturing the hearts, minds, and pocketbooks of those who might contribute.

3.  Keep the "size of our stomach" in line with our "appetites"; unless we are fully prepared to follow through, we cannot commit to something we won't be able to deliver.

GOAL THREE: *Model Cultural Diversity*

*Actively engage in purposeful dialog and culturally changing situations to spread appreciation for the diversity in our cultures throughout the world; we are a divine tapestry.*

OBJECTIVES:

1.  Ensure the foundation involves a culturally diverse set of leaders in designing our strategies.

2.  Develop thought-leadership related to appreciating each other's differences. Don't wait for only "safe" or politically correct moments; start the dialog ourselves whenever possible.

3.  Be courageous and positive. Don't let the limitations others may try to place on us influence our decisions on this subject.

GOAL FOUR: *Enlist and Empower Others*

*Develop and nurture on-the-ground groups throughout the world who look for places where new educational opportunities for children would have profound benefits.*

OBJECTIVES:

1. Move the activities of the foundation as far away from Loveland as possible and as close to those we are serving as possible.

2. Invite a wide variety of perspectives. Resist myopia at all costs.

3. Actively remove barriers from our ability to succeed. Remember that leaders are "chosen" by those whom they lead. We will be servant leaders.

GOAL FIVE: *Balance Opportunity and Accountability*

*Continue stressing the balance between equality in opportunity and the need for strong personal accountability related to the decisions and actions we make.*

OBJECTIVES:

1. Reinforce the fact that the foundation is based on the principle of offering hand-ups, not hand-outs.

2. Define and clearly articulate what we mean by accountability. We will actively work to help those who are helping themselves.

3. Develop a comprehensive set of tools and processes to help families understand and develop high levels of accountability in their lives.

GOAL SIX: *Bond and Serve Together*

*Provide relevant and motivating opportunities for individuals, groups, and organizations to connect with each other and to support each other as they support our abilities to deliver significant and ongoing financial, volunteer, spiritual, educational, and emotional support to families throughout the world.*

Objectives:

1. Leverage technology to create a massive "exchange" where needs are matched with resources.

2. Build never-before-seen synergies where infinite possibilities are perpetually manifesting themselves in powerful solutions.

3. Foster and develop a sense of "team" throughout all aspects of the foundation's work.


One more thing . . . The objectives shown above from the Moby workshop are not complete in that they need to be made S.M.A.R.T. (Specific, Measurable, Achievable, Relevant, and Time-Based). Jennifer didn't ask the attendees to finish "smart-izing" their objectives at Moby. That's the next job for the Falcon executive team.

# A FINAL THOUGHT

Some of the content in the Falcon Foundation story is based upon real experiences I have had. One of them, Ernesto's snowmobiling trip on the glacier in Iceland, is based loosely on an afternoon snowmobile outing I had with eight or 10 others on a real glacier in Iceland. Although our guide didn't fall into a fissure and we weren't stranded, the experience was incredibly intense. The Langjökull Glacier is a long way from civilization, and NASA selected that part of Iceland as the training ground for the first moon landing. I completely understand why: There's just mile after mile of gray rocks and gray soil—gray, gray, and more gray.

It was during the drive to the glacier that I saw one of the most incredible examples in nature of "making it real." As we were creeping along the road after driving for what seemed to be an hour or more, seeing nothing that hinted of life, I saw something breathtaking. Standing by itself, a single white flower was craning its bloom to catch the limited sunlight. It was regal and majestic—even if it was maybe only eight inches tall.

I asked our tour guide about it, and he replied, "That's the HOLTASÓLEY. It's the national flower of Iceland." (Yes, he shouted the name of the flower at me. He was enthusiastic!)

I can understand why Icelanders chose that flower to be their national flower. It is spectacular, and it is evidence that nature will always find a way to bring life to even the most inhospitable places. I have used the image of that flower on many occasions to remind myself that manifestation of ideas, of change, of new ideas, of innovation is possible—always. Nature is passionate about bringing forth life, and the JUMP! Innovative Change Model is all about helping you move forward, farther, faster.

Go forth and JUMP!

# APPENDIX

"Work for something because it is good,
not just because it has a chance to succeed."

—*Vaclav Haval*

# Character Summaries

### *Franklin Falcon*

Franklin is a private, controlling, and charismatic person whose character in the fable is a surrogate for anyone who has been successful in the past only to find him- or herself "stuck" in an unsatisfying status quo. Franklin realizes that change is inevitable, but he is unsure about the most appropriate direction, timing, and approach for the change. The fable follows Franklin's transformation from being the "hub to every spoke" in the foundation to being a trusting, vulnerable, collaborative leader in his JUMP! forward.

### *Jennifer Boyle*

Jennifer has worked for the Falcon Foundation for more than 20 years, originally starting as a case manager, who then ascends to the positions of executive director and eventually president. Jennifer is a respected, clear-headed leader with excellent communication, organization, and facilitation skills and is someone who isn't afraid to cast a big vision and then work to deliver it. Jennifer's courage is a key element in getting the foundation to create real outcomes from the Aha! moments they experience.

### *Ernesto Martinez*

Ernesto is a bookish scientist (who specializes in quantum mechanics) whose character offers the experience of a survival journey as well as insight into the mysteries of quantum stuff. His character is virtually egoless, and as a former Falcon Family "kid," his motivations are focused simply on assisting Franklin and the foundation. He also offers some comic relief through his nerdiness and self-effacing humor.

## Marty Wright

Marty passed away a few years ago, but his memory is strong within the Falcon Foundation. Marty represents a source of trusted wisdom even after his death, and his influence continues to accelerate the energy of those around him. His legacy was to always bring out the best in the situations in which, and the people around which, he found himself. The members of the foundation team refer to Marty's vestigial influence in improving things as "being Wrighted."

## Jo Falcon

Joanna (Jo) Falcon is a pragmatic, decisive, and strong person who has an affinity for simple, powerful philosophy. She is the yin to Franklin's yang, as she balances his brooding nature with her direct manner. She clearly loves and supports Franklin unconditionally, but she's not afraid to say what needs to be said when it needs to be said.

## Angela Liu and Liu Ping

Angela is a high school senior from Eden Prairie, Minnesota, whose family has been served by the Falcon Foundation for about 10 years. Angela is a genuinely compassionate and caring person who was raised by her parents to "do the right thing." Her self-less nature leads her to ask her social network to help Mr. Falcon. Angela's mother, Ping, is a loving, highly spiritual woman and is someone who isn't afraid to ask the hard questions. Her pro-active and positive question of Mr. Falcon begins the entire process of transformation for him and the foundation.

## Marissa Grant

Marissa Grant is a TV personality from New York who is driven by her ego, her need to be important, and her anger. She's a bitter, bullying person who is bent on avenging the fact she and her family were rejected by the Falcon Foundation due to her cheating on the admissions essay. She has not forgiven Franklin or the foundation, nor has she taken accountability for her actions.

## Greg Sullivan

Greg has worked for the foundation for many years and eventually finds himself promoted to the role of CFO, replacing Marty Wright. I'll admit that Greg is a stereotype—but his character is one that I see in almost every organization, no matter how large. He is stuck, he knows he's stuck, and yet he is completely committed to being stuck. He has no interest in looking at things in new ways; he just wants to do more of the same. He also takes no accountability for his role in the problems encountered by the foundation; instead, he's quick to blame others.

## Nicole Fargas

Nicole is relatively young (late 20s) but is someone who possesses extensive success in the world of non-profit fund-raising. Her upbringing in a tough Philadelphia neighborhood gave her a no-fear attitude that she tempers with a dry sense of humor. She also has an affinity for philosophy, as she introduces the executive team to the energy-based message in *Monsters, Inc.* Her youthful enthusiasm and can-do attitude assist the executive team in moving forward.

## Terrence Kennedy

Terrence is also a member of a former Falcon Family (who like Ernesto is one of the "kids"). Terrence's family comes from rural Georgia (USA), and he is descended from the sharecroppers who became landowners following the Civil War. He focuses on serving the needs of the Falcon Families and has difficulty in separating himself from his role at the foundation at times. He is conflicted in the fable—clearly he is someone who has benefited from the history of the foundation, but also someone who knows the foundation's old approaches aren't sustainable into the future.

## Elaine Gustavson

Elaine is an experienced HR professional who grew up in the American Midwest. Her Swedish heritage gives her a solid work ethic and a practical approach to solving problems. She was brought to the foundation by Franklin with the intention of establishing a new culture wherein each employee would reach his or her maximum potential. However, Franklin's controlling nature thwarted Elaine's efforts. She also brings to bear her experience from a former employer, an organization that ultimately failed due to its inability to transform.

## Betty Agassi

Betty is Franklin's personal administrative assistant and is an immigrant from Iran. She is a caring, dedicated person who takes pro-active steps to do the right thing. While for much of the book she seems to be almost in a subservient role, she, too, undergoes a personal transformation. Her character becomes overtly assertive as she demonstrates her conviction to do the right things. She steps out of the background to act as a powerful leader.

## Rebecca Anderson

Rebecca Anderson is in her mid-to-late 20s and is a shy, intelligent, and caring schoolteacher from a small town in eastern Australia. She traveled to Colorado to attend her sister's wedding and found herself at the La Quinta Inn in Loveland after becoming stuck in the snow. Her character shows the power of non-locality through the fact that she and her students back in Australia become part of the solution.

## Jack and Jason Miller

The Miller family was traveling from San Antonio, Texas when they got stuck in the snowstorm in Loveland. Jack introduces the readers to Destination ImagiNation (read more in the next section of the Appendix) and brings forward the concept of making unexpected connections. Jason Miller is 12 years old, clearly very familiar with the tools of social networking, and able to help the adults in the story make sense of the information coming from Facebook.

# DESTINATION IMAGINATION

I used Jack Miller and his son, Jason, to introduce Destination ImagiNation (DI) to you as part of the Falcon Foundation story. I've been involved in one way or another with DI (and other creative solution-finding programs) since 1985. As Jack's character said, DI is the best after-school program. Period. Why?

Combine the public pressure being placed on academic performance in today's education (yes, we need to know the basics; I'm not arguing that), along with the tighter and tighter restrictions on budgets today, and often the more esoteric skills like leadership, communication, planning, and innovation tend to be put at a lower priority. I'm not criticizing public education—far from it. It's just that school districts have to make choices, and sometimes these choices leave gaps.

We're preparing our kids for a future where they'll be doing jobs we've never heard of, using technologies that haven't yet been invented, and in a world where borders are being erased and competition is increasing. Augmenting their "classic" education involving reading, writing, arithmetic, science, etc., DI prepares kids to see the world's challenges as a series of steps to understand, solve, and move through. They're undaunted. They're confident. They're successful in life.

There are some 1.3 million DI alumni worldwide, and about 35,000 volunteers support DI's activities annually. Here's more information from DI's international organization website:

## Building Tomorrow's Leaders:
## One Challenge at a Time

*Destination ImagiNation, Inc. is an extraordinary non-profit organization that provides educational programs for students to learn and experience creativity, teamwork and problem solving. Every year, we reach 100,000 students across the U.S. and in more than 30 countries. Destination ImagiNation, our core program, is an exhilarating after-school activity in which students work in teams to solve mind-bending Challenges and present their solutions at Tournaments. Teams are tested to think on their feet, work together, and devise original solutions that satisfy the requirements of the Challenges. Participants gain more than just basic knowledge and skills—they learn to unleash their imaginations and take unique approaches to problem solving. (Source: Destination ImagiNation)*

I'm donating a portion of the profits from *JUMP!* to DI at three levels: the South Metro region in Colorado (a geographic area representing the southern suburbs of Denver in which I live, and other rural parts of south-central Colorado), Colorado Extreme Creativity (the overall DI organization in the state of Colorado), and the international Destination ImagiNation organization as well. I'm doing this so that more kids, both here in the US and in the developed and developing world, have the chance to participate in DI. I believe it's one of the best ways to help our kids become prepared for the complex challenges they'll encounter later in life. Like, next week.

For more information about DI, please check out their website. Better still, become involved. It's a great way to touch the future.

South Metro: SMetro.ExtremeCreativity.org

Colorado: www.ExtremeCreativity.org

International: www.IdoDI.org

# JOIN THE JUMP! COMMUNITY

Let me share my appreciation to you for reading *JUMP!*. I value your interest and commitment in getting all the way here to this final page. Thank you!

However, there's much more to JUMP! than just this book. My vision for JUMP! includes a vibrant, passionate community of those on a transformational journey, and I'd like to personally invite you to become part of that community. We need to hear your stories, share your successes, and benefit from your Aha! moments, as we all continue to deepen our experience with being clear, getting unstuck, and making magic.

Please join us at the JUMP! community website and become part of the conversation. I look forward to meeting you there.

www.OurJUMP.com

# About The Author

Most everyone calls me Bob, so if you've read this far, I hope that you'll do the same. I live in the south metro-Denver area in the beautiful state of Colorado with my wife, Debi, our two younger kids, Spencer and Grace (our two older kids, Amanda and Parker, are on their own and living in the Denver area as well), four cats (Sophie, Ozzy, Indiana Jones, and Dexter), our dog (Cinnamon), and various other critters and people here and there—some invited, some not. Our home is in a constant state of buzzing, so if you like it quiet and relaxed, it's best if you stay outside.

You can find out more about me and what's currently going on around here, book me to speak to your group, ask me to facilitate a workshop, or have me perform a consulting assignment for you or your organization by visiting my website at:

www.RobertSTipton.com